Just Below the Line

Disability, Housing, and Equity in the South

KORYDON H. SMITH, JENNIFER WEBB, AND BRENT T. WILLIAMS

With Contributions by Nancy G. Miller and Darell W. Fields
and a Foreword by Edward Steinfeld

The Fay Jones School of Architecture

The University of Arkansas Press
Fayetteville
2010

ISBN-10: 1-55728-923-9
ISBN-13: 978-1-55728-923-0

14 13 12 11 10   5 4 3 2 1

Designed by Liz Lester

⊚ The paper used in this publication meets the minimum requirements of the American National Standard for Permanence of Paper for Printed Library Materials Z39.48-1984.

LIBRARY OF CONGRESS CATALOGING-IN-PUBLICATION DATA

Smith, Korydon H., 1977–
        Disability, housing, and equity in the South / Korydon H. Smith, Jennifer
Webb, and Brent T. Williams ; with contributions by Nancy G. Miller and
Darell W. Fields and a foreword by Edward Steinfeld.
            p.   cm.
        Includes bibliographical references and index.
        ISBN 978-1-55728-923-0 (cloth : alk. paper)
        1. People with disabilities—Housing—United States. 2. People with
disabilities—Dwellings—United States. 3. Housing policy—United States.
4. Home ownership—United States. I. Webb, Jennifer, 1964–   II. Williams,
Brent T., 1964– III. Title.
        HV1569.2.U5S65   2009
        363.5'9870973—dc22

                                                    2009040549

The research and production of this book was supported in part by the Arkansas Universal Design Project (AUDP). The AUDP was funded in part by P.L. 108-364, the Technology Related Assistance for Individuals with Disabilities Act of 2004 under the auspices of the Increasing Capabilities Access Network of the Arkansas Department of Workforce Education, Rehabilitation Services Division (ARS), via grant H224A890020–04 from the U.S. Department of Education, Rehabilitation Services Administration (RSA). The AUDP was also supported by the Arkansas Department of Human Services (ADHS) and the University of Arkansas for Medical Sciences (UAMS), Partners for Inclusive Communities. The contents of this document do not necessarily reflect the views of ARS, RSA, ADHS, or UAMS; and the contents do not imply endorsement by the U.S. Government. The views expressed herein are those of the authors and do not necessarily reflect the official policies of the sponsoring agencies. Likewise, the guidance provided in this document does not supersede local, state, or national laws, codes, or regulations. It is the responsibility of the individuals utilizing this document to ensure compliance with all local, state, and national laws, codes, and regulations. The authors, contributors, sponsors, and publisher of this document are not liable for any claims for any special, direct, indirect, or consequential damages, including loss of revenue or profit, loss of opportunity, personal or bodily injury, or any other actual or perceived losses.

CONTENTS

We tend to look at issues of design of housing from the perspective of our own disciplines and professions, but barriers between these social worlds obscure our understanding of reality. By breaking down the "silo effect" and using a regional perspective as a lens, the authors of this book present a cogent and powerful argument on the importance of understanding the relationship between housing policy and housing design. They illustrate how housing and health are intertwined and how federal policy plays out differently from region to region due to cultural, historical, and geographic differences. And, by simultaneously taking a phenomenological perspective, they demonstrate the importance of understanding how the home is not only a reflection of self but also shapes the opportunities that people have to manage the presentation of self to others.

The concept of universal design emerged in the design fields from criticism of the "barrier-free design" paradigm. Leaders in this field recognized that the goals espoused in barrier-free design were universal goals. They asked, "Doesn't everyone want a more accessible, convenient, and safer environment?" And, if the world were designed to meet these universal needs, wouldn't people with disabilities benefit more than if only minimal conditions needed to eliminate discrimination for one group of citizens were addressed? Couldn't the principles behind barrier-free design be applied on a larger scale? Furthermore, they argued, if everyone benefited from improved design, wouldn't there be a much greater constituency for better design? In other words, the design goals for persons with disabilities are goals that are relevant for all citizens. This has prompted, over a period of ten to fifteen years, a growing worldwide movement. The authors take a critical perspective on these questions and ask if, in fact, they make sense and how the answers may play out within a regional context. This results in a more sophisticated argument and the identification of a broader agenda for this nascent field.

Rather than a one-size-fits-all concept, universal design is about providing universal benefits in ways that respond to the diversity of the human population. It is a way of thinking that can be applied in many contexts but should reflect the unique characteristics of place and culture. In many ways, Arkansas is a good proving ground to test the value of the universal design paradigm and how it gets played out in a regional context. Demographic indicators demonstrate that Arkansas has an older population than the United States as a whole, more people receiving social security disability payments, and a higher poverty rate. While viewed from one perspective, this seems like the state is behind the rest of the country. Viewed another way, however, it is a state that is *ahead* of the country in at least two ways. Projections show that the rest of the country will eventually catch up with Arkansas in terms of aging population and social security disability recipients. The high rate of poverty and the age of the population together not only demand action but also present a challenging context in which to test the assumptions of inclusive design. Using Arkansas as a case study can help us understand how context influences the implementation of universal design on one hand, and what lessons can be learned to improve the universal design paradigm on the other.

As the reader will find, the authors broaden our understanding of universal design to include two new dimensions: self-determination and health. They approach the subject from the multidisciplinary field of environment and behavior studies in housing. This literature demonstrates that housing both provides and constrains the opportunities for self-determination and also determines social identity. Thus, someone who has to relocate from an independent free-standing home where they have lived for most, if not all, of their adult life to "housing for the elderly," due to the inaccessibility of the former gives up a symbol of independence and self-reliance, losing, perhaps a piece of themselves. Likewise, the need to modify a house with limited funds and technical knowledge results in an awkward and ugly solution that stigmatizes the resident. Change in health status, whether related to aging or not, is not easily accommodated by contemporary housing design. But, does this have to be the case? In the design of housing, it is possible to anticipate health needs across the life span and incorporate features that would support independent living without compromising self-determination and social identity.

In looking to the future, the authors identify a paradox inherent in universal design. On one hand, universal design is intended to benefit all. On the other, it tends to be associated with disability due to the incorporation of features that address the real needs of persons with disabilities; for example, ramps and grab bars. So, universal design seeks to promote liberation from the stigma of disability but its practice often brings more attention to it. The authors argue, therefore, that it is not enough that we change our built environment to address the realities of disability, we need to change our perspective on disability as well. Disability is generally viewed as a health issue and is addressed primarily through health policy and services. They argue that the separation of health and housing policy amounts to a false choice. Rather, the two are closely related. Without accessible housing, the options for delivery of health services are constrained.

Rethinking disability as a universal experience will lead to a different view of the role of housing. In fact, it is not very difficult to see that disability is merely part of a continuum of functioning and that all people experience the full range of this continuum through their life span. Some of us may spend more time at one end than another, but there is no way to predict when, if, and how long we will find ourselves at any point. If we conceive housing policies and designs that support function along the entire length of the continuum, design for disability and its related stigma doesn't even enter into the equation. We are simply designing for a range of functional needs, for all of us. In fact, recent studies indicate that there is a one in four chance that at least one person with a mobility impairment will live in every new house over the course of its life span. So, there is good evidence to put this way of thinking into practice. Academics and practitioners both complain that no one listens to them. There will always be a gulf between theory and practice. Theory is an exercise in detached perception that comes from studying things with psychological distance. Practice is dominated by the demands to get on with things and live with the constraints of familiar modes of behavior. They are not mutually exclusive enterprises but it requires some effort to bring them together. Sometimes academics come along who are willing to listen. The authors of this book want to help bring theory into practice. Rather than imposing the "one best way" on policy makers, developers, and designers, they ventured out into their communities and studied them well. The extensive photographs of the Arkansas rural landscape demonstrate how seriously they have immersed themselves in the actuality of housing conditions in the state. They concluded that there are many ways to address the problems they found and they developed concrete strategies for doing so that make sense in the real world.

Through this book, they build a bridge from theory to practice, showing us how theory can contribute to practical solutions in the real world.

Perhaps the most unusual aspect of this book is how the authors incorporated design exploration as an important part of the argument. The prototypical houses included in the book show that it is possible to use universal design as a foundation to reinterpret the vernacular of the region and produce handsome, dignified dwellings that support changes in health status and their related social adjustments. Moreover, the attention given to affordability and sustainable design practices demonstrates that universal design in housing is not only realistic but can be integrated with other important contemporary design goals. The prototypes are convincing in their detail and presentation method. They demonstrate that the limitations of current policies and design practices are not insurmountable. In fact, they demonstrate that, with creative thinking, the paradox of universal design can be overcome. They embody the premise that redefining disability as a universal experience can lead to solutions that are both innovative and rooted in regional values that connote sense of place and belongingness with a cultural tradition.

Policy initiatives and design practices must address these fundamental experiences of dwelling to be effective in meeting real needs; otherwise, they simply create new barriers to the experience of domestic life or perpetuate obsolete approaches. We need to understand both the big picture and the details. We need to understand theory as well as practical matters. We need to learn how to understand the vernacular and its limitations and how to transition from that to a new vision that is still rooted in the culture of a region. Thus the idea inherent in this book, that region matters greatly, is a lesson that others all over the world can learn from and emulate. Universal does not mean that choices and differences are not valued. Rather, it means that choices and differences are valued even more.

EDWARD STEINFELD
Professor of Architecture
Director, IDEA Center
University at Buffalo

ACKNOWLEDGMENTS

The authors want to acknowledge several supporters of this work. First, thanks go to Arkansas Rehabilitation Services, the Arkansas Department of Human Services, and the UAMS Partners for Inclusive Communities for their sponsorship of the Arkansas Universal Design Project, which assisted in the research and publication of this book. Likewise, our gratitude goes to Jeff Shannon, dean of the Fay Jones School of Architecture at the University of Arkansas, for his support throughout this project. We also want to thank Zack Cooley, Cari Paulus, Rachel Smith, Matt Hagler, and Noah Updegraf, graduates of the Fay Jones School of Architecture, for their contributions to contents of this book. Their assistance with photography, design, and production, as well as providing keen, critical feedback, was most valuable. Thanks also go to Debbie Self for her thorough editing of this manuscript. Lastly, we want to thank our spouses, families, and friends for their critical advice, poignant witticisms, and tenacious encouragement during our work on this book.

Johnny Cash's Boyhood Home
in Dyess, Arkansas.

INTRODUCTION

Just Below the Line: Housing and Marginalization in the South

KORYDON H. SMITH, BRENT T. WILLIAMS, AND JENNIFER WEBB

I come from just the other side of nowhere,
To this big time lonesome town.
I've seen about enough to know where I'll bound.
Give my best to anyone who's left who ever done me,
Any lovin' way but wrong,
And tell 'em that the pride of just the other side
of nowhere's goin' home.

> —JOHNNY CASH, *country singer and native Arkansan,*
> *excerpts from the 2003 release of "Just the*
> *Other Side of Nowhere" (original lyrics by*
> *Kris Kristofferson, native Texan)* [1]

With the first wave of baby-boomers entering retirement in 2008, significant media focus has been placed on healthcare, retirement financing, and creating leisure activities for retirees. Simultaneously, an equal amount of press has been given to the economic slump and deceleration in housing production over the first decade of the twenty-first century. Relatively little attention, however, has been paid to the social and economic effects that the more than seventy million aging boomers and more than fifty million people with disabilities will have on the housing in the United States. Compared to the previous generation, it is expected that baby-boomers will live longer after retirement, will seek out widely varying housing designs upon retirement, and will be more outspoken regarding their preferences. The largest percentage of boomers will live in states throughout the South. Upper-income boomers will have the greatest access to choices in both healthcare and housing, while middle- and lower-income boomers will have far fewer options, especially in the rural South. The lack of suitable housing has become a glaring dilemma in the South and will fast become acutely problematic throughout the United States over the coming decades if housing policies and practices are not relined.

The problem is not merely an issue of an aging society, though the baby-boomer cohort exemplifies the dilemma. A "perfect storm" has emerged. The rate of disability continues to soar, while the rate of housing construction to meet these demands falls. At a time when many boomers would be trading in their lifelong residences for both a smaller home and a profit, housing values have plunged and retirement savings have dwindled. Likewise, the historic economic downturn of the early twenty-first century has highlighted the affordable housing crisis for people with disabilities. In the South, the situation is most severe.

First, the residual effects of Hurricane Katrina are not yet fully realized. There was a pervasive and well-publicized incidence of poverty and disability among New Orleans's Katrina victims.[2] Despite the fact that much of this population has been disbursed throughout other impoverished areas of the South, the primary spotlight remains on New Orleans. Little attention has been given to states such as Arkansas and Alabama who have absorbed thousands of Katrina victims, further stretching already strained healthcare and housing systems.

Second, the Southern region maintains both the greatest total population and the highest rate of population increase.[3] The United States has seen several eras of migration throughout its history. The initial push was to the West, with the proclamation of "manifest destiny." The Great Migration during the first half of the twentieth century, on the other hand, resulted in large numbers of rural Southern African Americans moving to industrial cities in the North in search of greater social, political, and financial freedom. The current era is also proving to possess significant migration trends, as Northerners and Midwesterners seek a more hospitable economy and climate in the South. The notion of "moving to a better place" parallels the dreams sought by the mass nomadic culture of the Great Depression, in which there was no specific destination, simply a search of a better place than the last.

Third, a large percentage of Southerners live in rural areas. Rural America has less variety in employment, lower wages, and less access to educational opportunities. Rural areas possess fewer housing options, inadequate or nonexistent public transportation, and few readily available amenities (e.g., shopping, healthcare, and entertainment). Poverty and the lack of services exacerbate many problems for persons with disabilities living in rural areas.

Millions of U.S. residents remain dependent upon state and federal resources, because little focus has been placed on the role of housing. The primary focus still remains on health services and medical intervention. The current support system relies heavily on nursing home care and various forms of assisted living. This type of living environment is problematic for two reasons: cost and perceived quality of life. Nursing home care is more than double that of in-home care. Estimates suggest that, by 2030, one-third of the U.S. gross domestic product will be spent on healthcare costs, largely contributable to expenditures for assistive housing facilities. In 1985, Medicaid expenditures for nursing home care were $14.7 billion. In 1998, nursing home care cost Medicaid $40.6 billion. Nursing home care now costs the federal government more than $150 billion annually.[4] These costs will continue to rise without adequate housing solutions. In the United Kingdom, research has shown that supportive services for independent living are 30 to 40 percent cheaper than assistive living costs. In addition, the majority of people worldwide perceive a decreased quality of living associated with nursing home life. Not surprisingly, people who live independently in the community affirm higher life satisfaction than people living in nursing homes.[5]

Although independent and assisted living have been touted as less costly and more affable alternatives to nursing homes, the design and construction of affordable, accessible housing remains the greatest barrier to independence. The housing and healthcare dilemma is exacerbated in the South for several reasons. The South maintains the highest percentage and number of people in poverty; the South has the highest percentage and number of persons with disabilities; and the South holds the largest and fastest-growing population of retirees. Age is the greatest predictor of disability. Fifty-three percent of U.S. residents age sixty-five and up live with at least one disability, while only 19 percent of residents ages fourteen to sixty-four and 9 percent of residents ages birth to fourteen have a disability.[6] By 2030, the number of people in the South that are sixty-five and older will double, which will result in a large increase in the number of persons with disabilities. The same is true across the United States. Developing housing that supports the needs of this population will be crucial, especially when considering that more than

85 percent of the (noninstitutionalized) older adult population in the United States lives alone or with a spouse (usually of similar age).[7] The trend of living alone will continue, while "fewer family caregivers for aging baby boomers could have large *proportional* effects on the demand for" housing alternatives.[8]

There is an urgent need to transform both national housing policies and local housing practices. "One of the government's biggest tasks in the new millennium will be an extensive education campaign to increase awareness of the wide range of alternatives to nursing homes."[9] Just as the concept of "green building" ("sustainability") emerged from a growing awareness of environmental concerns, the concepts of "barrier-free design," "universal design," "life-span design," and "inclusive design" have emerged from the perceived need to create environments and products that are usable by people across a broad spectrum of abilities. Many local and national building codes have been transformed to align with these environmental and social movements. Yet these concepts—"sustainability" and "universal design"—have not had broad impacts in housing policy, design, and construction; policy makers, designers, and builders have been slow to adapt. There is a need for a more comprehensive, holistic, inclusive approach to housing, quite simply: a need for better design.

Good design is ergonomic. Good design is aesthetically beautiful. Good design is affordable. Good design is efficient. Good design is environmentally responsible. Good design is socially responsive and recognizes diversity. Good design goes far beyond the mere provision of special features for marginalized segments of the population. Good design is creative in its effort to be more inclusive and comprehensive to the variety of needs and preferences of society. Designs resulting from this approach serve a wider array of people, including children, ethnic minorities, older adults, and persons with disabilities, establishing a better "fit" between a family and their home, between an individual and her/his community.

Johnny Cash, "The Man in Black," was popularly known by his all-black garb, Arkansas brogue, and sober-yet-catchy bass-baritone libretto. These outward characteristics, however, were simply extensions of Cash's life experiences, underscored by the duality—the pride and angst—of growing up in rural Arkansas and other areas of the South. Like "The Man in Black," the South is characterized by many diverse and deeper things. The importance of family and hard work, value in spirituality, a warm social

Modified Home Entry. The prevalence of disability in the South commonly results in ad-hoc ramp solutions.

and environmental climate, and the affirmation of cultural history—counterbalanced by prevalent rural poverty, racial tension, and a reliance on convention and the status quo—are often ascribed to the region south of the Mason-Dixon Line. These ephemeral traits are made visible in the housing across the South. The various sizes, shapes, colors, and styles of Southern housing articulate these lines of division—between black and white, between "abled" and "disabled," and between the "haves" and the "have-nots." Country music, much like country housing, serves as physical evidence of otherwise invisible ideological forces, racial attitudes, political jurisdictions and motives, economic states, and personal values, needs, and desires. A house is a billboard.

Housing design and construction, nonetheless, is a deceptively complex enterprise (see Appendix 1); the economic, sociological, technological, and environmental factors affecting housing design and construction are diverse and interrelated, further complicated by an increasingly diverse population with a widening range of needs and preferences and by the increased focus on equitable, just housing. Extraordinary demographic trends (e.g., the aging baby-boom generation and the increase in single-parent families), the lack of housing that fits the impending physical and psychosocial needs of the population (e.g., privacy, status, self-expression), and the housing industry's reliance on convention and inability to adapt quickly is resulting in a nationwide crisis. This dilemma is most apparent in the South, where there is a severe disjunction between the demographic makeup of the South and the housing stock available.

As such, in *Just Below the Line,* we explore this largely

overlooked predicament in housing. We seek to reveal the hidden issues that affect housing in the South, illustrate the urgent need to transform the culture of housing in this region, and provide solutions to the needs of an increasingly diverse population. For the reasons outlined below, Johnny Cash's home state of Arkansas is used throughout this book as a case study. U.S. census data, for example, reveal that of the ten states with the highest percentage of residents with disabilities, seven are also among the top ten in poverty rate. Arkansas makes that list. All but one county in Arkansas exceeds the national average in percentage of residents with disabilities.[10] Arkansas has the third highest disability rate,[11] highest rate of poverty, highest rate of increase in poverty,[12] seventh highest percentage of residents sixty and older, and the fifth highest percentage of Social Security recipients.[13] Arkansas is the only state in the union among the top seven in all of these categories.

As unique as Arkansas may seem, however, it is illustrative of national trends, a demographic exemplar of the United States in 2015. Because of the rapid rate of construction, growing number of persons with disabilities, and high percentage of older residents, Arkansas is a fertile ground for investigating current social trends and proposing solutions to the state's, region's, and nation's housing needs. If you can solve the housing crisis here, you can solve it anywhere. The South, in general, is worth a deeper look.

Arkansas and the South: Stereotypes and Realities

Arkansas holds some of the highest rates of disability, poverty, and aging in the country. This is not new. Yet the state may be most known for being the punch line of any number of redneck, back-woods, hick, or chawbacon jokes across the country, not only ranking number one in poverty but also topping out the charts in Leno and Letterman jokes (or so it appears). Arkansas is not a place to go, but a place to flee. According to Ray Charles, raised in the panhandle of Florida, if you "don't do right," they "send you back to Arkansas."[14] Arkansas seemingly typifies the mind's eye of the South: rural and agrarian, poor and languid, racially segregated, and conservative. But to what extent are these conceptions true? What is the difference between North and South, between Northerners and Southerners? Commensurately, what is the common ground? Why, more than seven score after Gettysburg, is America still preoccupied by the supposed chasm of the Mason-Dixon Line?

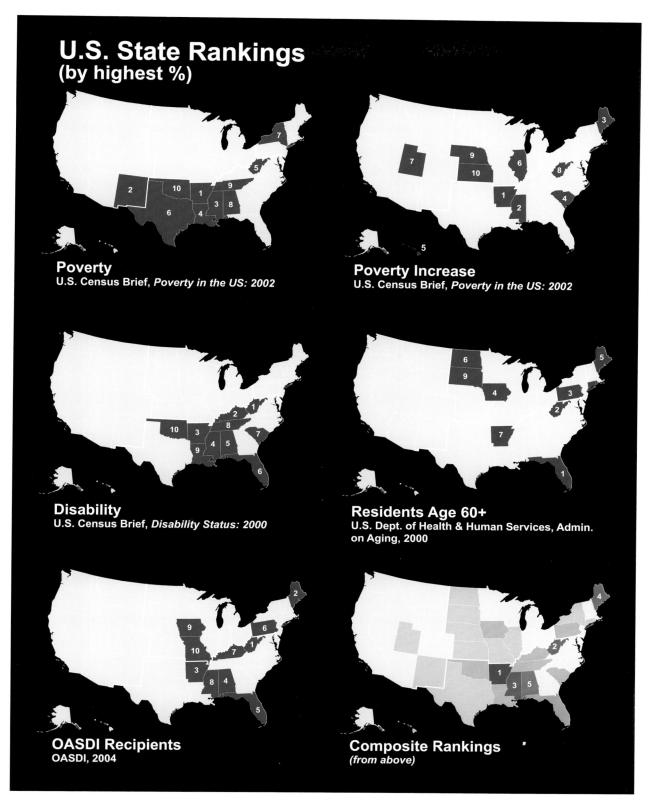

U.S. State Rankings
(by highest %)

Poverty
U.S. Census Brief, *Poverty in the US: 2002*

Poverty Increase
U.S. Census Brief, *Poverty in the US: 2002*

Disability
U.S. Census Brief, *Disability Status: 2000*

Residents Age 60+
U.S. Dept. of Health & Human Services, Admin. on Aging, 2000

OASDI Recipients
OASDI, 2004

Composite Rankings
(from above)

Poverty, Poverty Increase, Disability, Age, OASDI Status, and Composite Rankings by State. There is a high concentration of poverty and disability in the South and Arkansas.

According to the author and humorist Roy Blount Jr., "the North isn't a place . . . It's just a direction out of the South."[15] The sociologist John Shelton Reed defines the South as "that part of the country where the people think they are Southerners."[16] Both definitions illustrate the slipperiness of delineating the boundaries and characteristics of each region. The longitudinal studies on Southern identity conducted by Reed do shed further light, however. According to Reed's work, there are definitive differences in the political, racial, familial, and religious attitudes of Southerners versus non-Southerners. For example, Reed found, in 1987, that white Southerners most characterized themselves as "tradition loving," "courteous," and having "loyal ties to family," while the same group characterized white Northerners as "aggressive," "materialistic," and "loud."[17] This aligns with many conventional definitions of Southerners and Northerners. Likewise, in 1958, a Gallup survey revealed that 72 percent of white Southerners objected to sending their children "to a school where [a few] of the children are colored/Negroes/black," compared with 13 percent of residents of the non-South. By 1980, however, the distinction in attitudes had been erased, as only 5 percent of both Southerners and non-Southerners voiced objections.[18] In many ways, the schism that characterized the division of a "South" and a "North"—racial ideology—has evaporated, but other distinctions may still exist.

The renowned Southern historian James Cobb sums up the Southern stereotype of hospitality as such: "Never miss an opportunity to host a brunch and remember that a meal without cheese grits or a broccoli casserole is like a liquor cabinet without Jack Daniels or Maker's Mark."[19] Nevertheless, Cobb later states "that this obsession with idiom and idiosyncrasy threatens to turn the South of popular perception into nothing more than a home-grown caricature of itself"[20] and that "this may seem no more serious than going to a costume party dressed as Gomer Pyle or Scarlett O'Hara. The problem here is that complex and often unwieldy identities are being reduced to trendy and attractive lifestyles which, if not exactly up for grabs, are certainly up for sale."[21] This is exemplified by the growing popularity of NASCAR, born in the South and exported to the rest of the country. The important lesson here is that the South is "a mirror in which the nation can see its blemishes magnified."[22]

Population 65 and Over: US and Arkansas

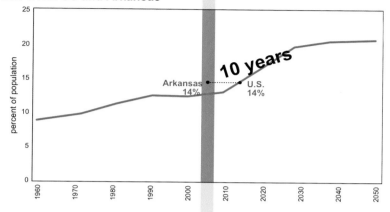

OASDI Recipients: US and Arkansas

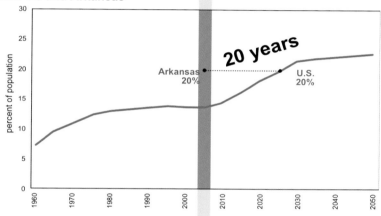

Poverty Rates: US and Arkansas

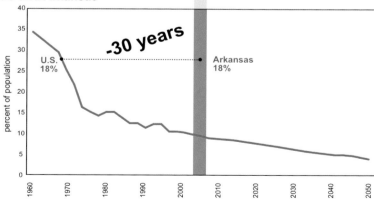

Comparison of Arkansas
and U.S. in Age, OASDI,
and Poverty Trends.

Those very qualities long attributed to the South as special possessions are, in truth, *American* qualities, and the nation reacts emotionally to the South precisely because it subconsciously recognizes itself there . . . Because the South embarrasses us, we try to disown it, apologize for it, hold it at a distance.[23]

The imageries of the South—whether accurate reality, exaggerated truths, or outsiders' perceptions—illuminate only a small, homogonous tract of Southern culture, for nowhere is the complexity of identity more evident than in the South. Southern identity is multivalent and contradictory, evident in both the momentous and the mundane aspects of the cultures found there.

Though Roy Blount Jr. asserts, "They don't have live bait / video stores in the North,"[24] we assure you that they do. It is as if saying, "they don't have rednecks in the North." Anyone who has grown up or traveled in the rural Northeast has seen plenty of evidence to the contrary. The reader may ask, "Why are you using Arkansas as the center of the discourse?" We could answer, as a variation on a Waylon Jennings joke, "Well, that's where Jesus was born, isn't it?"[25] But the reason we are looking at Arkansas is both because of its idiosyncratic reputation and its universality. Arkansas has great poverty and great wealth; Arkansas contains areas of racial diversity and areas of homogeneity; Arkansas possesses both a rolling landscape and a flat landscape, areas of urbanity, suburbia, and rural living. As hard as it may be for some to stomach, Arkansas is America.

Structure of This Book

Just Below the Line is divided into two major parts: "Part 1: Toeing the Line" and "Part 2: Redrawing the Line." Part 1 outlines the major sociological, economic, environmental, and technological factors that impact housing and disability in the South. Part 2 proposes solutions to meeting the current and impending housing needs of the South.

Part 1: "Toeing the Line"

The popular, scholarly, and legal definitions of "disability" have changed dramatically over the past four decades. As such, chapter 1, "Definitions of Disability," utilizes existing disability classification systems as a foundation for discussing cultural- and self-perceptions of persons with disabilities in the South. The author also introduces the notion that health and ability are transforma-

Southern Icons. The home expresses both belonging and autonomy.

tional and discusses the economic and sociological challenges encountered by persons with disabilities. The discourse on disability and identity introduced in chapter 1 is then broadened in chapter 2, "Definitions of Home," to explore the interrelationships between individuals and the built environment. This includes discussions on the multiple definitions and scales of home and the role that homes and communities play in extending, transforming, or subjugating personal identity and choice. Chapter 3, "Definitions of Equality," draws parallels and discusses differences between race-based and disability-based discrimination and equality. Changing perceptions of disability have resulted in numerous changes to wellness services, employment, and environmental design, as well as the legal structures that underpin them. In addition, the author discusses the interrelationship between legal statutes and social mores, as well as how legal and cultural changes impact housing and residents in the South. Chapter 4, "Definitions of Policy and Practice," reveals the impacts that legislative policies and home-building traditions have on Southern residents, especially persons living in poverty with disabilities. The construction industry—especially single-family housing construction—is grounded upon shared conventions of building and is

KORYDON H. SMITH, BRENT T. WILLIAMS, AND JENNIFER WEBB   xxiii often slow to respond to technological advances or social change. As a result, the single-family housing industry is a "culture" in itself, separate from (though not without significant influence on) the culture that it serves.

Part 2: "Redrawing the Line"

The second part of this book proposes solutions to the aforementioned issues regarding disability and housing in the South. The chapters of part 2 parallel those of part 1. Chapter 5, "Redefining Disability," utilizes previous theories regarding the relationship between person and environment to examine the continuum of human functioning and the diversity of environmental attributes. A new model for understanding the dynamic range of person-environment fit is presented. Chapter 6: Redefining Home discusses the transformation of "accessibility" and "barrier-free design" and the emergence of "universal design." This chapter discusses both the benefits and criticisms of "universal design" and makes the argument for a change in both terminology and thinking. In "Redefining Equality," chapter 7, the authors propose a series of single- and multifamily housing prototypes that are both site specific and inclusively designed. The authors outline the major site factors that influence housing design and illustrates how standardized prototypes can be deployed in a variety of topographic, climatic, cultural, and economic settings. Chapter 8, "Redefining Policy and Practice," discusses the major transformations that have occurred in housing policy throughout the past half century and the effects of these policy changes. The authors provide recommendations for future housing policy at the national level and how to influence housing practices at the local level. We conclude the book with a set of primary recommendations. In addition, we have provided a set of appendices and encourage the reader to review these appendices before and during the reading of this book.

Just Below the Line

The line that separates North and South, like the line that separates terms, is not a straight line running east-west. Instead, it is a line that is curving and broken, a smudge, thin at times, thick at others. The line dividing poverty and wealth, ability and disability, black and white is much the same. It is hard to locate—swerving, fuzzy, arbitrary, sometimes invisible. W. E. B. DuBois, in "The Forethought" to his famed *The Souls of Black Folk,* published at the dawn of the then-new century, stated that "the problem of the

Nowhere Road. The paradoxical South is (a) isolated and idiosyncratic and (b) representative of American history and trends. The South is both "nowhere" and "everywhere."

Twentieth Century is the problem of the color-line."[26] Here, at the dawn of the new millennium, we are arguing that the problem of the twenty-first century is the problem of the disability line. Regardless of what idiom we use—"poverty line," "race line," "familial line," "luck line," "battle line," "bottom line," "out of line," or Cash's "walk the line"—the importance of dignity, of dignified housing, is universal in America.

The American Dream is a slippery and complex concept to define; yet if anything exemplifies the fulfillment of this concept, it is the attainment of the American Dream Home. The average American moves every five years. In parallel, according the National Association of Home Builders, Americans spent $215 billion in 2005 on home renovation projects. These statistics exemplify the relentless pursuit of fulfilling the Dream, of achieving an ideal fit between the design of one's actual home and the mind's eye image of the Dream Home. A bigger home or a smaller home; a home in the city, country, or 'burbs; a newer home or older home; a home closer to work or school; shinier and brighter, or more rustic; more modern or less modern; a big lawn, a small garden, or a view of the park: size, shape, style, cost, performance, and "location-location-location" all affect home-buying and home-renting decisions.

Housing has romantically been seen as the purest creative domain and most unencumbered expression of the architect, designer, builder, or do-it-yourselfer; and it is the attainment of the Dream Home that remains an essential milestone for the realization of the American Dream. Popular television—*Trading Spaces, Town Haul, While You Were Out,* and *Trading Spaces: Family*

(TLC), *Extreme Makeover: Home Edition* (ABC), *Monster House* (Discovery), and various programs on HGTV—has reinforced this mindset. But the phrase *Dream Home* is a misnomer, a marketing strategy of politicians and the real estate and construction industries. In most cases, the Dream Home is never achieved. Seldom, if ever, does a homeowner (or renter) find his/her dream house; he/she settles for an approximation of it. Constrained by parameters of location and cost, the buyer/renter negotiates numerous factors in addition to aesthetic and functional preferences and available choices. As a result, Americans are constantly transforming their homes and themselves, attempting to more closely align one's image of home with one's physical home, inevitably changing both the Dream and the reality.

In order to provide housing solutions with a broad impact for middle- and lower-income boomers, it is critical to understand both the physical needs and the housing preferences of this exemplary cohort. Although "accessibility" will be central to housing and residential care planning, it will not be the only issue. The diverse psychosocial needs, attitudes, and preferences of boomers illustrate the necessity for a wider range of housing solutions. The example of aging boomers merely highlights the needs that already exist in the rural South. Social and environmental isolation is a significant dilemma for families confronting disabilities and/or poverty. Inclusive housing design is one step. Neighborhood and community design—access to employment, services, transportation, and recreation—also need to be considered. Housing design for persons with disabilities is not merely an issue of pragmatism, of doorway widths, grab bars, and sink heights (although these are essential); housing design is not merely about the technical or economic act of building. Housing is also about identity. Arguably the foundational component of identity is dignity. Without dignity, the greater development of a person's character cannot mature; and true independence is unachievable without it. Homes provide protection and enable people to accomplish tasks necessary to their personal, familial, and social needs. Homes are also a reflection of culture, geographic location, and status. Some spatial functions may be reallocated, walls can be painted, temperature can be adjusted, and personal objects can be displayed, but the home may still fall short in many ways. If the home does not allow physical access or one cannot bathe independently, the resident will be dissatisfied. If the home does not allow appropriate separation and connection of public and private spaces, a person may not be able to practice his/her religion. If the home is separated from its neighbors by several miles, individuals may feel isolated if accustomed to interacting with their community, friends, or relatives. In each of these cases, the home does not "fit" the person.

Every individual has a unique set of variables that include things such as age, gender, abilities and disabilities, culture, geographic origin, and past experiences. Each of these variables determines how comfortable someone will be in a particular setting. *Just Below the Line* seeks to define these variables, including disability, and examine them in the context of the South. The purpose is to provide readers with a better understanding of why good design is important, why design often does not suit people's needs, and how "fit" can be achieved between an individual and her/his home and community. The overarching goal of this book is to enable policy makers, housing designers, home builders, realtors, advocates, and consumers to increase their focus on the demographic make-up south of the Mason-Dixon Line and their consequences on creating equitable housing. We seek to understand both definitions of the term "just." This book seeks to grasp what it means to live *"just below the line"* and what it means to make housing *"just,* below the line."

Toeing the Line

Defining Disability

BRENT T. WILLIAMS

Call me whatever you want . . . I don't care . . . somebody
probably will. All I want is to be included, to have the same
opportunities everybody else has. It's not about labels, it's
about dignity.

—STEVE WILSON, *when asked by a local television reporter
about his reaction to his community's recent declaration of
nondiscrimination for the "crippled" and the "handicapped"*[1]

The complex nature of defining and understanding disability is
captured in Johnny Cash's remembrances of his childhood
friend Pete:

> Pete was an inspiration in more ways than one. I'd never been
> close to somebody playing the guitar except my mother when
> I was very small, and I thought he was the best guitar player
> in the world. To me he was wonderful, the sound he made
> purely heavenly. One day I said to him, "You know, Pete,
> you've got infantile paralysis, but you sure can play that gui-
> tar." His reply made a deep impression on me: "Sometimes,
> when you lose a gift, you get another one." From then on I
> didn't think of him as a cripple; I thought of him as having a
> gift. It hurt me when the other kids made fun of him. They'd
> see him hobbling the two or three miles from his house in
> town, and they'd start imitating him. I imitated him, too, of
> course, but not that way: he's where I got my guitar style,
> playing rhythm and leading with my thumb. Pete was crazy
> for music the way I was—he was the first person I knew who
> was that way—and we were both crazy for the radio.[2]

Johnny Cash described Pete paradoxically as "crippled" and
"gifted." The nature of Pete's disability, "infantile paralysis," is
the predominant characteristic through which Johnny initially
understands and relates to Pete. However, as John came to know
Pete better, he ceased to regard Pete as disabled, but as talented,

even gifted. Though the evolution of how Johnny came to regard Pete is itself inspiring, perhaps nothing is more telling than Johnny's description of Pete as being crazy for music, "he was the first person I knew who was that way—and we were both crazy for the radio."[3] In this description, John no longer describes Pete in terms of his disability or along a continuum of crippled or gifted. Here, Pete is understood in terms of his sameness to John: their mutual love of music. Johnny Cash, as do most of us, at some level understood disability, particularly with regard to Pete, in terms of a vague intersection of physical and social variables.

Over recent decades there has been growing recognition that our awareness of social issues is influenced by the concepts and language we use. For most people, the meaning of disability would seem to be clear and simple: It means "the inability to do something." However, in disability and social science as in design and architectural discourses, there is no consensus on what constitutes disability. There are no commonly accepted ways to define disability. Disability has been subject to many definitions in different disciplines. It has been described from medical, sociological, and political perspectives, and definitions of disability have been developed and used in different contexts for very different agendas.

Part of the difficulty in defining disability is that disability is a complicated, multidimensional concept. Because of the extensive variety of the nature of a disability, a universal definition of disability that fits all circumstances, though very desirable, is in reality nearly impossible. Attempts have been made to define disability with simple statements, classification schemes, and even through different forms of measurement. This has contributed to the confusion and misuse of disability terms and definitions, particularly when measures of disabilities are interpreted and used as definitions.[4] Defining disability is not simply an exercise; alternate definitions of disability can have far-reaching social, economic, and political implications.

Disability Models

The development of theoretical models designed to clarify and define disability has been driven by this vagueness. Theoretical models and the ensuing debates about the nature of disability have, however, been predominantly characterized by perspectives that view the body and society as separate spheres of human existence. In particular, disability theories have tended to

Disability Signifier 1. The wheelchair is the stereotypical signifier of disability and underscores the problems of conventional housing design.

revolve around the dichotomy of medical and social models of disability. Medical models rely on a conception of disability where biology is at the root of impairment. Social models define disability as a construct through which society oppresses, or at the most benign level, marginalizes, persons with disabilities. Both models, while capturing aspects of the lives of persons with disabilities, are incomplete and fail to recognize that biological, psychological, and social variables are entwined in an inextricable, dynamic relationship.

Medical Models

The medical model considers disability a problem of the individual that is directly caused by a disease, an injury, or some other health condition and requires medical care in the form of treatment and rehabilitation. The medical model attributes the problem to the individual, who has a condition that is unwanted and that places him or her in the "sick role."[5] "If a person has a permanent impairment which results in using a wheelchair to move around, that person will never get 'well.'"[6] This model is strongly normative: people are considered disabled on the

Disability Signifier 2. The limitations of adaptive technology and reliance on the medical model results in social isolation.

basis of being unable to function as a "normal" person does. Rehabilitation has an important role to play in bringing the person back or close to the norm. The major concern of the medical model at the political level is to provide healthcare and rehabilitation services. This model has been criticized on different grounds, including its normative focus.

Social Models

The medical model is often referred to as the old paradigm and stands in contrast to the social model of disability. In general, social models see disability as a social construct.[7] Disability is not the attribute of the individual; instead, it is created by the social environment and the mitigation of disability requires social change. Disability activists in the Union of the Physically Impaired Against Segregation (UPIAS) developed the United Kingdom social model, at the heart of which lies the concept of societal oppression. The core definition of the British social model comes in the UPIAS document *Fundamental Principles of Disability:* "In our view, it is society which disables physically impaired people. Disability is something imposed on top of our impairments by the way we are unnecessarily isolated and excluded from full participation in society."[8] The United Kingdom social model is quite Marxist in its view of disability, a view not often found in the United States.

The second version of the social model, that of the oppressed minority, says that persons with disabilities face discrimination and segregation through sensory, attitudinal, cognitive, physical, and economic barriers, and their experiences are therefore perceived as similar to those of an oppressed minority group. The marginalization experienced by persons with disabilities is similar to that encountered by other disenfranchised groups, such as high rates of unemployment and poverty; inadequate education, transportation and housing; and exclusion from many community activities.[9]

Biopsychosocial Models

Drawing the overall picture of disability models is not as simple as presenting a dichotomy between a medical model and a social model. There are other models that have developed on their own, as extensions of the medical or the social model or as integrations of the two. In the following section, two of these models are discussed: (1) the Nagi model, which has wielded substantial influence for the last three decades at the policy-making level in the United States and in the economics of disability in general, and (2) the recent International Classification of Functioning, Disability and Health of the World Health Organization, the worldwide scope of which gives this model a strong potential role in global policy development in the years ahead.

The biopsychosocial models attempt to integrate the medical and social models of disability. In the biopsychosocial model, disability is viewed as an interaction of biological, personal, and social forces. The interactions among these various factors result in disability. The biopsychosocial model of disability represents the dominant perspective behind contemporary definitions of disability in use today.

Nagi Model

Nagi's model has its origins in the early 1960s as part of a study of disability commissioned for the Social Security Administration and in his work on concepts and issues related to rehabilitation. Nagi constructed a model that differentiated among four distinct, yet related, phenomena that he considered basic to the field of rehabilitation. He referred to these as active pathology, impairment, functional limitation, and disability. This conceptual model has become known as the Nagi model.[10]

For Nagi, active pathology involves the interruption of normal cellular processes and the simultaneous homeostatic efforts of the organism to regain a normal state. Examples of active pathology are the cellular disturbances consistent with disease processes such as arthritis or stroke. For Nagi, impairment refers to a loss or abnormality at the tissue, organ, and body system level. Active pathology usually results in some type of impairment, such as the impairments associated with spinal cord injury or amputation.[11]

At the level of the individual, Nagi uses the term functional limitations to represent restrictions in the performance of the person. For example, functional limitations that might result from multiple sclerosis include limitations in the performance of tasks such as walking or transferring from a sitting to a standing position. These functional limitations might or might not be related to specific impairments secondary to the disease itself and thus are seen as distinct from disturbances of the organ or body systems.

According to Nagi's model, disability is the expression of a physical or a mental limitation in a social context. Nagi viewed the concept of disability as representing the gap between a person's intrinsic capabilities and the demands created by the social and physical environment—a product of the interaction of the individual with the environment. This is a fundamental characteristic of Nagi's thinking that is consistent with the biopsycho - social school of thought. For Nagi, disability is a limitation in the performance of a task that is associated with a specific role within a sociocultural context. Likewise, roles are organized within distinct activities such as those of the family or work. Since persons with disabilities assume different roles in different contexts, similar functional limitations may result in very different manifestations of disability.[12] This is true of all members of society.

Nagi's definition stipulates that a disability may or may not result from the interaction of an individual's physical or mental limitations with the social and physical factors in the individual's environment. In Nagi's terms, the physical impairments of a person with arthritis, for example, would not invariably lead to a disability. For example, two people with spinal cord injuries may present with a very similar clinical profile. Both may have similar physiological impairments such as paraplegia, paralysis of the lower extremities, and restricted range of motion and muscle weakness in the upper body. Their pattern of function also may be similar, with a difficulty grasping objects and fatigability. Their disability profiles, however, may be radically different. Environmental constraints may work toward differentiating their disability profiles. One, a resident of Dallas, Texas, knows how hard it is to push her chair across the street on hot summer days. She has learned the hard way that her manual wheelchair bogs down in melted asphalt and that outings are seldom worth blistered hands. Another, a resident of Madison, Wisconsin, knows that on the coldest of winter days the batteries of her power chair run down much more quickly. There are errands to run, yet with only a few hours of battery life, it simply is not worth the risk of being stranded in the snow. Though faced with similar physical limitations the environment imposes disabling conditions in different ways at different times of the year for each of these individuals.

Resources and personal preferences may also differentiate disability profiles. One individual may restrict or eliminate her outside activities, require help with all self-care activities, spend most of the time indoors watching television, and be unemployed and depressed. The other may fully engage in her social life, receive some assistance from a spouse in performing daily activities when needed, be driven to work, and be able to maintain full-time employment through workplace modification. Two persons with disabilities with very similar underlying pathology, impairments, and functional limitations may present very different disability profiles. Furthermore, similar patterns of disability may result from different types of health conditions.

The Nagi model has been extended to include sociocultural factors (e.g., social and physical environment) and personal

Man on Lawnmower Pulling Wheelchair. Environmental constraints necessitate ingenuity to achieve personal mobility.

factors (e.g., lifestyle behaviors and attitudes).[13] This was an attempt to attain a full biopsychosocial model of "disablement," which they defined as the impact that chronic and acute conditions have on functioning of specific body systems and on people's abilities to act in necessary, usual, expected, and personally desired ways in their society. "Process" is used to characterize the dynamic and changing nature of disability (i.e., variation in type and severity of functional consequences over time and the factors that affect their direction, pace, and pattern of change).

Nagi's concept of disability and the subsequent elaboration defines disability as a broad range of role behaviors that are relevant in most people's daily lives. Five commonly applied dimensions of disability evolved from this elaborated model:

- Basic activities of daily living (BADL), including basic personal care
- Instrumental activities of daily living (IADL), including preparing meals, doing housework, managing finances, using the telephone, or shopping
- Paid and unpaid role activities, including occupation, parenting, grandparenting, and student roles

- Social activities, including attending church and other group activities or socializing with friends and relatives
- Leisure activities, including sport and physical recreation, reading, day trips, et cetera[14]

This elaboration of the disability concept highlights the varied nature of role task behavior, from fairly basic self-care activities to advanced and complex social, work, and leisure activities.

A further elaboration of Nagi's conceptual view of disability is contained in Pope and Tarlov's *Disability in America*.[15] In 1991, the British Government's Institute of Medicine (IOM) report uses the original main disablement pathways put forth by Nagi with minor modification of his original definitions. The IOM report provides two important additions to this biopsychosocial model: the concepts of secondary conditions and quality of life, both of which are discussed later in this chapter. In an effort to emphasize Nagi's view that disability is not inherent in the individual but rather is the result of the interaction of the individual with the environment, the IOM issued another report, titled *Enabling America,* where they referred to disablement as the "enabling-disabling process." This effort was an explicit attempt to acknowledge within the disability model itself that disabling conditions not only develop and progress but they can be reversed through the application of rehabilitation and other forms of explicit intervention.

Many Southerners reside in manufactured housing, often referred to as "trailers." The standard design of these houses imposes intrinsic accessibility barriers. Not only can entry and egress be problematic, but the bathroom may be all but unnavigable for persons with mobility impairments. Frequently, residents with mobility impairments remove the tub stall and install a large grated drain in the center of the bathroom. With a little additional waterproofing the entire bath is converted into an adaptive shower stall that also provides improved access to the sink and toilet. These interventions demonstrate an understanding of the interaction between the individual and the environment. In these homes persons with disabilities make modifications reflecting Southern traits of self-reliance and ingenuity.

ICF Model

In 1980, a similar process was underway in Europe, which led to the World Health Organization's (WHO) International

Classification of Impairments, Disabilities, and Handicaps (ICIDH).[16] Like Nagi's disablement model, the ICIDH model differentiated a series of three distinct concepts related to disease and health conditions—impairments, disabilities, and handicaps. This original ICIDH model was designed to become part of the WHO family of international classifications, the best known of which is the International Statistical Classification of Diseases and Related Problems, which provides an etiological model for the classification of diseases, disorders, and other health conditions. The ICIDH was conceived as a complementary model, classifying function and disability associated with health conditions. It failed, however, to receive endorsement by the World Health Assembly.

Sensitive to criticisms of existing models, the WHO released a major revision of the ICIDH in 2001, called the International Classification of Functioning, Disability and Health (ICF), which, like the Nagi model, attempted to provide a coherent biopsychosocial view of health states from a biological, personal, and social perspective.[17] Like prior models, the ICF portrays human function and decreases in functioning as the product of a dynamic interaction between various health conditions and contextual factors. Within the ICF, contextual factors include aspects of the human-built, social, and attitudinal environment that create the lived experience of functioning and disability as well as personal factors such as sex, age, coping style, social background, education, and overall behavior patterns that may influence how disablement is experienced by the individual. Within the ICF, the term "health condition" is used to represent diseases, disorders, injury, or trauma, aging, and congenital anomaly. The terms function and disability are used as general or umbrella terms in the same fashion that the term "disablement" is used within the Nagi model.

Though this semantic quibbling may seem trivial, words matter. Perhaps no Southerner is more notorious for his word choices than Mark Twain, who is credited with saying that "the difference between the *almost right* word and the *right* word is really a large matter—'tis the difference between the lightning-bug and the lightning."[18] Arcane and inaccurate descriptors perpetuate negative stereotypes and reinforce incredibly powerful attitudinal barriers, which are often the greatest obstacle facing individuals with disabilities. Johnny Cash described the watershed moment when he ceased to look at Pete as "crippled." It was important for John to remove the burdensome label of "cripple" from someone he respected. You do not have to visit too many Southern diners, farm and ranch coops, or churches to hear the like of "Aw, he ain't crippled, he just can't see," or "my momma's not disabled, she just can't walk, but she gets around just fine." Paralleling Nagi and the ICF models, many Southerners strive to separate those they love and respect from terms that demean and marginalize.

The ICF identifies three levels of human function: functioning at the level of body or body parts, the whole person, and the whole person in their complete environment. These levels in turn contain three domains of human function: body functions and structures, activities, and participation. The term disability is used to denote a decrement at each level (i.e., impairment, activity limitation, and participation restriction).

The first domain of the ICF model includes physiological functions and anatomical structures of the person. Impairments, therefore, are "problems in body function or structure as a significant deviation or loss." Impairments are "deviations from generally accepted population standards in the biomedical status of the body and its function and can be temporary or permanent." The second domain of the ICF model includes activity and participation. Activity refers to "the execution of a task or action by an individual," while participation refers to "involvement in life situations."[19]

The main concepts included within the Nagi and ICF models are strikingly similar although the terms used to represent them are quite different. The ICF organizes the domains of activity and participation into subdomains. The subdomains include the following:

- Learning and applying knowledge
- General tasks and demands
- Communication
- Mobility
- Self-care
- Domestic life
- Interpersonal interactions and relationships
- Major life areas
- Community, social, and civic life

For the ICF model to capture descriptive information about functioning and disability in each subdomain, the model uses qualifiers that identify the presence and severity of a decrease in functioning at each domain of the ICF (i.e., body function, activity, or participation). In the domain of body function and structure, for instance, the primary qualifier is the presence and degree or severity of a specific impairment. A scale is used to record the severity of impairment as one of the following: no, mild, moderate, or severe impairment.

Within the activity and performance domains, the ICF advocates the use of qualifiers to assess performance or capacity. A performance qualifier is used to describe what a person does in his or her current environment, including whether assistive devices or other accommodations may be used to perform actions or tasks and whether barriers exist in the person's actual environment. Capacity qualifiers, however, are used to describe a person's inherent ability to execute a task or action in a specified context at a given moment. The capacity qualifier identifies the highest probable level of functioning of a person in a given ICF domain in a standardized environment without the use of specific assistance or accommodations. In essence, the performance qualifier captures what a person actually does in their typical environments, whereas the capacity qualifier describes the person's inherent ability to function without specific environmental impact. The gap between capacity and performance reflects the difference between the impacts of current and uniform environments as well as personal factors, the second part of the ICF model.

The ICF model includes two contextual factors: environmental and personal factors. Environmental factors are defined in the ICF model as the physical, social, and attitudinal environment in which people live and conduct their lives. The subdomains included within the domain of environment include products and technology, natural environment and human-made changes to the environment, support and relationships, attitudes, and services, systems, and policies. The environmental factors, once defined, identify specific features of the person's actual environment that act to facilitate or hinder a person's level of function. This classification can also be used to standardize specific testing environments where capacity in activity and participation are able to be assessed.

Personal factors are the particular background of an

Ad-hoc Ramps in Arkansas. Home modifications in the South are ubiquitous, but reflect individual resources and circumstances.

individual's life and living, and are composed of features of the individual that are not part of a health condition or health states. Personal factors can include sex, race, age, health conditions, fitness, lifestyle, habits, upbringing, coping style, social background, past and current experience, character style, as well as other psychological assets. Although environmental factors have been elaborated upon within the ICF model to facilitate their classification, personal factors have not.

Existing models present the process of disability as a linear progression of response to illness or consequence of disease and/or trauma. One consequence of this traditional view is that disabling conditions have been viewed as static entities. This traditional, early view of disability failed to recognize that disability is more often a dynamic process that can fluctuate in breadth and severity across the life span. It is anything but static or unidirectional. More recent elaborations of earlier models have explicitly acknowledged that the process of disability is far more complex. These more recent elaborations all note that a given process of disability may lead to further downward spiraling of functional loss and limitation.

The adoption of the ICF model by the WHO was an important moment in the conceptualization and subsequent defining of disability. It represented a reaction to the impasse of debates couched in accepting either a medical or a social account of the determinants of disability. In contrast, far from reducing the understanding of disability either to physiology or social and attitudinal barriers, the ICF model seeks to develop a relational understanding of the determinants of disability. This emphasizes the interplay between the body, the person, and broader social and environmental factors in determining the content of disability. In doing so, the ICF model notes that any understanding of functioning and health has to incorporate insights from both sociological and biological inquiry. This represents the ICF's commitment to a pluralist and consensual approach to theory building that seeks to cross the divides and differences between disciplines and offer a deeper and more complex understanding of human functioning.

The South is a region characterized by broad contrasts in demographic and geographic variables. The South is as varied as any region in the United States. This diversity intensifies as one more closely examines the complex and often contradictory notions of what is it to be "a Southerner." With the highest rates of poverty and disability and the lowest rates of higher education and employment, the interplay between functioning and "Southerness" has often resulted in conflicting definitions of disability. Though not a problem unique to the South, these conflicting definitions of disability have not been resolved from within the traditional binary understanding of human functioning: "disabled" versus "nondisabled." To understand disability within the broader social and environmental contrasts of the South, human functioning must be understood as existing along a continuum.

Conclusion

The biopsychosocial models have undoubtedly been the dominant paradigm in researching and understanding disability in recent years. In spite of this paradigmatic shift, there remains a gap between individual needs and wants and a corresponding response in the constructed environment. The redefinition of disability in terms of a disabling environment, the recognition of persons with disabilities as citizens with rights, and the reconfiguration of the responsibilities for overcoming prejudice and marginalization demand responses that consider the interaction of the person and the environment on a new level.

The discussions of the different disability models recognize that many different philosophical positions focus on a tension between the body and society. The ICF model has the great merit of producing a dynamic construct of disability with responsibility shared by all parties. The argument is that ICF and other models of disability provide a radically incomplete version of the "experience" of persons with disability. Although useful within many contexts, for the purpose of design, the ICF model is conceptually underdeveloped in the sense that it fails to specify in any detail the nature and adequacy of the interaction between the factors. Most persons with disabilities want to live in the community as independently as possible. The extent to which that can be achieved depends to a large extent on the accessibility of the built environments at home and in public. Few homes are built with any real thought for more complex individual needs of the people who may live or use them.[20] It is in this sense—the failure to meet these requirements to provide designers with useful insights into the social life of the persons with disabilities—that previous models and definitions of disability have fallen short. By excluding personal experience from the analysis of disability, a vacuum is left, which may in turn be filled by those who adopt an individualistic and decontextualized approach to design.[21]

We do not need a model to tell us that getting a wheelchair up steps is difficult. However, this is not to critique previous models for stating the obvious. The problem of design rests not on theoretical notions of how we define disability, but on how to ensure that the needs of all people—disabled or temporarily able bodied—are translated into appropriate, or simply "good design" that should be empowering to all. Poor design can present dramatic compromises in social activities, role definition, and identity, whereas good design can facilitate individual actualization and integration.[22] Consequently, the challenge is to design inclusively rather than create new forms of accommodation. This sensitivity toward the social implications of good design is itself informed by detailed investigation into the everyday life of those for whom the design is intended. Previous models of disability have failed to see the ambiguities and rhythms with which a person relates to their environment, and the attendant choices concerning what to look for in the social setting that are central to inclusive design. As James Cobb observed in *Redefining Southern Culture: Mind and Identity in the Modern South,* the "central theme" of the writings of the New South historians was "the concept of triumph over adversity, of steel will and impeccable character overcoming staggering problems, often against what seemed impossible odds. The South depicted in most of these early histories rose from the extraordinary devastation of Reconstruction to a glorious plateau of achievement." Models that ignore such cultural implications make the mistake of attempting to imposing fit rather than including good design.

In the South, the environment is paradoxically perceived as both benevolent and indomitable. The same floods that enriched the soil of the deltas for hundreds of years may very well force you to abandon your home in the middle of the night and head for higher ground. Southerners do not begrudge the environment for being the way it is; instead, Southerners prize resilience and ingenuity in coping and overcoming obstacles. This, again, is exemplified in Johnny Cash's description of his childhood friend Pete.

> He had what we called infantile paralysis, later known as polio, which had crippled his right leg and withered his right arm to about half the length of his left. He'd adapted well. I

wrote about him in the liner notes for American Recordings: with his left hand he made the chords as he beat a perfect rhythm with his tiny right hand. I thought if I could play the guitar like that I'd sing on the radio someday.[23]

John did not make any observations with regard to the injustices of Pete's environment; John only wished for the abilities Pete did have.

Housing design, like popular definitions of disability, is entrenched within out-dated notions of how people fit into their environment. In no place is good design and establishing person-environmental fit more important than in the home. Few industries are more tied to convention and tradition and resistant to change than the housing industry. The need to redefine the concept of disability as well as the design of communities and housing is especially significant to those living with disabilities in the South.

2 Defining Home

JENNIFER WEBB AND NANCY G. MILLER

> A new house is a new life . . . A house is an expression of who you are. It says something not just about the place where you have come from, your family roots, or even your social status; it is also an expression of your identity as an individual . . . Today it is expected that you will be able to look at a dwelling and tell something important about the person who lives there.
>
> —CARL ELLIOT, *Better Than Well: American Medicine Meets the American Dream*

In the first chapter of Jimmy Carter's book, *An Hour before Daylight,* the former president describes memories of his home in Plains, Georgia. From the physical environment, "flat and rich," to the cultural environment, "separate but equal," Carter learned that the land provided daily sustenance and that hard work garnered respect and financial success. For Carter, home was further defined by the human relationships constructed over generations, the memories of events long past, and the place to which he returned at the end of the day and at pivotal points during his life.[1] Through his work with Habitat for Humanity, Carter has been reminded of these differences and inequities.

> "Habitat has opened up unprecedented opportunities for me to cross the chasm that separates those of us who are free, safe, financially secure, well fed and housed, and influential enough to shape our own destiny from our neighbors who enjoy few, if any, of these advantages of life."[2]

Semantically, there is confusion in today's culture about the use of the word home. Consider the differences between the terms shelter, dwelling, house, and home. Anthropologists use the term shelter to describe any structure devised by

Jimmy Carter Working with Habitat for Humanity. *Courtesy of HFHI/Steffan Hacker.*

man/woman for use as protection against the elements. Abraham Maslow suggested in his "Hierarchy of Needs" that shelter was a necessity of survival.[3] In today's culture, the term shelter is further used to refer to the physical form of temporary protection: emergency shelter, homeless shelter, and battered women's shelter.[4] For most purposes, the term dwelling is used interchangeably with shelter. Dwelling, however, involves a long-term commitment. At its foundation, dwelling has a meaning that is more emotional than that of a simple, short-term shelter. For academics studying the role of shelter and its economic considerations, the terms house and housing are prevalent. A house is the physical manifestation and is generally considered to be the "bricks and mortar."

Today's cultural context, however, has superimposed the term home over most of these other terms. Home is used in reference to the physical structure of the house or dwelling and simultaneously in reference to the set of relationships between the physical structure or location and the individuals. Home conveys an emotional investment that is constructed over time and implies a shared history with memories of people and events. Historically, individuals constructing the physical manifestation have been called house builders and realtors have sold houses. Instead, common language today suggests that builders are constructing and realtors are selling homes with the relationships and memories already intact. The word home has at its roots some degree of meaning with regard to family, security, and belonging. A home is "where one starts from" and serves as a reference for its residents. Home can occur without a physical place and instead can be generated from the fire, both figuratively and literally, around which the family gathers. The fire represents the preparation of food and the provision of safety and warmth shared within a communal group. [5]

The common interchange of the terms house and home confounds the discussion and investigation about home. [6] A home is defined as the center of activities,[7] a set of relationships,[8] items moved from place to place or a specific place such as a house or a country of origin. Activities and relationships that define home, however, can also occur outside of the physically constructed residence. The physical home can be comprised of a geographic location, structure, climate, or street. The home is further defined culturally through religion, economy, family structure, ritual, belief systems, and so on.[9] Ironically, the term home has also been used when referring to residential care options for persons with varying levels of functioning[10] and has been applied to housing facilities of all scales, inhabited by any number of persons that are not related, and controlled by a roster of employees (e.g., nursing home).[11] The simple use of the term home for such a facility does not make it so. The purpose of this chapter, therefore, is to define some of the many roles homes play in people's lives (see Appendix 3) and describe how houses, through human efforts to manipulate self, objects, and environment, become homes.

Homelessness

Any discussion about home and its associated definitions must include both the concept and reality of homelessness. In its

American Dream Homes.
Emotional marketing strategies
are reflected in the language
used by realtors, builders, and
developers.

most common form, the U.S. Department of Housing and
Urban Development (HUD) defines a "homeless person" as
someone "lacking a fixed, regular, and adequate nighttime residence" as well as those who reside in public or private shelters,
temporary institutions, or places not intended to regularly
accommodate sleeping arrangements.[12] While it is not intended
to disparage the serious plight of persons without shelter, it is
important to explore homelessness in a different context.

The legal definition of homelessness equates home with
the physical structure providing nighttime shelter. However,
consider the earlier definitions of house as physical structure
and home as the relationship to family, safety, and belonging.
Service providers and agencies suggest that shelter alone
becomes a home. A person without a fixed nighttime residence
may be more accurately described as houseless or shelterless. A
physical structure that does not support the psychological or
social needs of individuals will not become a home to its resident. Most important, a house, a shelter, or an institution can

result in feelings of vulnerability, isolation or crowding, and loss of social relationships—feelings of homelessness.

Homes occur on a variety of scales and homelessness can occur in the same manner. This is especially true for people who are without shelter and for people in transition between life stages (e.g., retirement, divorce, or student). There can be a loss of a geographic setting through immigration, war, or natural disaster. A known and loved structure can be lost through, among other reasons, financial mishap or fire. Personal objects significant to our self-identity can be lost for many of the same reasons.[13] The loss of home negatively influences individuals' and social groups' identity, places physical well-being at risk, and removes feelings of familiarity and comfort. The mortgage lending crisis that began in 2006 is an important illustration in understanding the impact loss of home at any scale can have. While national foreclosure rates are higher than those in the South, Arkansas home foreclosures have increased significantly over the last two years, placing many families at risk.[14] Evidence suggests that these events can result in post-traumatic stress syndrome and loss of home further results in loss of stability and a decrease in self-esteem.[15]

Regardless of how home and house are defined, some houses become homes while others do not. Some families, though housed or sheltered, remain homeless. There is the pragmatic perspective in which the house fulfills the physical needs of individuals but there is also, and perhaps most overlooked, the role a home plays socially and emotionally. Providing physical shelter can be straightforward. Providing a house that has tangible and intangible qualities contributing to feelings of home is difficult. Homes fulfill broad social and psychological roles: home is an expression of self-identity, personal tastes, and values; home is a defensible and safe dwelling for self and family; and home is a connection to the greater community.[16] Jimmy Carter, through his work with Habitat for Humanity, helps residents find not only a house but also introduces them to the emotional bond one has with a home. As he states, "we give them the keys to their own house, and we all cry."[17]

Home and Identity

Human interaction with the physical features of an environment infuses a place with emotional significance and the interaction is necessary in developing a sense of place.[18] These same actions that create sense of place also contribute to creating one's own identity. Expression is sought for one's personal identity and for one's shared identities such as family, social groups, and nationality. Through expression of identity, territory is also claimed by individuals and groups thereby contributing to feelings of safety, security, and belonging.[19] This process is a careful balancing of individual and shared identities.

The interior of the home can be most easily altered to fit personal needs and preferences. These actions include manipulating, constructing, and embellishing interior spaces, arranging furniture, and displaying personal objects. Spaces are shared or private, formal or casual. A window is covered or uncovered, a chair is oriented to a favorite view or the television, a hobby is allocated prime space, and favorite objects are displayed. In the most intimate spaces, carefully selected colors, objects, and the most personal memorabilia are used to define the self; this identity is the one shared with a spouse or partner, children, or very close family members.[20] Even from these most intimate people, some objects or memorabilia might be hidden.[21] In public areas, an identity to be shared in more formal interactions is created. The display of family portraits, removal of clutter, and formal arrangement of furniture make spaces more acceptable to share with visitors and presents a less intimate identity.

Interior space is also the most private and carefully guarded. Residents have ownership and control and feel free from surveillance[22] and have a sense of privacy.[23] The home is enclosed by a door and window coverings in varying amounts intended to communicate the degree of welcome to outsiders. At this level of privacy, invasions of territory are the most unwelcome. Whether a parent investigates a child's room or a caregiver assists with activities of daily living, the loss of privacy can erode one's perceived self-efficacy.

Several studies suggest that the inability to express one's ideal self limits a residence's ability to be homelike.[24] People indicated that in their homes they could manipulate the environment to reflect themselves and that they could behave or act as they believed reflected their identity.[25] The ability to change the residence and to add desired décor or memorabilia is paramount to the house becoming a home. Even for visitors, the ability to discern something about the resident's personality is strong when the resident believes the dwelling is a strong reflection of him/herself.[26]

In the South, porches not only provide a method of coping with the heat but also provide a transition from the exterior to the interior of the residence. This extension provides for a wide range of social interactions. As secondary living spaces, porches and verandas reflect the more public image of the residents. People may visit on the porch but, just as frequently, conversations are held between the porch and sidewalk or a neighboring home. Being invited onto the porch is akin to being invited into the living room of the home. The social significance of the porch in the South may be best illustrated in one of the South's newest and most prevalent housing types: the mobile home. The first modification usually made is the addition of a makeshift porch or transition. That this spatial mediator is addressed first illustrates the importance of transitional space; it serves to not only facilitate entry to the home but also provides an additional barrier between the casual or uninvited guest and the most private domain.

Not only do people have a need to transform the immediate spaces around them as a way of expressing their self-identity, they also define themselves in a larger context. Just as t-shirts and bumper stickers act as billboards for group membership and belief systems, the immediate surroundings of one's home such as lawn art and the car parked in the driveway communicate identity as well. The community may be constructed around a core system of visual components that include size, materials, density, and so on. Different communities value variation in each of these physical qualities. Houses, and therefore homes, are typically selected on the basis of perceived fit: uniform appearance or freedom to personalize, close neighbors or relative isolation, or other values or characteristics.

Rural settings typically come unfettered by neighborhood covenants and freedom of expression is valued by many of its residents. The use of a front porch for storage, the random parking of vehicles, and the collection of objects for an unknown purpose is observed in many rural settings. While membership in this rural setting is often unimportant, communication of freedom and of values is essential. In parallel, apartment dwellers believe their home to be safer from crime when the boundary is gated and speaks to the role of territory in perceived well-being.[27]

Home, whether an apartment or a farm, fits into a community with defined points of interaction. A community may offer a social environment prized by its residents or may, both through physical design and social context, provide little interpersonal interaction. Public places such as plazas and parks contribute to a sense of community, including culturally important symbols and activities. A sense of community or the feeling that home extends beyond the physical house to include either a social milieu or a definable physical space, contributes to a sense of belonging and a larger concept of home.[28] A great proportion of Southerners live in small towns; in Arkansas, approximately 35 percent of the residents live in small towns.[29] This setting, between the urban and the rural, binds its residents with shared values and identity further solidified by a relatively flat social hierarchy.[30] The town square becomes the unifying place around which residents participate in long-term relationships. The town square in Fayetteville, Arkansas, is the location of the Farmers' Market. Several times each week for half of the year, residents purchase food, flowers, and crafts but, more important, participate in activities that create a sense of belonging and closeness with other community members. If you are running for a local public office, this is the place you campaign.

Communities also contain places over which an individual or group may lay temporary claim that is acknowledged by the larger group. These secondary territories include a particular stool at the local diner or the corner bench at the town park, recognized as "belonging" to a community member or group. These space-claiming behaviors contribute to a sense of belonging and ownership, and communicate some degree of status in the community.[31] An individual's visible presence in the community is the only way to be assured any degree of status. When communities do not allow for transportation other than private car and public spaces are inaccessible, some individuals will be unable to achieve a role within the community simply due to lack of presence. Participation in the community is important for everyone and this must be facilitated through the design of homes, neighborhoods, and transit systems.

Home is the touchstone to which a person returns each night, but home may also be the city or state of the formative years or a homeland left behind. The idea of homeland is strong for many and is well exemplified by celebrations such as St. Patrick's Day. Although many Americans participate in these celebrations, it is very likely that their family emigrated from the home country many generations previous. Many emigrants

Porch as Storage. Rural dwellings offer freedom in the utilization of space.

choose to live in enclaves where language, food, and culture can be perpetuated. The heritage of Scotland in North Carolina, France in South Carolina and Louisiana, and Spain in Florida is reflected in food, architecture, language, and religion and have been carefully maintained. Across the South, the rich variety of African cultures are clearly observable.

It is not widely known or expected, but Springdale, Arkansas, is home to the largest population of Marshallese outside of the Pacific Ocean islands. Arkansas represents opportunities in the modern world but the large Marshallese community allows the celebration of their culture and recreation of a distant home.[32] The emergence of this enclave indicates that the South is not the purely homogenous population commonly characterized. Further, this cultural enclave also suggests individuals and groups choose homes that facilitate both individual and group identities and fosters a sense of inclusion.

Autonomy

While some individuals work to establish a shared identity in a larger context, other individuals work to create an identity separate from one's family or social context. In a home, identity is continuously negotiated between spouses or partners, between parents and children, or between housemates.[33]

When individuals are in transition from one life stage to another, the need to develop autonomy may be stronger. Claire Cooper Marcus found that women removed expressions by a departed spouse in order to reestablish herself as the home-owner.[34] Students' personalization of dormitory rooms is another example. The degree to which students personalize space is directly correlated to the length of time they will remain in school and is indicative of their commitment to this new, autonomous role.[35] Young adults still residing in parental homes report that parents set the standard of behavior, self-expression, and access to resources within the home. When values do not match, conflict inevitably results. The young adult invariably saw the only way to achieve his or her personal expression and identity was to leave and establish an independent residence. In the United States, lower socioeconomic status may inhibit young adults from establishing an independent residence thereby foregoing this form of self-expression and the establishment of autonomy. [36]

Balancing feelings of belonging and independence begins in childhood and continues throughout the life span. The environment provides both a palette of expression and a physical mechanism of control that contributes to individual and shared identities. Identity is maintained and developed over the life span and interruptions to this identity through loss of home can carry long-term consequences.[37]

Memory

Homes have unique qualities of light, sound, smell, and thermal properties. These qualities contribute significantly to sense of place and of home. Jimmy Carter stated that he did not remember the heat of his childhood home but that he remembered the "shivering cold days" when he would rush to dress in his parents' bedroom near the early morning fire.[38] The feel of the cold, the smell of the fire, and the frantic rush through the house contributed to his memories of home and family.

Memories of smell, sounds, and light evoke strong reactions to physical spaces that can be both positive and negative. Odor memory, in particular, enables humans to remember past events and experiences.[39] Many individuals have powerful impressions of places through sensory memories: a fire in a home, a nearby chicken farm, the light flooding a room, or the feel of a table under hand. As Charlayne Hunter-Gault, civil rights activist and journalist, describes so eloquently in her memoirs[40]:

> . . . the evocative sights, sounds, and smells of my small-town childhood, the almost overpowering smell of honeysuckle and banana shrub . . . clouds of black starlings producing shadows wherever they flew over the dusty red clay haze. This was the part of the South that I loved, that made me happy to be a Southerner.[41]

These sensory memories last throughout a lifetime. The smallest cue can release emotions believed to be forgotten or unimportant until they are experienced at a later time.

Individuals gather, organize, and retrieve this sensory information about environments. This information is held, in part, in the form of cognitive maps and includes information about spatial relationships and the attributes of the environments.[42] This knowledge allows people to visualize the space even when they are not in it. In the case of arriving home at night after curfew, these maps allow people to navigate the home without sight and even to avoid the squeaky step. Much of the information contained about environments is stored as tacit knowledge.[43] Tacit knowledge is carried around in a person's mind and they are often unaware of possessing this deep wealth of knowledge. Scholars often call this imbedded knowledge context and laypersons may think of this as experience.

Tacit knowledge and cognitive maps significantly impact human interactions with the built environment. This knowledge, because it can be recalled and visualized, can be shared with others. These mental images of places and especially of homes allow individuals to return to a place and navigate successfully, to execute tasks without thinking, and to communicate information about these places to others. It is this knowledge upon which memories are founded. Because of the imbedded nature of the information, it is a powerful element of home. Tacit knowledge is created over time; cognitive maps are continually revised and amended as environmental exploration and interaction becomes more extensive. Over time, the knowledge may become less accurate but it does not become less meaningful.

Barriers to Forging Identity

There are multiple roles that each person fulfills and each role is encumbered by desirable characteristics as well as demands. As a component of identity, the home requires the individual's actions and resources applied over the life span. When actions or resources are unavailable, the creation of identity suffers. For persons with disabilities, actions and resources are allocated over a greater range of demands. The creation of home and identity, therefore, is much more tenuous for persons with disabilities.

Housing tenure and available resources play significant roles in self-expression. If a home is not under the direct ownership and control of the residents, desired transformation can be prevented or limited.[44] Rental properties often restrict activities and physical alterations. Some rental housing restricts particular outdoor activities such as barbequing, playing music, and decorating the exterior. The interior is equally restricted with regard to spatial sequencing, aesthetic finishes, and activities such as pet ownership. Self-expression must be achieved through the collection of objects and furniture displayed. Financial resources, available time, and requisite skills necessary to facilitate environmental changes can result in a residence not expressing an individual's unique identity. Inability to express one's identity at any level inhibits the creation of home.

Because identities are communicated to both the self as well as to others, it is important to understand the role of a potentially negative identity. Even more important, the home environment can communicate and reinforce an identity that may be unattractive or undesirable to the individual as in an "impaired role." If the functional role of the environment revolves around the need for medical or human intervention, the desired identity of the individual can become secondary or even lost. Further, the home that does not support the individual's unique abilities can further facilitate the acceptance of an impaired role. One of the main effects of accepting the impaired role is in tolerating a lowering of expectations with respect to various aspects of home.

As do all socially prescribed roles, the impaired role includes both responsibilities and privileges. Thus, the individual is not held responsible for his or her condition and is granted exemption from fulfilling "normal" social obligations; in return, the individual is required to accept limitations and barriers in exchange for abeyance for those same social obligations.

. . . the impaired role is easy to maintain and difficult to leave for it is meant to be permanent, but it carries with it a loss of full human status. It is true that the impaired role does not require the exertions of co-operating . . . but the price for this is a kind of second class citizenship.[45]

The preferred identity is not necessarily the true identity. Individuals, in their effort to negotiate status and social exchange, create the identity that will achieve the best fit within the community.[46] This preferred identity is created through their homes because "members' sense of significance, solidarity, and security" define a psychological sense of community.[47] This may well be especially true in the South where outsiders are viewed with suspicion and in rural areas where strangers garner unwarranted attention. The unprecedented growth in "do-it-yourself" television shows and retail outlets are significant, as it enables many individuals of a lower socioeconomic range and skill level to undertake projects necessary to achieving a preferred identity through the creation of home.[48]

The physical act of adjusting a space, and particularly a residence, to reflect one's personal needs and preferences can be difficult to achieve. Manipulating the environment to reflect a desired identity may be more difficult for individuals with disabilities. Additionally, if a person is unable to act independently, the changes facilitated by an outsider may or may not accurately reflect the individual and do not contribute to a sense of self-efficacy. Scarce resources may require that other priorities be placed ahead of the desired changes. Persons with disabilities may also have a more difficult time establishing and maintaining autonomy and sense of self as, in a marginalized state, others overlook what would ordinarily be perceived as clear expressions of identity and of territory.

The ad-hoc design process observed in rural settings is indicative of the limited resources available for home personalization and modification. A ramp is a good example of the isolation of a rural environment combined with limited financial resources resulting in less-than-optimal changes. Necessary for access to the home, a ramp can be constructed of material scraps from the farmyard or storage shed, thereby solving the access dilemma. However, there may be a lack of knowledge for optimal ramp width, slope, and length. The materials may be hazardous when wet. And more important, the ramp itself communicates a weakness on the part of the resident. The resident may now feel vulnerable or that the circumstances of one's existence has been communicated to the entire neighborhood, whether that was desirable or not.

Home, as a tool to create and maintain identity, is complex and, at times, unwieldy. The need to balance a sense of independence along with feelings of belonging requires a continual reassessment of values, beliefs, and needs. Because a sense of belonging is important, the individual identity can sometimes be subsumed by larger, shared identities. An individual's ability to affect change is, ultimately, indicative of that individual's ability to create home and self. The characteristics of home are subtly nuanced and often unconscious until cued by some long-forgotten memory. In the remainder of this chapter, the creation of home through more tangible means, objects and activities, will be explored.

Home as Objects

In addition to the physical structure, home is conveyed by the objects in the home. A number of studies have examined the role of objects or possessions in respect to the home. Claire Cooper Marcus explains that people use objects to turn a specific place into a home.[49] Objects serve to create comfort and familiarity for the resident, to define self through personal values, accomplishments, and relationships to others, to claim territory on a permanent or temporary basis and to position one's self within time.

The display of objects can make an uncomfortable place seem more homelike. For some, comfort may be achieved through a familiar object such as the traveler with a favorite pillow or a child with a favorite stuffed animal. Objects also serve as reminders of family and friends, those who are distant or deceased, and for events in personal history. These connections to other places, people, and events transform a new residence; indeed, these objects allow "old homes" to inhabit "new homes."

For persons without traditional homes, the role of objects is significantly different; possessions or the lack of possessions further accentuates the absence of home. Homeless persons used scavenged objects to replace lost symbolic elements.[50] Three categories of objects are important to homeless women: items maintained despite homelessness, items that suggested a better future, and items that had been lost but whose memories served as a touchstone.[51] The opportunity to select and retain objects allows an individual the ability to maintain a sense of

Colors of the South. Personal
preferences are often revealed
in the application of color.

control and a sense of identity during difficult times. An evaluation of images from the Astrodome in Houston following Hurricane Katrina illustrates the rarity of personal possessions following the disaster.[52] This loss results in a diminished sense of security and may be one of the reasons for the tension and conflict reported in these settings.

Objects are also used to define self. By displaying documents of accomplishment, souvenirs of travel, and other objects, the individual is telling viewers of interests and personal achievements.[53] Display of photos often communicates relationships with other people and also conveys values such as family and friends. As important symbols of the self, furniture, photos, books, and musical instruments are some of the most frequently cited cherished objects. With increasing age, more importance is placed on furniture, irreplaceable photographs, and other items associated with meaning. Objects are so linked to identity that the dispersal of these items at end of life is difficult. Older adults fear that when valued objects are given away, they will experience a loss of identity.[54] People's interactions with objects also change as their capabilities change. A photograph that was prized for the image of a place or people is later identified by touch, recalling the memory. The feel of a piece of furniture, the chime of a clock, the scent of an object stimulate memories where visual identification was once the primary method of interaction.

Of all possible objects, photographs are most often indicated as a necessary feature in the creation of home.[55] Many individuals cite family photographs as the one possession they would miss the most if forced to evacuate their home quickly. Photographs rekindle memories of significant and everyday experience, marking the norm for the viewer. Portraits are common family possessions at all economic levels and are used by families to record family history at particular moments. Families with greater resources hire professional photographers to record prized possessions and pets, significant events, and everyday life. For families of limited means, this would be an uncommon luxury and these artifacts assume even more importance.

For most individuals, home reflects objects of one's own choosing. When the objects filling a space are added as a necessary part of life such as mobility, hearing, or visual devices, the home takes on a less than personal meaning. Medications lined up on a window sill, grab bars in the shower, an amplification

Astrodome after Hurricane Katrina. The loss of home and the loss of personal possessions contributes to a loss of self identity. *Courtesy of FEMA/Andrea Booher.*

Collection of Personal Photographs. Displaying photos and collectibles reinforces a sense of home and self.

system for the telephone, digital magnifiers for reading: all place the emphasis on the level of functioning and not on the individual. A significant challenge in designing living environments is to facilitate each person's ability to communicate their (1) sense of self, (2) connection to family, and (3) role in society effectively. An effective design solution allows the individual to control how the self, via the home, is understood by others.

As individuals transition between homes, objects are used to define home and may be moved from one location to another. Often, relocated objects are placed in an arrangement similar to the previous arrangement to further emphasize the establishment of home. Special objects, pieces of furniture, and photographs are transported with the individual, and while they serve as a connection for the individual leaving, in some scenarios they result in a void for those left behind. Students, divorced households, older adults, and people who are homeless represent diverse groups for whom objects serve as the primary way of creating a sense of home.

College students create their first homes when they move into residence halls. Objects are carefully selected due to limited space and the possibility of theft. Image is critical as the young adult establishes his or her own identity; inherent conflict exists between the desire to create familiarity and comfort without appearing childish. In a similar context, divorced persons take objects from the marital home and relocate to a new residence.[56] These divided possessions represent an earlier, shared identity and must be morphed into the new identity. Both students and those reestablishing their adult household communicate independence and often find themselves in conflict as to their new identity.

Creating a homelike space is a primary goal for older adults who transition into congregate living settings. Originally, nursing homes provided hospital-like furnishings and limited the types of personal possessions or alterations allowed in the individual's room. Today, personal furniture and accessories are encouraged in a variety of care settings for older adults, especially in more individual-oriented care facilities. Door decorations, memory boxes, and doormats are used at the entry to the private living space to denote territory. Nevertheless, interior finishes, furnishings, and personal objects are recognized as forming both a physical and emotional framework of home for residents of all ages and abilities.

Limited by economics, increasing family size, or the inclusion of assistive devices, the role of displaying personal objects assumes a higher order in establishing identity. One researcher believes that we should be more amazed at what one's cupboard contains than when we discover one empty.[57] The cherished, little-used objects are tucked safely away, while objects for daily need are in easy reach. Whether reserved for ritual use or enjoyed daily, objects embody the concept of home. The ability to possess or display an object that reflects one's identity and that communicates roles, values, and relationships is critical to the establishment of home. The opportunity to both possess and choose the objects is a statement of personal choice and independence.

Home as Activities

Just as home can be defined by the physical context and the objects within, home can also be defined by the events and activities that occur within its boundaries. The home is characterized not only by its physical qualities such as structure and objects, but is "defined by . . . a system of activities."[58] These activities may be related to, for example, personal care, hobby and leisure activities, food preparation, and, increasingly, employment driven tasks. Homes are also comprised of personal relationships.[59] Family rituals, whether daily or annually, are important ways in which people sharing a home confirm and recommit to relationships and shared values. The social aspects of home, family, and community are driven by the relationships that exist within and outside the home. Individual levels of functioning influence the performance of each these activities.

In the South, there are a variety of activities that enjoy special positions within households and that, more than many other activities, define home. First, food is an important component of Southern culture where personal recipes and concoctions are fiercely guarded and are also served with great fanfare to family and friends. Rural cooks parade their best products at county fairs and at chili or BBQ cookoffs. Religion is yet another significant component of Southern culture; the Protestant, evangelical church plays a large role in many families where prayer and Bible study occurs not only in the community church but is also shared in the home as a family activity in addition to private worship.

Home activity categories have historically been based on traditional family structures and gender roles. For example, the amount of time spent in different parts of the house varies on the basis of gender, employment status, and marital status.[60] Fully employed, married women spent more time interacting with other people than other respondents. There is evidence that indicates that residents of the South and rural areas in particular retain fairly traditional attitudes about gender roles. Most Southerners have a more conservative view of women in politics and working women as mothers. While there is the suggestion that these differences are growing smaller, the changes have been slow.[61] These traditional views may impact the distribution of household tasks despite the individual skills.

The home is the location of some of the most important activities undertaken by individuals as well as those that are most private and autonomous.[62] It is in the home that the shared identity and work of the family is negotiated. That said, not all scholars agree on the role of the home in a variety of activities. One perspective is that home is defined as the place where childrearing, caring for the sick, and rest and relaxation occur, and that the home is the center of family activities.[63] These activities make a house into a home. The opposing perspective is that a home cannot be defined by its functions because other specialized environments such as hotels, schools, and hospitals perform the same functions more efficiently.[64] This contrast is perhaps clarified from the perspective that relationships with and caring for others are expressed through these activities.[65] This display of emotional investment is the line of separation between home and institution and is the further definition of family. Rising rates of single parenthood and divorce in the South, as well as the high incidence of poverty, challenge traditional family and home life. More important, however, is that the South leads the call to renew traditional family life and, concomitantly, traditional family work.[66]

Activities, for the most part, have a predictable schedule. The daily activities of bathing, dressing, and meal preparation are fairly short-term tasks that occur with great regularity and frequency. Alternately, activities associated with rituals such as birthdays and religious holidays are generally more lengthy and occur with great regularity and predictability but with much less frequency. Other activities, such as work crises, school projects, or illness are much less predictable in duration and frequency. Predictability is further a function of the environment. As the disjuncture between the environment and the person's needs increase, more effort (i.e., time or expended energy) is required to achieve the desired outcomes. As individuals age or as a particular level of functioning changes, predictability is further eroded.

In evaluating the impact of these activities, one must determine the resources necessary to manage each. While some activities are highly predictable, they can result in stress. For example, a particular person might have responsibility for preparing dinner each night. This preparation requires planning, budgeting, and shopping that precede actual meal preparation and clean up. These seemingly manageable tasks are more difficult with pressures of time, money, preference, and external factors. Even predictable activities result in stress on families without coping mechanisms or with resources spread too thin.

Patriotic Wedding. Home is a canvas for celebrating family and national values.

For persons with disabilities, these tasks may require even more time and planning due to environmental constraints.

Not only may the division of labor differ within households but the labor itself may differ. For individuals of varying levels of functioning, activities of daily living may become more central to the functioning of the household. Some activities may be more difficult for individuals with disabilities to accomplish or may require resources needed for activities of daily living, thus changing the nature of the activities as well as the division of labor. Simple tasks such as bathing, meal preparation, and dressing may dictate scheduling and assistance from a household member or someone outside of the home. Such activities may consume time otherwise spent on leisure or hobby activities or time spent with others in the home.

Findings from the 2006 Arkansas Health and Housing Survey indicate that entertaining friends, participating in games/hobbies and community activities, and providing child-care for friends and family was important to Arkansans of all ages.[67] In addition, Arkansans with a range of disability types were less likely to participate in a variety of activities outside of the home (dining, visiting, shopping, religious activities, etc.) and inside the home (entertaining, hobbies, and leisure activities). Participation in activities may be curtailed because individuals are not able to access the location, because resources are not available, or the social or physical context may not meet a family's needs or preferences.

For some, a home can be a prison. Simple actions such as arrival and departure have a tremendous influence on other activities. A door becomes a barrier due to a narrow width or a change of grade requiring steps or a steep walkway. Navigating such a barrier may require alterations both inside and outside of the home. Participation in the community can be further influenced by the ease of arrival and departure from residence as a function of transportation and neighborhood design. Shopping, healthcare, education, and neighborhood activities take place in the larger community and are critical to the perceived level of fit. Accessing a workplace is central to the well-being of most families; neighborhoods and cities that do not support walking and public transport can significantly limit a wide range of individuals' participation in necessary and desired activities. The Arkansas Health and Housing Survey also suggests that female Arkansans believe the design of their neighborhood will influence their ability to live independently compared to men.[68] This is perhaps significant to the historical role women have played as the mediator between home and community. Facilitating independence, participation, and environmental fit is central to the concept of home.

A wide range of private and social activities is important to each individual. These activities contribute to self-identity and perceived autonomy and further fortify relationships with others. Not only do many of these activities occur in the home, but being cared for and caring for others also contributes to feelings of home. At the same time, when these roles are unrelenting, feelings of imprisonment or servitude can become debilitating.

At the root of all activities is the idea of participation and inclusion. To create home, individuals need to participate in activities at all scales: completing personal care, taking part in familial routines and rituals, patronizing local businesses, enjoying a neighborhood walk. When one is unable to participate in those activities, the individual becomes marginalized and excluded. If good design occurs nowhere else, it should happen at home. More accurately, "home" is impossible without it.

Home as Belonging

While the definition of home, through context, scale, objects, and activities, varies from one individual to the next, feelings of attachment, warmth, identity, familiarity, consistency, resiliency, and security are universally associated with one's home. Nowhere is this more true than in the rural South. Southern people are tenacious in their quest for survival and continue to maintain their unique identity and to overcome limitations in resources and opportunities. A sense of community and home is tied to particular places because "where we are [is] an inextricable part of who we are."[69]

John Cash sums up his attitude about one of his homes and the wealth of opportunity that it provides to him:

> This is a great place for pottering. I can cook my own food, read my own books, tend my own garden, and wander my own land. I can think, write, compose, study, rest, and reflect in peace. . . . I can talk to myself. "Okay," I can say, "Where do you want to put this book of eighteenth-century hymns you found at Foyle's in London? Is it going to go in with the poetry books, or with the antiques you never look at?"[70]

He reflects upon his ability to engage in activities, control desired privacy, and act upon or change his environment. Cash's comments communicate feelings of security and independence. His home, in part, defines a significant component of his private self.

Sense of Place

Sense of place is comprised of the physical characteristics and subsequent emotional connections unique to a particular location or structure. Place can be defined as a location, position, or duties within society,[71] or even where people view themselves in relation to others (i.e., context), creating a "collective sense of place."[72] These definitions can be applied thus: the place as the house, the duties as the responsibilities assumed within the household, and the context as the relationships shared within the household and the community. At a smaller scale, sense of place could, therefore, be termed "sense of home."

Place has been defined as a product of human interaction with the physical features of an environment; interaction infuses a place with emotional significance and is necessary in developing a sense of home. Phenomenological investigations suggest that while all individuals experience sense of place, or in this instance sense of home, it is defined uniquely for each individual.[73] These two thoughts underscore the idea that a house, in order to become a home, must be malleable and changeable so that the resident can act within and upon the environment in order to achieve one's unique sense of home. A house becomes a home and a neighborhood becomes a community when it is a canvas for self-expression and belonging and when fit is an achievable goal. In the South, sense of place is particularly acute as "a result of . . . dramatic and traumatic history and their rural isolation."[74]

Temporal Aspects of Home

Home, for most individuals, is not created instantaneously but is carefully crafted over time.[75] Connections to the past occur to the temporal nature of home. As Alice Walker once said of Martin Luther King Jr.: "He gave us back our homeland, the bones and dust of our ancestors, who may now sleep within our caring and our hearing. . . . He gave us continuity of place, without which community is ephemeral. He gave us home."[76] This perspective underscores the role time plays in the creation and maintenance of a "sense of home."

Making place is a process of carving or claiming space by first marking the space, usually followed by naming the place, thereby allowing it to collect a history. For some, the physical home is a place to which children and grandchildren will return to in the future. On the University of Arkansas campus, each graduating student has his or her name carved on the sidewalk with the rest of their class. During summer orientation for new students, parents seek out the names of grandparents as well as their own name as a way of creating a sense of home and belonging for the newest generation of Razorbacks. Homes are shared with others today and are places to which children and other family members will return in the future.[77] Objects and rituals are passed from one generation to the next and the oral histories that accompany these objects ensure preservation of home. These collective histories connect people to the past and allow them to anticipate the future. Homes, therefore, transcend time.

Conclusion

Continuity in personal and environmental characteristics contributes to basic life needs and social relationships supported by

Signs of Home. Conveying
ownership contributes to the
personalization and defense
of home.

Demarcating Territory. Claiming and defining of space around the home establishes distinctions between public and private.

physical environments.[78] The ability to create layers of identity over time is realized when the home serves as a canvas for self-expression. Selections of finishes, the addition of memorabilia and personal objects over time, and the arrangement of furniture until it is "just right" are part of the process of creating a home. Shared experiences with friends and families also occur over time and it is the establishment of ritual that constitutes the deeper meaning of a place. Knowing which neighbor one can call in an emergency, which pharmacy stocks a preferred item, and which bus or train will go to a desired location contribute to community inclusion and to an improved quality of life. Central to each of these characteristics is the individual's ability to act upon the environment; without the ability to engage with the environment there is a concomitant loss of identity, belonging, and self-efficacy.

In Arkansas, the challenges of creating a home in all of its many facets may be more difficult than in other parts of the country. The high incidence of disability and poverty in the state, as well as the prevalent rural setting, results in isolation and decreased access to services and other resources. There are many individuals who experience lack of home as a result of any of these constraints and the dilemma is not uniquely Southern. "As would be true of any demographic group in a pluralistic society, we should not expect traditionally southern characteristics to be completely absent among non-southerners or uniformly present among southerners."[79] The role of the South in general and in Arkansas in particular, however, as an exemplar of demographic trends should not be underestimated as the lack of fit is likely to increase in prevalence if attitudes, policies, and practices do not adapt to radical demographic shifts and needs.

Continuity is a significant factor in houses and neighborhoods becoming homes.[80] To consider a home a disposable or replaceable commodity is failure to recognize the role environments play in security, autonomy, and emotional comfort. John Cash speaks lovingly of his Nashville home and the protection it has offered him over the years:

> I'm sitting in my library, looking out the westward-facing window at the strengthening rain and the blackening sky above the deep green fields of this beautiful place, and I feel good. This log house is a warm, strong, secure little cocoon. Short of a tornado, nothing could hurt me in here.[81]

The ability to just "be yourself" with all of the foibles and eccentricities should, if nowhere else, be allowed at home. However, people experience exclusion in his/her own home because participation in family activities may be severely limited or impossible. Home is also comprised of relationships with other people and the ability to include the whole host of friends and relatives that comprise family is critical to sense of home. Homes should be places where you are welcomed and where you can welcome others.

When the home is the site of renewal and protection, the home is a haven. A house or a neighborhood or a city thoughtfully designed so that a whole range of individuals can participate in it is, quite simply, good design. Any environment that does not facilitate participation in the activities of living is inadequate and unjust. Resources to create good design for all individuals, whether rich or poor, young or old, abled or disabled, white or black, Northern or Southern, are the outcome of a just society.

3

Defining Equality

KORYDON H. SMITH

The most interesting aspect of a society's world view is that its individual adherents are . . . unconscious of how it affects the way . . . they perceive the reality around them. A world view is successful to the extent that it is so internalized . . . that it goes unquestioned.

—JEREMY RIFKIN, *Entropy: A New World View*

Ensuring equality, presumably, is among the highest missions of democracy in the United States. As the disability scholar Douglas Baynton states, "Since the social and political revolutions of the eighteenth century, the trend in western political thought has been to refuse to take for granted inequalities between persons or groups."[1] Nevertheless, as the population of America has grown more diverse—economically, ethnically, religiously, and in age—ensuring equality has become an evermore difficult task. A series of questions have emerged: What demographic factor carries the most weight—race, gender, class, geographic location, age, (dis)ability, education? Which factors are most likely to foster increased social advantages? Inversely, which facets are likely to lead to discrimination and oppression? Amy Petersen, a special education professor at the University of Northern Iowa, tackles these questions in an extensive set of interviews with Krissy, a black female college student with a learning disability.[2] What affects college life and socialization most: being black, being female, or having a learning disability?

The case of Krissy illustrates both the similarities and the divergences of gender, race, and disability identity development. Krissy's remarks also illustrate the struggles of social acceptance and of self-acceptance. Like Cross's second stage of Nigrescence, where black identity is called into question and often viewed to be a liability, Krissy questions her race and gender, and sees disability as a negative label. She embraces Afro-centrism, but resists disability classification, especially detesting the physical and socio-academic space that articulates it, the "resource room":

> It [high school] was horrible, there were no black boys; so of course, when one came we all fought over him. We were like oh, he's so cute, but then we found out he was in resource and then he wasn't cute anymore. We were so mad to find out. We finally get a black boy and he turns out to be in resource. He was dumb after all . . . So I didn't like being in there . . . I didn't want to be in resource . . . When I turned 18, I signed myself out.[3]

One of the most well-known theories of Nigrescence, the process of African American identity development, is attributed to William Cross. According to Cross, the development of black identity contains five sequential stages, moving from a lack of awareness, through stages of heightened awareness, toward self-respect and activism.[4] Cross's work in the area of race identity is paralleled in gender studies by the work of Ruthellen Josselson, among others. Rather than "stages" of development, Josselson defined four identity "types" in women, each with varying degrees of self-realization and self-confidence and diverse views toward familial relationships.[5] Analogous theories of identity development can be found regarding gay, lesbian, bisexual, and transgender identity, but there is less cohesion regarding theories of identity development among persons with disabilities. Much of the scholarship in this area has borrowed from the literature on sexuality.[6] One cause is the relative newness of disability studies disciplines. A second cause is the diversity found among the category "disabled," including persons with visual or hearing impairments, learning or cognitive disabilities, mobility impairments, and so on. As one might expect, the personal experiences of deafness, depression, or impaired mobility, for instance, like the personal experiences of upper-class versus lower-class blacks, or rural versus urban homosexuals, likely vary a great deal.

So, the debate continues about the benefits and drawbacks of specialized education, employment, housing, and services. How is identity development fostered or hindered? How is equality cultivated or subdued by the way education and housing are designed? In any case, it is clear that design plays a central role in socialization, identity development, and perceptions of equality. This chapter explores these questions—paying special focus to the interrelationships and trajectories of federal legislation, architectural regulations, and cultural values—in an attempt to reveal the influence that changing social mores have on housing production in Arkansas, the South, and throughout the United States.

Further Parallels between Disability and Race

In 1890 Louisiana passed the Separate Car Act, which stated that intrastate rail companies had to provide "separate but equal" accommodations for black passengers and white passengers. Explicit in the legislation are two paradoxical directives: (1) a mandate for segregation of whites and blacks, and (2) a counter-directive for equality. The Separate Car Act and the premises of "separate but equal" were upheld in the 1896 U.S. Supreme Court decision of *Plessy v. Ferguson,* giving legal sanction to certain social attitudes and mores prevalent in the South at that time. Not without significant social strife, "separate but equal" was overturned in 1954 by *Brown v. Board of Education.*

Segregating social practices have not been restricted to issues of race, however. There are numerous parallels between race, gender, sexuality, age, religion, and disability discrimination.[7] Nevertheless, caution must be exercised in drawing parallels between race and disability rights; the risks of oversimplifying the distinct facets of race-, gender-, disability-based struggles and so on should be self-evident. At the root of each type of discrimination—racism, sexism, ageism, "ableism," and so forth—is a struggle for power between some in-group (e.g., white, male, able bodied, etc.) and a corresponding out-group (e.g., black, female, "disabled," etc.). Two brief yet decisive examples illustrate the efficacy in drawing further parallels between race and disability rights.

The first example resides in the statistical relationships between disability, poverty, and race. Arguably the most intertwined demographic correlation in the South resides in the interrelationships between disability, poverty, and race. Among the working-age population, the rate of poverty for persons with disabilities (18.8 percent) is nearly double that of individuals without disabilities (9.6 percent); African Americans have among the highest rates of disability (26.4 percent) of any race in the sixteen to sixty-four age range, considerably higher than whites (16.8 percent); and overall poverty rate is highest among African Americans (greater than one in five) and lowest among

Contrasts in Race, Disability, and
Resources. Access to resources
differs across races and abilities.

non-Hispanic whites (fewer than one in thirteen).[8] The strength of these correlations is exceeded only by the relationship between age and disability.[9]

The second example exists in the emergence and enforcement of the Fair Housing Act, which sought to end numerous types of discrimination in the construction, sale, and rental of housing. Race and disability, more so than gender or familial status, have become the primary foci of Fair Housing initiatives. Partially as a result of Nixon's "Southern Strategy" and the structure and proceedings of the U.S. Supreme Court during Nixon's administration, Title VIII (Fair Housing) was the most protracted component of the Civil Rights Act in terms of implementation and enforcement.[10] As a result, inter-group conflict and discrimination based on disability, race, and income persist in the housing and real estate industries.[11]

> Disability has functioned historically to justify inequality for disabled people themselves, but it has also done so for women and minority groups. That is, not only has it been considered justifiable to treat disabled people unequally, but the *concept* of disability has been used to justify discrimination against other groups by attributing disability to them.[12]

Disability-based and race-based discrimination are often simultaneous; and the disability and civil rights movements have been as well. James Meredith, an African American student escorted by U.S. marshals, "integrated" the University of Mississippi in the fall of 1962, while, in the same academic cycle, Ed Roberts, a student with quadriplegia, "integrated" the University of California at Berkeley.[13] The former received greater press than the latter, but their coincidence and kinship cannot be ignored. The parallel extends further, as the government's practices regarding both, disability and race, has resulted in segregated housing: institutions for persons with disabilities and "projects" for lower-income African Americans.

Social Identity and Inter-group Conflict

Social identity theory[14] provides a means to understand the common ground between various social movements of the nineteenth, twentieth, and twenty-first centuries, including the women's rights, civil rights, gay rights and disability rights movements. According to this theory, identity resides more in inter-group relationships than in personal qualities. Identity is an intricate construct of belonging to (or not belonging to) any number of social groups, including observed demographic classifications—gender, age, race, religion, economic status, place of birth, education, disability status, et cetera—and less apparent categories such as career, political beliefs, sexual orientation, personal preferences, et cetera.

Social identity theory illustrates that inter-group conflict is tempered by the worldviews of the individuals who reside within, on the fringes, and outside the dominate group. In essence, there are two means, binary in nature, by which individuals view themselves relative to society: a belief in "social mobility" or a belief in "social change." Individuals who maintain the assumption that social strata (e.g., economic status or educational attainment) are permeable and can be negotiated by the individual are said to hold a belief in "social mobility." In opposition, individuals who hold the assumption that it is difficult if not impossible for individuals to change relative status, that the larger society possesses most of the control regarding status structures, believe in "social change." At the risk of oversimplification, believers in "social mobility" assume that individuals hold the power to change position in the social strata, while "social change" believers think that individuals are effectually powerless and change in social position results haphazardly from changes in the society at large. This binary, however, operates on a continuum where some belief in each philosophy is usually at play.[15]

It is also important to understand three additional aspects of identity. First, identity, rather than singular, is multifaceted. Identity is interpersonal as well as intrapersonal, socially defined as well as self-reflective. The prevailing religions of the South and throughout the United States illustrate this well, as spirituality is both a group activity and an individual pursuit. Second, identity is ever changing. A person's worldview and behavioral responses change over time and from one socio-environmental setting to the next. For instance, though one's central personae may remain, the behaviors one exhibits in home life, work life, in an educational setting, or in recreational activities with friends may vary significantly. Quite simply, in the rural South, where economic and social challenges are ever present, "there are countless ways of 'making do'" with the situations one confronts.[16] Lastly, there is a perpetual struggle between preserving the current identity and adapting that identity to better fit one's social and environmental circumstances. Dana Felty, for example, one of the dozens of "regular folk" interviewed in the 2001 PBS documentary *People*

Like Us: Social Class in America, described the challenge of return-ing home to Morgantown, Kentucky (with a population of fewer than three thousand) for a visit after living in urban Washington, D.C. She had become an educated urbanite, or what the locals to Morgantown referred to as "gettin' above your raisin'," striking at the heart of the tradition versus change phenomenon. The trans-formation of social ideology, therefore, is often multigenerational, as evidenced by the century-plus history of civil rights debate and legislation.

Stages of Social Change

Just as Cross describes the phases of identity development at the micro scale, four sequential stages of social change may be extrapolated from the preceding discussion. These stages include (1) the lack of awareness that there is inequity or differ-ence, (2) the emergence of a definable group identity and the formation of in-groups and out-groups, (3) the materialization of inter-group conflict and a struggle for power, and (4) a shift in power (i.e., increased or decreased rights, status, etc.). During the first stage, as in Cross's first stage of Nigrescence, there is little awareness that differences and inequities exist. As the open-ing quotation to this chapter suggests, members of a given soci-ety are unconscious to the way that their worldview *colors* the way they see the world. In this first stage, it is not that differ-ences between groups do not exist, but simply that they go unseen. In fact, the concept of race did not always exist.

The second stage results from the classification of domi-nant in-groups (e.g., white males of the late 1800s) and out-groups (e.g., blacks and women of the same time period). This "emergent" stage is paralleled, for example, in *Madness and Civilization: A History of Insanity in the Age of Reason,* where Foucault reveals that the materialization of "insanity" in seven-teenth and eighteenth-century Europe was more a process of social categorization than a truly new emergence of mental ill-ness. According to Foucault, mental illness existed for centuries prior to the Age of Reason, but was so engrained as part of soci-ety and entertainment—such as in Shakespearean plays—that it went unquestioned. Prior to the Age of Reason, madness was integral to daily life. Oddly, the institutionalization of "the mad," as Foucault describes, resulted in part from the virtual eradication of leprosy in Western Europe following the Middle Ages. As leprosy was eliminated, a large number of leprosaria became vacant; so too was a vacancy left in one strata of society: the deviant. The need to fill both the institutions and the social void perpetuated the marginalization and confinement of the mentally ill. The leprosarium became the insane asylum, which subsequently housed criminals, debtors, and the physically ill, often concurrently.

It was not the advance of medicine that promoted institutionalization, but the transformation of the surrounding social structure. The shifting economic and employment structure of the industrial revolution contributed to institutionalization as well. Prior to the emergence of mass-production and assembly-line jobs, employment was often individualized and self-run: baker, blacksmith, et cetera. The mass standardization of employment had sociological effects. Mental and physical illness became more apparent against the datum of a standardized labor force. Discrimination, in both the general sense (i.e., identifying differences) and the negative sense (i.e., injustice), and the stratification of in- and out-groups became easier. Historically, the South was widely agrarian, composed on enclaves of farming and livestock communities. The South, like much of the rest of the world, has seen increased industrialization, commerce, and non-agribusinesses over the past two centuries.

The third stage, the materialization of inter-group conflict, results from an actual or perceived imbalance of power or status between groups. This is often the most discernable and most lasting stage of social change. This is exemplified in the continued prevalence of racial discrimination in housing. Although Title VIII of the Civil Rights Act of 1968 ensured equal rights and criminalized discrimination based on race, gender, and age in the purchase, sale, lease, and rental of housing, the National Fair Housing Alliance estimates that 3.7 million cases of racial discrimination and an even greater incidence of disability discrimination in the sale and rental of housing occur annually.[17]

Inter-group conflict is not always resolved and the final stage of social change—a shift in power—does not always come to fruition, nor is it always readily evident. In addition, a shift in power often cycles back to the previous stage numerous times. This continues to be the case in the Fair Housing laws. Many of the states in the South (e.g., North Carolina and Georgia) enacted fair housing laws throughout the 1980s and 1990s to be commensurate with the federal legislation of 1968, while some other states have made numerous revisions to their policies. Still others have struggled in their attempts to comply with the federal guidelines. Arkansas, for example, did not enact its Fair Housing Act until 2001, while Mississippi's attempt to draft a commensurate bill in 2006 died in committee and did not make it to vote. In addition, many of the state agencies empowered to assure compliance with fair housing statutes and handle claims of housing discrimination have lost significant portions of funding in recent years. Both Foucault's discourse on the transformation of the leprosarium into the asylum and the continued expansion of Fair Housing laws illustrate an almost cyclic surge and counter-surge of discrimination.

This was clearly the case in the desegregation attempts of Little Rock Central High, among the most famed incidents following *Brown v. Board*. The Little Rock Nine—as the first group of nine black students to gain access to the school were later known—were scheduled to attend school on September 3, 1957. The night before, then Arkansas governor Orval Faubus ordered the Arkansas National Guard to blockade the entrance and deny the nine students access. After federal judges reinforced the *Brown v. Board* ruling and demanded the students be admitted, Faubus ordered the closing of all Little Rock schools, opting for "access for none" rather than face desegregation. The U.S. Supreme Court later ruled the school closings unconstitutional and the schools were reopened. Ernest Green, one of the Little Rock Nine, became the first black graduate of Little Rock Central High in May 1958 and the Little Rock Nine did not appear publicly together as whole until 2007. Civil rights are often not achieved through consensus building; rather, civil rights are typically propelled by a few tenacious individuals in concert with forward-looking legislation.

Despite its infamy, this example does not necessarily typify Arkansas's role or attitudes regarding civil rights. Counter to popular belief, in the 1960s, Arkansas tended to be among the most progressive Southern states regarding desegregation and civil rights. Arkansas governor Winthrop Rockefeller, for example, was the only Southern governor to publicly honor Dr. Martin Luther King Jr. following his assassination in 1968.[18] What about the progress of disability rights in the South?

The Resurgence of "Separate but Equal"

The Education for All Handicapped Children Act of 1975 and the Individuals with Disabilities Education Act (IDEA) of 1990 (amended 1997 and 2004) parallel the 1968 Civil Rights Act. Combined, these acts set out to ensure access to public education for children with physical, cognitive, and developmental disabilities. Although legally enforced, not all states and schools currently comply. Noncompliance with disability rights laws in education is one example of the resurgence of "separate but equal." The disability rights movement exemplifies the reemergence of "separate but equal" dogma and practices, vetoed by *Brown v. Board of Education,* but implicitly sanctioned by contemporaneous accessibility legislation and building codes. Separate entrances for ambulatory and nonambulatory occupants, separate restroom facilities, separate paths of travel, separate (but "equal") employment and housing amenities seem hauntingly similar to the socially prescribed separate drinking fountains of the 1950s. As Elaine Ostroff states:

> Accessibility features that are thoughtless add-on(s) after the basic design of a place . . . have a stigmatizing quality not unlike the segregated "back of the bus" practices that were once the norm in the United States.[19]

Although the Architectural Barriers Act (ABA) of 1968 and the Americans with Disabilities Act (ADA) of 1990 sought to advance rather than impede civil rights, the ABA and ADA implicitly permit "separate but equal" practices. Public buildings are merely required to be "accessible," but not necessarily integrated. Many architectural responses to the ABA and the ADA have provided separate entries—often in less prominent, more cumbersome locations—for persons with disabilities (especially users of wheeled mobility devices). Many buildings, though possibly well intended, segregate ambulatory and nonambulatory users, often requiring nonambulatory occupants to enter through the back door. This is especially the case for renovations of historic buildings, where it is often costly and/or prohibited by historic preservation guidelines to provide "universal access" (i.e., a single entry for all users).[20]

Segregated access is also prevalent in new-build construction. This includes works as recent as *Living Tomorrow: Home and Office of the Future,* completed in December 2003, designed by UN Studio, and located in Amsterdam (a city popularly considered to be among the most socially progressive places in the world, the antithesis of the popular conception of the American South). The signage located at the main entry to *Living*

House of the Future Front Entrance Signage, Amsterdam, Netherlands. Contemporary prototypes continue to reinforce the status quo of "separate but equal" design for persons with disabilities.

Tomorrow indicates that the entrance for the "disabled," along with delivery services, is located at the rear. This is a common practice seen at government offices, college campuses, and multifamily housing throughout the United States as well. The segregated "back door" design approach to accessibility is currently legal, but the history of women's rights and civil rights provides precedent for future changes to accessibility in architectural design. "Separate but equal" is no longer a legal practice regarding housing and education for women and racial minorities; it may follow, then, that "separate but equal" could soon be outlawed regarding disability. As the first and fifth chapters in this book illustrate, the major dilemma is how (dis)ability is conceptualized. Designers and builders often plan for two distinct, unequal groups—"able" and "disabled"—and provide separate design solutions for each group, rather than designing for a continuum of abilities. This is where (dis)ability and race are most similar, as both are conceived categorically rather spectrally.

One major difference between race and disability regarding desegregation, however, cannot be overlooked. It was difficult for proponents of school segregation, for example, to argue that racial de-segregation of schools was going to be cost prohibitive. It was likely just the opposite, as services did not need to be duplicated: one school for whites, one school for blacks. Inclusion of persons with disabilities, however, could have both positive and negative ramifications dependent upon the service or amenity being considered. While fostering inclusive housing rather than specialized, institutional housing has been shown to be fiscally efficacious, other provisions, such as the design of public transit systems—trains, buses, and taxis, for example—may be cost prohibitive in some settings.

Nevertheless, many regions and municipalities spend a great deal of funds on "paratransit," specialized transit services for persons with disabilities and family members of persons with disabilities, such as dedicated vans and buses. Not only are many paratransit systems costly, they are often cumbersome and inconvenient, requiring advanced notice and are plagued by mechanical failures. As such, many regions and municipalities redesigned their primary systems to be more accessible, eliminating the need for paratransit.[21] Outside the United States, the taxis of London, England, are a notable example. What is apparent is that not enough research has been done to identify the cost and quality-of-life benefits of providing more integrated health services, housing, neighborhood planning, public transportation, employment, education, and amenities. The efficacy of the reallocation of resources needed to ensure disability rights is situational and needs to be assessed on a case-by-case basis. A second major difference between race and disability resides in social norms. While marginalization of persons with disabilities is often invisible, and, to some degree, culturally accepted, overt segregation based on race is seen as a serious transgression.

Broadly speaking, there is a reciprocal relationship between cultural attitudes and federal legislation. At times, federal legislation extends or formalizes broadly held social values; at other times, federal legislation seeks to impart a legal (if not ideological) position that may or may not be held by the culture at large. Moreover, architectural regulations (building codes) serve as an extension or further articulation of state and federal housing laws. The ABA, for example, formalized the awareness of the role that buildings played in enabling or disabling access to employment, education, and housing for persons with disabilities. This legislation stemmed from a report issued by the National Commission on Architectural Barriers to Rehabilitation of the Handicapped. Following its ratification, it was quickly revealed that the ABA—not unlike the Fair Housing Act and affirmative action, for example—was inconsequential without enforcement; the legislation did not change design and construction practices. As a result, the U.S. Access Board was formed in 1973 as an independent government agency with two primary charges: (a) investigating claims of noncompliance with the ABA (and, more recently, the ADA), and (b) developing and authoring guidelines and regula-

Paratransit. Older adults and persons with disabilities in the rural South often rely on restrictive public transportation.

tions for ABA (and ADA) compliance.[22] The Access Board published the Uniform Federal Accessibility Standards (UFAS) in 1984 and the ADA Accessibility guidelines (ADAAG) in 1991 to provide quantifiable, enforceable regulations for the ABA and the ADA, respectively. Other accessibility standards have also resulted from the Telecommunications Act (1996) and amendments to both the Fair Housing Act and the Rehabilitation Act (1988 and 1998, respectively). Due to the need for enforceability, building codes, in general, and accessibility standards, more specifically, have had a growing importance and impact on the legalistic aspects of housing.

Codifying Disability Rights

Housing design and construction is often seen as a simple enterprise, an assembly of materials and forms for purposes of shelter. Housing—and the individuals and agencies that design and construct housing—is often perceived as innocuous, if not benevolent. But, as the previous two chapters illustrate, this is an oversimplification. Housing (all of design, actually) is political; it is not benign and holds the potential to be liberating or caustic.[23] Housing typologies—such as the shotgun houses of New Orleans, the brownstones of New York City, or the California bungalow—not only emerge from the repetition of spatial arrangements and methods of construction, but also reveal the settlement patterns of various worldviews. Housing, as much as it is stylistic and material, represents social strata and values.

It seems that both American society and the contemporary popular media continue to romanticize housing as the primary

above and opposite: Contrasts in Housing. Divergent economic and social characteristics exist side-by-side in the rural South.

signpost in the fulfillment of the American Dream. This idealized view of housing, however, is being shaped more and more by increasingly stringent architectural codes and regulations, greater local and federal housing legislation, and the perceived design and aesthetic preferences of popular culture. Numerous legal and ideological trends have had and will continue to have tremendous influences on housing policy, design, construction, and purchasing in the United States. The civil and disability rights movements, for example, have resulted in a profusion of federal legislation affecting housing, including the Fair Housing Act (1968), the Architectural Barriers Act (1968), the Rehabilitation Act (1973), the Fair Housing Amendments Act (1988), the Americans with Disabilities Act (1990), and the Housing for Older Persons Act (1995). This legislation, coupled with federal judgments such as the *Olmstead Decision* (1999), has resulted in numerous changes to local and federal housing codes; and further changes appear imminent, as evidenced by the proposed Inclusive Home Design Act, which could have large impacts on the design of single-family housing, the bulk of the housing in Arkansas and the South.

A second major trend, an ideological shift between the silent generation and the baby-boom generation, exemplifies

changing attitudes about healthcare, housing, and lifestyle.[24] This trend has resulted in an explosion of diverse living arrangements for older adults—exercise-centered retirement communities, board and care facilities, assisted living facilities, continuing care retirement communities—and the condemnation of traditional nursing home environments. These, and other trends, will become more evident in future housing.

Again, legislation and culture often share ideological space, though legislation may not represent the desires and convictions of both in-groups and out-groups equally. Building codes illustrate this overlap in legal and cultural attitudes; architectural regulations and standards are explicit interpretations of these positions. For example, the guidelines and standards published by the American National Standards Institute and the International Code Council, the primary code authoring bodies in the United States, are developed through a process that includes (a) the synthesis of applicable research and know-how of scholars and practitioners in a specified field (e.g., electrical engineering), (b) synchronization with existing federal laws and industry standards, and (c) review of proposed changes submitted by the general public.[25] It follows then, just as buildings evidence the predilections and preferences of a given society, that a reading of the evolution of building codes may provide insight into the social and legalistic relationship between disability and housing. Lefebvre has argued that architectural space is the product of an underlying social or political agenda. Design professionals typically refer to building regulations as "codes," but Lefebvre refers to space itself as a "code." According to Lefebvre, architectural space can be deciphered; one may "decode" space to see an underlying meaning that may be socially or politically driven. In other words, the built artifact is a "code" and the underlying ideology is that which the code represents—that is, the building is the signifier and the ideology is that which is signified.[26] More specifically, legally enforced building codes inflect the design of architectural space, and as codes become more prescriptive, space becomes a more direct expression of the ideology that each code embodies. First, a general overview of the role of building codes in architectural design and construction is necessary. This synopsis is followed by a brief history of building codes pertaining to accessibility and usability.

Building Codes: A Brief Theorization

The legal, economic, and design implications of architectural codes and standards are readily apparent to design and construction professionals. Comprehension of these codes and standards (e.g., the International Building Code, LEED Standards, or ADA Accessibility Guidelines) is a significant prerequisite to obtaining and maintaining licensure or certification. The constraining effects and murkiness of these regulations, however, are often lamented. Navigating and conforming to requisite codes, nonetheless, are primary activities in the practice of housing design and construction. In the most general sense, codes can either be explicit written documents, enforceable by law, or general conventions or mores of design and construction.

> There is no art without rules to codify its practice. This truism has been consistently reaffirmed from antiquity to the present, and it rings true for architecture . . . buildings must obey an entire set of prescriptions that are as social as they are technological.[27]

Legal codes generally emerge from one of two broad realms: *technology* (e.g., structural codes and fire codes) or *social ideology* (e.g., ADAAG). Both of these realms are tempered by actual or perceived economic constraints. Technological codes emerge either from new innovations or from catastrophic failures. The great fires of Chicago and Seattle, for instance, resulted in vast changes to local and national building regulations and construction practices. Space and egress requirements, construction assemblies, and material uses: these have been the dominant features of building codes, with a primary emphasis on structural safety and fire protection. Codes were revised or augmented based on empirical research, such as materials testing, or from case studies, such as the code changes resulting from investigations following the Rhode Island nightclub fire of February 2003.[28] Codes, however, also stem from less scientific avenues.

Social ideology has had a growing influence on local and national building codes, yet there has been little discourse on the reasons for or ramifications of this change. Ideological shifts, whether localized to the discipline of architecture or generally present in the society at large, result in architectural shifts (and vice-versa). The disability rights movement is a clear example, inducing modifications to architectural codes, the built environment, and the legal system. Likewise, aging boomers have been responsible for driving code changes at the local level across the United States. Advocacy groups have a central role in code authoring, as illustrated by the aforementioned processes of the American National Standards Institute. The overriding mission of all codes is to ensure health, safety, and welfare of occupants, but this mission has been interpreted and proselytized in diverse ways. Insurance companies, lobbying for loss prevention, disability rights groups, seeking more stringent accessibility codes, environmentalists, promoting more "green" design and construction practices, among others, submit their agendas to code authoring bodies, which may accept or deny requests for changes. These advocacy groups often hold divergent, if not oppositional, goals.

There are also hidden, less formalized, though equally influential, codes. The preponderance of the gabled roof type among single-family housing in America, for instance, illustrates a shared aesthetic penchant which ultimately places constraints on the conceptualization and innovation of housing. (Further examples are discussed in chapter 4.) Antoine Picon refers to these constraints as "ghosts."[29] The aesthetic principles set forth by Vitruvius; the structural limitations of steel, concrete, or wood; and the accessibility guidelines developed by the U.S. Access Board: each is a specter that haunts the design and construction of architecture. The physical manifestation of architecture is an amalgamation of these underlying codes, whether culturally implicit or legally explicit. With such a heavy history, it stands to reason that these ghosts are occupants in every home in the South.

Accessibility Codes: A Brief History

Changes to building codes have always resulted in changes to the way that spaces, assemblies, and surfaces of architecture have been designed and constructed. With these changes, a new set of building conventions begin to take form. The emergence of "accessibility" in architectural codes has resulted in some of the most significant changes to building conventions (at least the design, configuration, and dimensions of space) in recent architectural history.

Despite the existence of standards since 1961 (ANSI A117), accessibility/usability regulations did not gain widespread influence on housing in the United States until the creation of the revised ANSI A117.1 and UFAS (Uniform Federal Accessibility Standards) in 1980. The publication of the ADAAG in 1991 further advanced the cause. Arguably, however, it was not until the creation of the International Building Code (IBC), developed by ICC/ANSI in 2000, that accessibility/usability regulations became commonplace and synchronous throughout the country. The IBC was a synthesis of the Uniform Building Code (used predominantly by Western states), the BOCA National Building Code (employed in the East and Midwest), and the Southern Building Code (utilized in the South). Though architectural, interior design, and urban design professionals continue to be vocal about recent changes and the need to clarify accessibility requirements and enforcement methods, the IBC was a major step forward not only in accessibility but also in the coordination of all facets of building codes across the United States.[30]

Beyond this generalized history, three other issues that illuminate the historical evolution of accessibility codes (including both the written codes and the ideologies that underlie them) are worth noting. First, the essence of "usability" (ergonomics)—the common ground between accessibility (specifically) and functionality (in general)—has been a part of architecture codes, including housing, since the postwar era. The 1946 UBC, for example, included two small but notable sections. The first, section 1405(b), specifies minimum spatial dimensions for living, eating, and sleeping spaces, as well as kitchens in residential occupancies. Presumably these minimum dimensions resulted from what the authors of the code defined as a minimum usable space given each relative function. The second, section 3306, defines the minimum width and slope, surface construction, and handrail requirements for ramps. Ramps are often equated as the primary architectural responses to the accessibility movement, but the basic code elements (size, slope, surface, etc.) were in place decades prior to accessibility codes. In essence, use and function were part of housing codes prior to the country's first major housing boom.

Second, accessibility/usability codes, primarily due to their newness, remain inconsistently enforced in the South. This happens both in housing, at the small scale, and infrastructure, at the large scale. In Fayetteville, Arkansas, for example, it is not uncommon to see utility poles moored in the center of sidewalks. This practice results from the contractual relationship between the city and the utilities companies regarding "right-of-way." In many areas throughout the city, the sidewalk is part of the utility system not part of the pedestrian realm (e.g., an eighteen-inch telephone pole in the center of a three-feet-wide sidewalk). As a result, there is increased inconvenience for ambulatory pedestrians and decreased usability for nonambulatory pedestrians. For both user groups, personal safety is put at risk, as the street is the only means of passage. Similarly, consider some small towns of the rural "Delta" (counties bordering the Mississippi River): construction permits and other regulatory systems may not be in place at the local level. Likewise, in comparison to more urban areas, enforcement may not be a part of the normal home-building culture. As well, home inspections for both new construction and existing home purchases may be spotty at best. The regulations and supervisions that might exist tend to focus on structural, electrical, HVAC, and plumbing systems not on accessibility.

Compliance with access/use regulations remains primarily the responsibility of the design and construction teams, while legal action (after the fact, after construction is completed) by public or private entities or individuals persists as the only recourse for noncompliance. This further isolates accessibility from the other factors that influence housing design and construction. While structural, plumbing, and electrical work is inspected throughout the construction process, compliance

Utility Poles in Pedestrian Paths. The infringement of commercial easements on pedestrian rights-of-way is common in many locales.

with accessibility regulations maintains little oversight. As such, enforcement of accessibility codes has been inconsistent across Arkansas and other Southern states, almost nonexistent in the single-family housing and manufactured housing industries, which make up the majority of the housing in the rural South.

Finally, there has been a transformation of the language used in accessibility codes. The terms "handicapped," "disabled," "person with disability," and others have been used at different times in architectural codes. In both the language of popular politics and in architectural codes, "handicapped" slowly transformed into "disabled," which has subsequently been substituted by "person with a disability" and, most recently, "person with a disabling condition" (though the transformation, presumably, has been prolonged in the rural areas throughout the country). This shift in language has been coupled with an increased recognition of the role of environmental design as an enabling or disabling factor in activities of daily living,[31] evident in the emergence of the concept of "universal design."[32] Historically, disability was seen as a unique, infrequent circumstance.[33] As a result, housing design for "the handicapped" was ad-hoc, resulted in specialized solutions, and frequently stereotyped the lived experiences of people with visual, hearing, mobility, and cognitive impairments. The disability rights movement, much like the equal rights movement of the 1950s and 1960s, has activated a reaction against these segregating, discriminatory design practices. Not only are these practices losing acceptance; they are also seen more and more as "bad design."

Changes in Design Ideology

Just as cultural values change over time, design ethos also changes. The transformation of aesthetic values, opinions, and predilections has been central to design and the pursuit of the avant-garde. Less apparent—especially to the general public—are the changes in design ideology that have resulted from technological advances in materials; research in human perception, sociology, and anthropometrics; changes to local and national building codes as a result of case studies or expert influences; and the emergence of new social, economic, or environmental dilemmas. As such, many design philosophies have experienced great difficulty in gaining both consciousness and traction in the general population. The emergence and advancement of the "green building" movement is one clear example.

The Analogy of "Green Building"

"Green building" (or "sustainability") has recently achieved heightened status in both the design professions—through the materialization of the LEED standards—and the general public —most notably through Al Gore's *An Inconvenient Truth*. Environmental concerns, however, have been a part of many design practices for decades. "Green" thinking has simply been protracted in its permeation of the collective conscious. Three major problems still remain.

First, the nomenclature "green building" as well as a general naiveté obfuscates many of the complexities and issues of designing and constructing more environmentally responsible buildings, landscapes, and environments. Some believe that "green building" is literally that: a building covered in green sod, moss, trees, et cetera.

Second, as much as the essential character or tenets of sustainable design might be understood by the populous, sustainable design has yet to be incorporated into practice at an equal scale. This is most evident in the design and construction of single-family housing and neighborhoods. As discussed in the following chapter, most of the materials, methods of construction, and design schemes employed in today's single-family housing developments are decades, if not centuries, old.

Lastly, "green building" is still seen as a specialized area, an autonomous practice for special-interest designers and consumers. This movement has not yet been synthesized into the general customs and conventions of design and construction. These issues serve as an analogue to the "enabler" design movements associated with disability rights: "universal design," "inclusive design," "life-span design," and so on.[34] The enabler movements have not yet penetrated and embedded into the culture of housing design and construction. As one Arkansas home builder in a public meeting on changes state housing standards said, "Who is going to want this universal design stuff?"—illustrating the perception that universal design is seen as a custom, market feature not a central tenet of all housing design and construction.

The Emergence of "Universal Design"

Universal design (UD) is a transformation and extension of the disability rights movement, accessibility, and "barrier-free" design. There are no explicit building regulations for UD, though UD is referenced by federal agencies such as the Department of Housing and Urban Development. Many experts in the field of UD argue that it is a way of thinking and designing and should not be explicitly codified. Nonetheless, the inclusion of UD language in documents/policies published by federal agencies such as HUD cannot be overlooked, as all current accessibility codes and guidelines originated from either federal legislation or federal funds. This begs the question as to whether or not UD will be (or should be) codified. (This is discussed more fully in chapter 6.)

Thirty years ago the initial focus on "de-institutionalization" and independent living shifted resources from state institutions to community-based programs. This focus was based on the precept that independent living increases the quality of life for persons with disabilities and decreases government spending. Despite federal legislation, millions of U.S. residents have remained dependent upon state/federal resources because little focus has been placed on the role of housing. It appears that primary focus still remains on individual health, health services, and medical intervention. This is true of both government spending and public perception.

Regarding government spending, currently one-sixth of the GDP in the United States is spent on healthcare—the largest of any expenditure category. In 2007, expenditures by the U.S. Department of Health and Human Services (DHHS) exceeded $672 billion; in comparison, expenditures by the Department of Housing and Urban Development were less than $46 billion (a difference of more than $626 billion). In addition, while DHHS expenditures continue to rise rapidly, budget allocations to HUD have dropped over the last three years.[35] In Arkansas, approximately one-fifth of the budget goes to health and human services, exceeded only by expenditures in general education.[36]

Regarding public perception, it is a statement of the obvious to say that people prefer to remain healthy and live at home as long as possible. Well over 90 percent of Arkansans believe they will maintain their independence as they age, though 81 percent also believe their health will decline. Fewer than half of Arkansans, however, believe that the design of their neighborhood will affect their ability to live independently.[37] This oversight is paralleled by federal and state governments who continue to place increased priority on healthcare financing and reduced emphasis on financing the design and construction of higher quality housing and neighborhoods. Nevertheless, a significant body of research has illustrated that performing home modifications for persons with disabilities (installing lever handles on bathroom fixtures, for example) increases self-care and reduces out-of-pocket and government spending by up to 20 percent.[38] As a result, UD is now endorsed by prominent federal agencies, including HUD, NIH, NIDRR, and DHHS. The vast majority of interventions in housing—such as accessibility renovations and the installation of assistive devices—however, have been extemporaneous, especially in the rural South.

The apparent aim of the ADA, and its reaffirmation in the *Olmstead Decision* of 1999, is the integration of persons with disabilities into the community to the greatest extent possible.

Integration, however, does not necessarily result in full access to nor does it ensure participation in the broader community. A house may be designed according to universal design ideals, but the surrounding community, in both its physical and social makeup, may not be. Inaccessible neighborhood design and/or the perception of an inhospitable social climate (e.g., "ableism") may result in isolation. Someone might reside in the community (be integrated) without the ability or willingness to participate (be included) in it. Integration and inclusion are two distinct concepts, illustrated by the first wave of African American adolescents "integrated" into previously all-white classrooms in the South who faced social and physical reminders in the hallway (such as taunting by white colleagues and segregated drinking fountains), it was clear that "inclusion" had not yet been attained. A critical question of this chapter, this book, and the civil and disabilities rights movements is, How are equality and inclusion achieved? The highest goal of civil rights is to establish "race blindness." A similar goal may be true of both disability rights and universal design: achieving "disability blindness." But is this possible?

Other Emergent Discourses

Countries and localities throughout the world have altered their urban policies and building codes to include greater emphasis on usability and accessibility issues. The United Kingdom's Part M is an exemplary instance, especially regarding this code's range of influence over housing. Part M was implemented in 1999 to increase the accessibility and usability of new housing construction and predominantly focuses on issues of mobility (rather than on issues such as vision or hearing), especially for users of wheeled mobility devices. This includes provisions such as ground-level, zero-step entries and ground-level water-closet facilities. It is estimated that 68 percent of new homes constructed since its inception incorporate Part M standards.[39]

In the United States, national legislation, similar to that of the United Kingdom, has been attempted. Among the most popularly cited examples is the proposed *Inclusive Home Design Act,* authored primarily by U.S. representative Jan Schakowsky of the Ninth District of Illinois in 2005. The bill was not passed, but continues to circulate and gain support, and was referred to the House Subcommittee on Housing and Community Opportunity on January 11, 2008.[40] Under the governing laws of 2008 (e.g., Fair Housing and the Rehabilitation Act), only a small percentage of housing units constructed utilizing public funds must meet basic accessibility requirements. This percentage is misleading, as single-family housing, for the most part, is unaffected by accessibility regulations; fair housing laws traditionally focus on multifamily housing. In addition, accessibility regulations have only been applied to housing developments where federal funding is direct; projects utilizing federally subsidized mortgage programs are not often influenced. As a result, an incrementally small percentage of homes currently being constructed in the rural South are fully accessible to persons with disabilities. The Schakowsky Bill, on the other hand, seeks to increase the accessibility and usability of residences constructed with the use of federal monies, and casts a wider net, impacting both multifamily and single-family housing, and includes housing that utilizes federal mortgage programs. The act, however, at the time of publishing of this book, has not made it out of congressional committee.

At the state and local levels, the spirit of the Schakowsky Bill has made some strides. The city of Tucson (AZ), along with Atlanta (GA), Bolingbrook (IL), Toledo (OH), Austin (TX), Scranton (PA), and others have established ordinances to increase the "visit-ability" of their housing stock. Advanced by initiatives such as Atlanta-based *Concrete Change,*[41] these cities, and the visitability movement in general, recognize that housing should not simply be designed for the residents but should also accommodate potential visitors—neighbors, friends, and family—each of whom may have a variety of physical and/or psycho-social needs. Similarly, this change in thinking about housing alters the percentage-based approach of most accessibility regulations by increasing the base-minimum of functioning, requiring that *all* homes meet a certain bottom line of access and use.

In addition to the aforementioned notion of visitability, there are two other major flaws with the percentage-based approach. First, it does not take into account resale and the fact that the average American moves every five years. Who might live in a residence next? Homes need to be considered over an evolutionary life span not simply for the first residents. Second, the percentage-based approach does not take into account the fact that disability/ability is transformational. Unexpected injury or unforeseeable health problems, or, inversely, new medical interventions can radically alter—positively or negatively—one's independence and freedom. Former president George Bush's New Freedom

Initiative appears to hold many of the same values of the visability movement, the ADA, and the *Olmstead Decision,* but has been criticized for its ties to increased subsidies for the pharmaceutical industry and a reliance on the "medical model" of disability rather than a focus on housing. What the commission that developed the ADA recognized, which the New Freedom Initiative does not, is the role that the built environment plays in fostering or hindering access to employment, housing, healthcare, education, and leisure activities. The bulk of the funding behind the New Freedom Initiative has been directed toward healthcare not housing and community design.

Conclusion

Specialized housing, like special education, remains the convention. In neighborhoods and high schools throughout the country, segregation remains the convention. For a previous generation, race was the central issue, as evidenced by the experiences of Charlayne Hunter at the University of Georgia in 1961. Hunter, along with Hamilton Holmes, were the first two African American students to attend that institution and faced verbal assaults by crowds of white students chanting "two, four, six, eight, we don't wanna integrate" and thought that a segregated educational system was the best model. Despite the unwelcoming hostilities of her peers, according to James Cobb, Hunter (later Hunter-Gault, the Peabody and Emmy Award winner and leader at CNN, NPR, and PBS) still felt the University of Georgia and the South in general was her "home."[42] For the current generation, disability is the focal point, while achieving a sense of home remains universal.

Segregation and discrimination have a history equal in length to the history of culture. As well, discrimination is ever transforming. Discrimination based on religion, race, gender, physical and cognitive ability, sexual orientation, and age have occurred at various times in the history of Western cultures. Disability discrimination is among the most recent, as "separate but equal" has moved from the train car, to the public school system, to the back of the bus, to the back door. Discrimination has been attitudinal as well as physical (e.g., separate drinking fountains and separate entrances). As "the material world and social identities are in some way an immediate reflection of each other,"[43] contemporary housing design and attitudes

Ad-hoc Ramp. Home modifications in the South are ubiquitous, but often unsafe and stigmatizing.

regarding disability mutually illustrate discriminatory practices. Yet, at the same time, the South has also held a sense of "unity," of commonality, if not solidarity, regardless of differences among its residents.[44] This is partly why the mythos of the South exists at all, and why other regions seem not to possess such a strong identity. This is also why, for repressed individuals (black or "disabled") it is important to return to or remain in "a region . . . fraught with pain and difficulty," because the localized South "provides a major grounding for identity."[45]

The disability rights movement is not simply an issue of pragmatism; it is not simply about access and use, or measurable allowances and tolerances. This is not to say that the functional design of an "accessible" door handle, sink, entrance, sign, alarm system, or drinking fountain is unimportant. But, as epitomized by the race-segregated drinking fountains of the 1950s, equal rights, especially in housing design, is an issue of identity and social parity. Furthermore, technological innovation, community planning, and environmental sustainability are inextricably linked to quality of life, affordability, and functionality in housing. Quality of life, affordability, and functionality, in turn, affect personal identity and self-concept. "Good design" requires an awareness and reconciliation of various social, pragmatic, technical, and aesthetic issues.

The major parallel between disability rights and race rights is the pursuit of "equal access." In both cases, the first materializations of access were provisional, segregated, and often unequal. In many places throughout the South this still remains standard practice. Although historically the greatest focus in the

South has been on race relations, it is arguable that today disability discrimination is more problematic, but also more hidden. Disability is often invisible. Although the image of the wheelchair user struggling to get in and out of a van with a lift comes to the foreground as an exemplar of disability, there are many more disabling conditions that are less perceptible. Hearing impairments, some arthritic conditions, early stages of multiple sclerosis, and certain visual impairments are but a few examples. Likewise, the lack of social integration—the inability, refusal, or reservations on the part of people with some disabling conditions to "go out in public"—results in a general lack of public awareness about the true prevalence of disability in the United States. While awareness of gender and racial discrimination has become part of America's collective consciousness, cultural awareness of disability discrimination remains minimal. The rural South is harbor to an unknown, though presumably large, number of "hermetic" persons with disabilities.

One major difference is that racial discrimination tends to be attitudinal and personal—such as denial of employment, homeownership, or education—whereas disability discrimination tends also to be physical and institutional—for instance, the design conventions that underpin the housing industry. A second major difference between integration of services regarding race versus integration of services regarding disability resides in the unknown fiscal ramifications. Intuitively (and frankly), as one Arkansan involved in disability rights points out, "It costs less to seat a black guy at a diner counter than it does to modify the door, counter, and restroom for someone in a power chair." Research is seriously lacking in this area. What is decidedly clear, however, is that current demographic trends will radically alter the policies and systems for health and housing services and will require new strategies for housing and community design. These trends will necessitate changes in resource allocation, greater public education about disability and the role the built environment plays, changes in strategies of providing health services, and alternative housing solutions and settings. As the demographic make-up of the United States, the South, and Arkansas changes, it will not be a minority population that will be affected. The percentages of the population affected by the aging of the boomers will create an ideological transformation about aging and independent living so significant that neither the federal government nor the housing and health industries will be able to curb the issues.

Defining Policy and Practice

KORYDON H. SMITH AND JENNIFER WEBB

Building cultures did not always have the form they do today. They have changed through history, sometimes slowly, sometimes quickly. But at any time, in any particular place, the building culture can be described as a specific configuration of knowledge, institutions, rules, and built results.

—HOWARD DAVIS, *The Culture of Building*

The housing industry is the largest economic force in the United States, and with it, for good or ill, goes the U.S. economy. The American housing machine is fueled by the collective value in homeownership, substantiated both by federal housing policy and by the behaviors of the American public. Homeownership rates have increased every decade since 1940 (excluding a minor dip from 1980 to 1990), from a 43.6 percent rate in 1940 to 66.2 percent in 2000.[1] Levittown, New York (1947), Levittown, Pennsylvania (1951), and Levittown, New Jersey (1955) marked the start of a new way of designing, constructing, and purchasing homes in the United States: suburban tract housing. The values and perceptions of suburban homeownership were clearly evident in Herbert Gans's well-known sociological study of Levittown, New Jersey. Levittowners exclaimed their newfound love of yard work. They also reflected on the freedom and privacy of their new homes, as one new resident said: "In a row house, you hear everybody's troubles. You are always hearing the other person's business and fighting about how much of the lawn and driveway is yours," but not so in Levittown.[2] Suburban life equated to happiness: "We have a new house and want to keep it up nice; this is not work but enjoyment. I've never been more content."[3] A house in Levittown signaled personal achievement, "something to show for all your years of living."[4]

This new housing strategy may have been born in the Northeast, but the value system that underpinned it was universal. Both homeownership and suburban living have been largely fueled by the concept of the American Dream, a phrase coined by James Truslow Adams:

> . . . the *American dream,* that dream of a land in which life should be better and richer and fuller for every man, with opportunity for each according to his ability or achievement . . . It is not a dream of motor cars and high wages merely, but a dream of a social order in which each man and each woman shall be able to attain to the fullest stature of which they [*sic*] are innately capable, and be recognized by others for what they are, regardless of the fortuitous circumstances of birth or position . . . It has been a dream of being able to grow to fullest development as man and woman, unhampered by the barriers which had slowly been erected in older civilizations, unrepressed by social orders which had developed for the benefit of classes rather than for the simple human being of any and every class. And that dream has been realized more fully in actual life here than anywhere else, though very imperfectly even among ourselves.[5]

According to Adams, the American Dream emerged and became possible because of the expansive frontier west of the newly born country, a wilderness perceived to be unburdened by the social and spatial hierarchies that characterized Europe (regardless of its native inhabitants). The dream surfaced with visions of what the vast expanses to the west might offer: the ability to own one's own land and, therefore, the chance to own one's existence, things largely unthinkable in the European ancestry. A series of events then allowed the dream to become real, including the 828,000 square miles of the Louisiana Purchase in 1803 (part of which was the future state of Arkansas), the Land Act of 1804, the Homestead Act of 1862, and the National Housing Act of 1934 (and its siblings) from which FHA home loans materialized.

Synonymous with suburbia, the bulk of the housing in the United States is made up of detached, single-family homes. As indicated by the 2000 U.S. census, of the more than 69 million owner-occupied homes in the United States, more than 56 million are detached, single-family units (greater than 80 percent), while more than 60 percent of the 116 million renter-occupied units in the country fall into this category. What is the second-most prevalent housing type? Mobile homes: they make up 8.4

House and Land. The desire to own home and land is essential to the historic pursuit of the American Dream.

percent and 7.6 percent, respectively, of the owner and renter housing stock in the United States. This may come as little surprise given the upsurge of suburbia and the role of the single-family home in achieving the American Dream. Yet, both American suburbia and the American single-family house are relatively new inventions and phenomena. As commonplace as they are now, neither typology existed in any significant manner in the United States prior to the twentieth century. In 1790, 95 percent of the population lived in rural areas, only 5 percent lived in urban areas. The 1920 census marked a turning point, where 51.2 percent of people lived in urban areas and 48.8 lived in rural areas.[6] By 2000, the gap between metropolitan and rural inhabitants grew considerably. A simple binary look at the distribution of the population, however, does not give the full story. In 1940, nearly 70 percent of the metropolitan population lived in cities, while just over 30 percent lived in suburbs. By 1980, the suburban migration was clearly evident, as nearly two out of three people living in metropolitan areas were suburbanites. Today, more than half of the country lives in the 'burbs.[7] So, does that equate to more than half of the U.S. population attaining the American Dream?

As content as some 1950s Levittowners—and neo-suburbanites—may have been, suburbia has also harbored discontent. In addition to the bored suburban housewife, Gans illustrated that suburban life was excruciating for teens. As one teen said, "After school hours, you walk into an entirely different world. Everyone goes his own separate way, to his homework, take a nap, or watch TV. That is the life of a vegetable, not a human being." Another concurred that, "In plain words, a boy shouldn't live here [in Levittown] if he is between the ages of 14–17."[8] Similarly, comedian George Carlin, in one of his stand-up acts, took a typically cynical tack, stating that the American Dream is an invention of the wealthy "owners of the country" to keep the working class in line. According to Carlin, "You have to be asleep to believe it." Carlin's cynicism appears to have some substantiation, as numerous books have explored the racial, gender, and economic disparities exacerbated by suburban planning and design. There has been less focus, however, on the burdens of suburban life for older adults and persons with disabilities. If the land-locked teen of Levittown waits anxiously for the day he gets his first car, does it not translate that someone with a mobility or vision impairment would hold similar feelings of isolation in the suburban landscape?

Here, suburbia is simply used as an example. It is an invention. Detached housing, the cul-de-sac, and attached garage are inventions as well. These features of the built environment, however, have become so commonplace that they become invisible. They become unquestioned conventions. No one any longer asks the simple question: are these appropriate for today's society? In addition, do the policies and practices that reinforce these conventions still make sense? Is it time to invent a new set of housing traditions?

The housing industry—composed of policy makers, financiers, designers, builders, and realtors—is a culture in itself, separate from, though not without significant affect on, the culture that it serves: home buyers and renters. The "housing culture" of the South, however, has been largely ignored by scholars and practitioners in housing, despite its deeply entrenched influence on American society. There is a cyclic relationship between social and legislative change, and they often work in tandem. The same is true of the relationship between *legislation, policy,* and *practice* [Table 4-1]. For purposes of this chapter (and for chapter 8), *legislation* refers to statutory law that has been confirmed by all necessary branches of government (or by the electorate in cases of referenda) such as to make it legally binding—including all directives, prohibitions, and funding associated with such statutes. *Policies,* as defined here, are the guiding principles; missions, goals, and objectives; and strategies and programs of an organized body—governmental agency or sub-agency, private organization, administrative body, et cetera.

Suburbia. Levittown initiated the ubiquity of modern suburban housing design prevalent today.

Policy may originate from legislation (explicitly or implicitly) or may originate from the organized body. This chapter utilizes the term *practice* quite simply to refer to the day-to-day conduct of the individuals and collectives that carry out or subvert legislation and policy. *Legislation* is what is required or prohibited by law; *policy* is the strategy for achieving those laws; and *practice* is what actually occurs and may or may not correspond to policies and/or legislation. *Legislation* is the most formalized; *policy* is less formal; and *practices* are the least formal, but most influential, of these activities, especially in the rural South.

The relationships among legislation, policy, and practice can be complex. Both overlaps and gaps exist between legislation and policy and between policy and practices. For legislation to be effective there needs to be congruency between policies and practices. Yet, by the simple virtue that different individuals are involved at each of these three levels, gaps will always exist. Sometimes gaps are small; sometimes they are large. Gaps may occur between legislation and policy. For example, the Individuals with Disabilities Education Act of 2004 requires public school systems to develop Individualized Education Programs (IEPs) for children with disabilities, but not all public school systems may currently be in compliance; Arkansas continues to struggle with equal rights in primary and secondary education. Gaps may also occur between policy and practice. A state housing authority, for example, might require a certain percentage of newly constructed housing units to be accessible to people with mobility impairments; a lack of understanding on the part of designers and builders, coupled with a lack of oversight on the part of the

Table 4-1. Definitions: Legislation, Policy, and Practice

	LEGISLATION	POLICY	PRACTICE
What it can include:	1. legal directives 2. legal prohibitions 3. funding	1. principles 2. missions, goals, and objectives 3. strategies and programs	1. activities that seek to fulfill policy/legislation 2. activities that seek to subvert policy/legislation 3. activities that neither fulfill nor subvert policy/legislation
Who can be involved:	1. federal, state, or local legislative bodies* 2. electorates 3. executive bodies 4. judicial bodies	1. federal, state, or local government organizations 2. public organizations 3. professional organizations 4. private organizations	1. federal, state, or local government organizations 2. public organizations 3. professional organizations 4. private organizations 5. informal groups 6. individuals

* Legislation is most typically established by federal, state, or local legislative bodies. In less frequent instances—and usually occurring in local rather than federal contexts—electorates and executive bodies may institute legislation. Technically, judicial bodies do not have the capacity to establish legislation. Some judicial verdicts, however, by virtue of the precedents they set, may affect legislative change.

housing authority, could result in a breakdown of meeting this requirement. Finally, gaps can also exist within legislation itself. This often occurs when legislation includes directives, but commensurate funding is not provided. The leading cause of critique of the No Child Left Behind Act (2001), for instance, is a lack of funding. An exemplar more directly related to housing is the disjunction between (a) the legislative sum of the Fair Housing Act (1968), the Americans with Disabilities Act (1990), and the *Olmstead Decision* (1999), which established decrees for community-integrated housing for people with disabilities and (b) the lack of funding to support the construction of such housing. Moving out of institutional settings and into the community is not possible with the current housing stock, which generally fails to meet minimum functional requirements for people with various types of disabilities. This is especially the case for people with mobility, visual, and developmental impairments. So, although legislation highlights the economic and sociological value placed on community living, funding structures and localized practices are not in place to facilitate it. Segregation and isolation of older adults and people with disabilities, therefore, continues. Utilizing the discourses of the previous chapters, this chapter explores the impacts that conventions in the housing industry have on residents with disabilities living in the South.

Single-Family Housing in the South

Before discussing specific conventions involved in housing, it is necessary to briefly discuss some of the major differences between single-family and multifamily housing as well as differences between the living arrangements found in the South compared to those in the North. The constituents, participants, regulations, and technologies commensurate with single-family housing versus multifamily housing are widely divergent, and the conventions associated with each can vary a great deal. In addition, the type of housing, family structures, and building conventions of the North and the South differ significantly due to climatic, cultural, and economic differences.

Because detached dwelling units contain much less variety in structure, material use, and spatial organization, and a smaller number of design professionals and craftspeople than large-scale multifamily housing, detached housing is more strongly rooted in convention, in knowledge passed on from one generation of builders to the next. Although the design and construction of multifamily housing is also largely rooted in convention, multifamily housing is more likely to incorporate newer materials, methods, and organizational strategies than single-family housing. Multifamily housing, however, is more stringently governed by federal, state, and local regulations and building codes, which may be either an instigator of or a barrier to change. National accessibility codes, for example, typically only apply to multifamily structures, though some local housing authorities and municipalities do require some accessibility features in detached housing. Manufactured housing and mobile homes, moreover, must adhere to a separate set of construction standards, different from single- and multifamily housing standards. Issues of accessibility have had little impact on the manufactured housing industry. In all cases, there is a gap between codes and dissemination; codes do not ensure knowledge or compliance.

Beyond regulatory issues, the greatest difference between single-family and multifamily residences is likely the predominant setting in which each resides: single-family housing exists primarily in rural, suburban, and small-town areas, while multifamily housing, by definition, is more urban. In order to understand the building culture and conventions that underpin

Table 4-2.

MULTIFAMILY HOUSING	SINGLE-FAMILY HOUSING
• is governed by extensive federal, state, and local regulations	• is governed by fewer regulations
• involves a multiplicity of design professionals and consultants (e.g., architects, structural and mechanical engineers, etc.) and trades-/crafts-people (e.g., welders, etc.)	• involves a smaller and less-trained construction and design team with fewer specialists and consultants
• is limited in location and size by local zoning ordinances	• is limited by neighborhood covenants, more so than zoning ordinances
• has a wide variety of unit types (e.g., loft, walk-up, etc.) and circulation types (e.g., single- and double-loaded corridors, gallery access, etc.)	• has a narrower range of types (e.g., ranch, bungalow, etc.)
• exhibits a broad range of structural systems (steel, heavy timber, concrete, etc.) and finish materials	• typically utilizes wood structural systems and a smaller palette of finish materials

single-family and multifamily housing in the South, it is essential to understand the broader culture within which each type resides. Housing is not merely about the house proper. Neighborhood, climate, local economy, and an expansive set of other contextual factors influence both settlement and migration patterns as well as design and construction practices.

In comparison to the Northeast, the South maintains a much greater reliance on single-family homes and mobile homes, and a much lower utilization of multifamily structures. In the Northeast region of the United States, 3 percent of residents live in mobile homes, 59.4 percent live in single-family housing, and 37.6 percent live in multifamily housing (two or more attached units), while in the South, 11.6 percent of the population lives in mobile homes, 66.5 percent live in single-family homes, and 21.6 percent live in multifamily structures. In Arkansas, the statistics in these three areas, respectively, total: 14.9 percent (mobile homes), 70.8 percent (single-family), and 13.9 percent (multifamily).[9] These statistics are intimately connected to the rural and agricultural temperament of the South and, commensurately, the more urbanized Northeast, although this has been shifting throughout the past several decades.

Beyond a simple indication of the corresponding context, the economic and social implications of a subculture predominated by rural single-family housing are immense. Employment is less accessible and less diverse, as is education. Access to

Mobile Home. Manufactured housing is common in the rural South, but is shaped by different regulations, financing, and aesthetics than traditional single-family housing.

health services—general healthcare, specialized healthcare, mental health services, and pharmaceuticals—also tends to be impaired in rural areas. Housing construction tends to be less efficacious in rural areas, as materials need to be transported greater distances and in smaller quantities. As well, construction labor is less predictable in both availability and skill, and there is less variety of construction technologies compared to urban areas. Real estate, financial, and legal services are fewer in number; and there is less housing variety. Although it is not certain that these limitations directly lead to higher rates of disability in rural (as compared to suburban) areas, it is clear that more restricted access to education, wellness, financial, and housing services is a major barrier to physical and financial independence regardless of disability status.

Although a great deal of data exists regarding racial and ethnic characteristics of single-family versus multifamily as well as renter versus owner residences, much less information is available regarding disability status and housing setting. However, two basic generalizations can be made: (1) all demographic sects occupy all types of housing; and (2) there appears to be little difference in the frequency of disability regarding urban, suburban, and rural areas. In Arkansas, of households in which one or more disabilities is present, 27 percent identify themselves as living in cities, 6 percent as living in suburbs, 37 percent as living in small towns, and 30 percent as living in rural areas. These numbers closely parallel those of households with no disabilities: 29 percent residing in cities, 7 percent residing in suburbs, 32 percent residing in small towns, and 31 percent residing in rural areas.[10] These statistics do, however, differ from other Southern states.

Historically Arkansas has been populated predominantly by small towns and rural enclaves as opposed to major urban centers and the suburban enclaves that typically surround them. Mississippi, Alabama, Louisiana, and the Florida Panhandle are quite similar in this respect. The Florida peninsula, as well as states like North Carolina and Maryland, inversely, withhold greater segments of the population in major metropolitan and surrounding suburban contexts. This difference is significant because of the demographics that typically occupy urban versus suburban versus small town versus rural areas. As is often cited in conversations about "white flight" or "the great migration," racial, political, and economic marginalization tends to occur at greater rates in remote rural areas and dense urban areas than in suburbs. Similarly, suburbs often maintain lower percentages of people with disabilities than do rural and urban areas.

Patterns regarding rental versus homeowner housing also affect design and construction decisions. The lowest rates of homeownership (i.e., highest rates of rental housing) are concentrated in three primary regions of the United States: (1) California and parts of the Pacific Northwest, (2) urban areas in the Northeast, and (3) the Mississippi Delta region, including eastern Arkansas, southeast Missouri, western Mississippi, and western Tennessee.[11] Low ownership rates on the Pacific and Atlantic coasts results primarily from high housing density and high real estate values. High rates of rental housing in the Delta, however, result from extreme poverty and the inability of a large percentage of the population to obtain housing finance.

Home values are also lower in the South than in the North. The median home in Arkansas ($72,800), the second-lowest home value market (Mississippi is the lowest: $71,400), is only half of the value of the typical home in the Northeast. So too are the economic gains of resale diminished in the South. Prospective sellers of rural housing in the South face added challenges due to lower numbers of potential home buyers and an imbalance of supply over demand. This is also coupled with differences in housing typologies. Mobile homes, with highest numbers in Southern states, have a median value of $31,200, as compared to multi-unit dwellings, most popularly seen in the Northeast, with a median value of $116,600. As such, there is added difficulty in making a profit in the rural South. This is an often-overlooked but major dilemma, as investment returns on housing is a primary means for advancing economic standing in America. But "cheap housing" is not ubiquitous in the South. Atlanta, for instance, among places in the United States with 100,000 people or more, has the ninth-highest percentage (2.6 percent) of single-family homes valued at $1 million or more, illustrating that there is an extreme disparity in the localized housing markets of the South.[12]

Finally, it is essential to understand the diversity of household structures that comprise Arkansas and the South. The traditional family is no longer the status quo. Households are more diverse than ever—for instance, single-parent families, multigenerational families, nonrelative households, interracial families, co-habitation households, and so forth. "The most noticeable trend is the decline in the proportion of married-couple households with own children, from 40 percent of all households in 1970 to 24 percent in 2000." Additionally, from 1970 to 2000, the percentage of "family" households dropped from 81 percent to 69 percent.[13] The building industry has been slow to recognize the increased variety of household types and continues to construct housing for a thinning population: traditional families. Traditionally designed detached single-family homes remain the most predominant housing type in Arkansas and the South. In addition to people with disabilities, the most underrepresented groups in housing are single men, single women, and older adults living alone, married couples without children, nonrelative households, older-adult married couples, families with young adults (18–24) living at home, and single-parent households. As chapter 2 suggests, a kind of "homelessness" results from this lack of congruence between individual needs and the housing available. Because of the reliance on single-family housing in Arkansas and the South—which lacks effective codes, design, construction, and enforcement—many older adults and persons with disabilities are forced into institutionalized living.

Home in the Mississippi Delta Region of Arkansas. Many rural Southern homes illustrate the restricted availability of material, labor, design, and financial resources.

Eight Dilemmas in Single-Family Housing

Despite demographic shifts and the improved efficacy of alternative housing types, it does not appear that detached single-family housing will be supplanted in the foreseeable future. The foothold that single-family housing will likely maintain results from numerous factors. One of these factors is the role that the detached home—complete with fenced yard, pitched roof, two-tone paint, and divided windows—plays in the collective mind's eye of the attainment of the American Dream. Secondly, the sheer number of Southerners who live in detached housing is extensive. Single-family residences make up the bulk of the existing housing stock in the South. There is nothing inherently problematic about the single-family archetype; it is the design features that have become present-day norms that are problematic. The single-family housing industry is grounded in convention. Not all conventions are necessarily flawed, but many features present challenges to older adults and persons with disabilities.

Eight conventions in single-family housing reinforce existing barriers to community inclusion for persons with disabilities. These eight facets of single-family housing—housing policies and codes, organization of the housing industry, demographic make-up, public perceptions, neighborhood planning and development, space-making conventions, construction conventions, and conventions in appliance and fixture design—are discussed below. These conventions are explored relative to the scale of their influence, from the macro (housing policies and codes) to the micro (fixture and appliance design). The goal is to illustrate the lack of fit in meeting the diverse and dynamic needs of the increasingly heterogeneous housing market.

1. Housing Policies and Codes

Although single-family housing has far less oversight and restrictions than multifamily housing (in general, single-family housing is far less technologically complex), designers, financiers, and builders of single-family housing must uphold a set of national, state, and local building codes. Plumbing, electrical, structural, and fire codes all influence how single-family homes are designed and constructed in the South, at least to the extent that these codes are implemented by builders and trades-people and enforced by local code officials. Most of these codes are "model codes"—written by a national code authoring body, such as the International Code Council or the American National Standards Institute (ICC/ANSI)—which are adopted by states or local municipalities. Accessibility codes, however, are not present in any of the model building codes for single-family housing (e.g., the broadly utilized International Residential Code) nor are accessibility codes present in most local building codes. Moreover, unlike plumbing and structure, most issues of access and functionality are not inspected by local building officials.

If codes are the "enforcement" side of housing, policies are often the "incentive" side. In tandem, codes and policies influence housing practices: the way people design, fund, construct, and market housing. Like codes, housing policies occur at national, state, and local levels. (A deeper look at housing policies, including the transformation of federal housing policies throughout the past century, is included in chapter 8.) For the most part, national housing policies focus on issues of income—i.e., "affordable housing"—rather than issues of disability. As has been previously discussed, income and disability are intimately linked; yet the bulk of the federal government's affordable housing programs—e.g., the HOME Program—place little, if any, emphasis on housing for persons and families with disabilities. The majority of these programs utilize capital incentives—such as tax credits, low or no interest construction loans, or other subsidies—to developers and builders for constructing, selling, or renting housing units to lower-income families.

In parallel, a great deal of legislation throughout the past eight decades has pointed to the substantive relationship between housing, poverty, and disability, including the National Housing Act (1934); the Housing Acts of 1949, 1954, 1956, 1959, and 1964; the Community Mental Health Centers Act (1963); the Civil Rights Acts of 1964 and 1968, including the Fair Housing Act; the Architectural Barriers Act (1968); the Rehabilitation Acts of 1973 and 1998; the Education for Handicapped Children Act (1975); the Fair Housing Amendments Act (1988); the Americans with Disabilities Act (1990); the Housing for Older Persons Act (1995); the Telecommunications Act (1996); and the Individuals with Disabilities Education Act (1997 and 2004). Disability, however, remains of cursory importance in these programs despite the higher rates of disabling conditions among lower-income residents. Quite simply, the incentives do not encourage an awareness or production of housing that supports diverse physical, emotional, perceptual, and cognitive needs, merely fiscal needs.

2. Sales and Rental

The average American moves every five years. From March 1999 to March 2000, 16 percent of the U.S. population (43 million people) moved to a different residence. A third of the rental population moved during this same period.[14] Such widespread migration can only lead to one thing: realtors. As of 2008, according to the National Association of Realtors, there were 1.3 million realtors in the United States.[15]

People move for various reasons, which may be work related, housing related, family related, or for other impetuses. The bulk of the aforementioned migratory population, however, sought out a new home in the same locale: 56 percent of those who moved remained in the same county and another 20 percent moved to another county in the same state. There are significant differences between short-distance and long-distance movers regarding the reasons each group decides to move. The bulk (65.4 percent) of short-distance movers relocate for housing-related reasons: more affordable housing or moving from rental status to homeownership, for example. In contrast, fewer than one-third (31.9 percent) of long-distance movers move purely for home-related purposes.

In parallel, long-distance movers are far more likely (31.1 percent) than short-distance movers (5.6 percent) to move for work-related causes. Comparatively, these two groups are equally likely to move for family reasons: 25.9 percent of short-distance movers and 26.9 percent of long-distance movers. Not only do reasons for moving differ between short- and long-distance migrants but there are also considerable differences in their demographic composition. Individuals holding a bachelor's degree are significantly more likely to move outside the county/state than individuals not possessing a bachelor's degree. In addition, much higher rates of moving occur among lower-income populations compared to higher-income households (21 percent of households with incomes less than $25,000 and 12 percent of households with incomes of $100,000 or more), and lower-income households possess a higher likelihood of remaining in the same county.[16]

So, how does this play out in the South, a place that lore would suggest has residents that hold great pride in their homeland? It seems fair to assume that Southerners would move less than Northerners, but this is not true. Nevertheless, "although census data show Southerners to be about as likely as any other Americans to leave their home states and region, there is abundant qualitative evidence from every juke box that they are much more likely to complain about having left."[17] It is not the act of moving that is important, but how the new location is perceived by the expatriate.

The typical starter home of approximately 1,500 square feet is intended to fulfill the needs of the stereotypical family of two parents, one or more children, and pets.[18] Additionally, these homes are designed for a fully-abled family. "Peter Pan housing,"[19] and spec housing in general, has been designed for a population that never grows old, never confronts short- or long-term disability, and is free from any specialized interest or need. Today's reality is that two in seven households in the United States report some type of disabling condition.[20] Even more important, most individuals will experience short-term disabilities throughout their life span: pregnancy, flu, chemotherapy, or a waterskiing accident. Accessibility in each of these scenarios is not simply design for permanent disabilities but is design for the life span and all that life brings, the concept that everyone is merely "temporarily able bodied."[21]

Accessibility is starting to enter the popular media as one of the most significant trends in the housing market. The arrival of the baby-boomers has propelled these concepts into the general population's consciousness through agencies such as the AARP.

Yet there remains a lack of understanding about fulfilling current and future market demands for accessible housing. An increase in client demands for accessible features that "include wider hallways, fewer steps, and more single-floor designs" for the "aging and handicapped" was reported by 62 percent of residential architectural firms.[22] Significantly, the reporting firms believed that "special" populations were intended recipients. Very few single-family residences, nevertheless, are designed by licensed architects. As with most services, households with financial resources are those that are able to obtain housing that fulfills their needs. For families seeking affordable housing, accessibility is a luxury that most cannot obtain. The previously mentioned design features, along with a wide range of other design elements, benefit all residents. The failure to recognize the role of a well-designed environment in the lives of all consumers is indicative of the design and construction industries.

One example of an attempt to encourage builders and salespersons to inform potential buyers about *visitability* options occurred in Irvine, California.[23] In 1999, the municipality implemented a program that required potential home buyers to be informed of design features that facilitated visitability. Builders ignored the required step in informing buyers about visitability options and model homes did not display any of the options available. Because the legislation only required informing the potential buyer and there was no enforcement component, compliance with the program was almost nonexistent. Builders must buy into concepts of visitability and inclusive design and see the opportunities provided to their business before promoting these options to potential clients. Increased public discourse needs to be a more central goal.

Just as builders and real estate representatives can be misinformed, landlords can be equally confused. In urban settings where individuals are better able to access services, landlords are more familiar with the wide variety of services and programs that support individuals living independently and can be more responsive to the individual's needs. In rural settings, and single-family dwellings in particular, landlords may lack basic knowledge concerning housing code, accessibility basics, and so on. Landlords may be unwilling to make changes to a residence if they perceive decreases in profit for a potentially short-term tenant. Even if the resident is willing and able to finance the accommodation, changes that may later reduce the marketability of the property are viewed as undesirable.

Landlords also experience the conflict between guaranteed income through vouchers and the potential quality of the renter; households that use vouchers can lower overall standards, increase maintenance costs, and increase potential for inspections.[24] While willing to help persons with disabilities, landlords often lack knowledge about disabilities or illness, about programs and resources available, and about ways of fostering community inclusion.[25] Some landlords may also have negative experiences with home modifications, as alterations may be "jury-rigged" not designed. Equally problematic is the unwillingness of many landlords to participate in the voucher program.[26] Educational programs and resources that can be effectively shared with landlords and residents alike can improve relationships and strengthen the community.

The real estate industry—a significant cog in the housing industry—holds a great deal more power than popularly assumed. Home builders and developers, engineers (e.g., civil and structural engineers), and the design professions (e.g., architecture, interior design, and urban design) are often seen as possessing the greatest clout in housing. The majority of home buyers and renters, however, never interact with these people, relying more heavily upon realtors. Realtors are more intimately involved in all aspects of renting/buying a home than any other member of the housing industry. Realtors are involved from beginning to end as far as most buyers/renters are concerned: marketing ("listing"), exhibiting ("showing"), and selling ("closing"). In contrast, it is estimated that only 2–28 percent of homes are designed by architects.[27]

3. Demographic Context

Not only are there legal and procedural systems that are influential but there are contextual parameters that affect housing as well. Social identities are influenced by demographics that include income, employment, education, gender, race, ethnicity, disability, and age. These elements are tightly interwoven. Income, the single largest factor in housing security and housing quality, is directly influenced by employment status and occupational type. These variables occur within the greater economic environment. Income is further defined by education, gender, and race. An individual's age and health/disability status are discrete variables that further influence household income. These identities are often unique to geographic areas as further influenced by regional resources and industries and individual community characteristics. These personal and environmental characteristics allow the identification of specific trends and, ultimately, facilitate the formation of potential solutions.

Homeownership, whether in the conventional economic sense or in the proverbial sense of feeling "at home," is a significant contributor to one's perceived quality of life. In terms of the various indicators of quality of life, the South has often been at or near the bottom,[28] often due (directly) to lower incomes and (indirectly) to lower rates of homeownership by way of income and occupation. Poverty has been synonymous with the rural South throughout history. Excruciating physical labor for long hours in dreadfully hot summer weather is often the pictorial of the rural South. This image does depict certain hard truths, but, more accurately, these images need to be understood as both geographically and historically situational, not universal. Moreover, the reader should be cautious about applying her/his own affects to the prevalence of poverty of the South. Impoverishment does not necessarily lead to unhappiness or the feelings of "homelessness" described in chapter 2. Many rural Southerners hold great attachment to where and how they live. Chalmers Archer reflected on growing up as a black child in rural Mississippi, stating, "I have many good memories of my experiences growing up in Tchula. After all it was 'home.' And it's just human nature to want to look back kindly on a place of which you were once so much a part."[29]

Homeownership, in every sense of the word, is central to being a Southerner and central to the American Dream. Between 1940 and 2002, homeownership levels in America increased from 44 percent to 68 percent.[30] In the mid-1800s, approximately one-third of Arkansans farmed land that they owned while the remainder "squatted" on government-owned land that they hoped to purchase one day.[31] In contrast, in 2005, 69.4 percent of Arkansans owned their own home.[32] Owning a home, however, does not mean that it fulfills the household's needs or that it meets current housing standards. Ownership, in addition, does not guarantee a return on investment, as housing values may recede for numerous reasons, including issues that are not in the owner's control.

Concerns grew rapidly during the first half of 2008, where it was estimated that nearly two million families would receive a foreclosure notice by the end of the year as a result of the housing crisis.[33] Estimates proved to be low as the late-summer/ early-fall credit crunch and historic plummet of the stock market sent home values downward and foreclosures skyward. In August 2008, 1 out of every 416 households in America received a foreclosure notice. This was an increase by 12 percent from the previous month.[34] In Florida, more specifically, the rate was more than double the national average. Not only do foreclosure surges affect the families of foreclosures directly but it also indirectly impinges on neighboring families who continue to make payments while home values depreciate. Families lose 1.14 percent of their own home value for every foreclosure that occurs on their block.[35] As of October 2008, it was projected that more than 7.5 million households owed more on their mortgages than what their residence was worth.[36]

INCOME   For a majority of households, income is the most obvious determinant in maintaining stable residency. Nationally, the median household income is $44,334 annually while in Arkansas it is significantly lower at $35,295.[37] Low household income in Arkansas is underscored by the fact that 15.6 percent of the state's population lives below the poverty level, 3 percent higher than the national rate.[38] Additionally, 47 percent of Arkansans eighteen and older report that, for a variety of reasons (e.g., retirement, full-time student status, or unemployment), they were not working for pay.[39] In the context of housing security, the national average rent for a one-bedroom unit was $715 per month in 2006.[40] In Arkansas, for the average household (2.49 people),[41] this translates into one quarter of the total pre-tax income.

Many households are severely housing cost-burdened, defined as spending more than half of their income on housing. In 2001, it was reported that one in seven households were severely housing cost-burdened and that number increased between 2001 and 2005 in 47 states.[42] Those most affected are in the very lowest income bracket. The bottom quartile of the income represents those households earning less than $23,000 and represented 78 percent of the severely housing cost-burdened.[43] While renters represent the majority of the severely housing cost burdened, homeowners are not immune from the pressures of housing costs. Harvard University's Joint Center for Housing Studies reported that 5 million low-income homeowners, through 2006, had severe burdens and that delinquency and foreclosure rates increased while ownership rates decreased.[44]

A generally positive economy has not offset the demand for affordable housing either.[45] Housing demand is always local, dependent upon local economies, local demographics, and local housing supply. In the Southeast, between 1997 and 2005, the economic growth rate was nearly 3.1 percent.[46] Five of the ten states with the lowest per capita gross domestic product (GDP), however, are in the South. Arkansas was ranked forty-eighth in per capita GDP in 2006.[47] Arkansas ranks first in poverty level and increase in poverty, something intimately understood by the state's residents. Each year, between 2000 and 2005, the economy was ranked as the most pressing problem facing the state by approximately 30 percent of Arkansas residents.[48] The availability of suitable, affordable housing, therefore, is a main concern, as a generally healthy economy does not reflect the dichotomy of households in the United States.

EMPLOYMENT   Income is directly linked to employment status. A primary predicting factor in welfare dependency is the absence of work experience.[49] "High unemployment and limited opportunities for the meaningful employment for residents" was one of the most salient problems facing residents of the nation's most distressed public housing.[50] During 2007, the national unemployment rate was 4.5 percent, while in Arkansas the rate was 5.1 percent.[51] More specifically, across the state of Arkansas, there has always been significant variation in unemployment rates. In northwest Arkansas, average unemployment rates have been 3.74 percent while in Pine Bluff, the rate is more than double (7.6 percent).[52] Lower than average incomes and higher than average unemployment rates place state residents at risk with regard to not only housing but also food, childcare, and healthcare.

EDUCATION   Employment status is most directly linked to education and, therefore, income. The Bureau of Labor Statistics reports that, in 2006, individuals with a doctoral degree experienced a 1.4 percent unemployment rate and earned on average $1,441 per week. In contrast, those without a high school diploma experienced a 6.8 percent unemployment rate and earned only $419 weekly.[53] Even basic educational skills make a difference in a household's independence. Confidence in basic math skills and, to a slightly lesser extent, computer skills, is significant to being self-sufficient.[54] Low education attainment has been correlated to housing and food vulnerability. More specifically, as education levels decrease for those in poverty, housing vulnerability increases, underscoring the need for policy that addresses local education.[55]

If education contributes significantly to an individual's ability to earn a reasonable income, reduces unemployment, and decreases housing vulnerability, then the state of education in Arkansas must be considered. Fewer than 17 percent of Arkansans (compared to 24 percent nationally) hold a bachelor's degree and only 75 percent (compared to 80 percent nationally) have a high school diploma.[56] This is a problem throughout the South. In 2008, the EPE Research Center analyzed a person's "chance-for-success" in each state. With indicators such as early childhood programs, public education, and educational and economic attainment in adulthood, the center found that residents of Massachusetts, New Jersey, New Hampshire, Connecticut, and Vermont had the best "chance-for-success," while residents of Mississippi, Louisiana, New Mexico, Nevada, West Virginia, Arizona, and Arkansas had the lowest "chance-for-success."[57]

Equal access to education has been debated in Arkansas courts for many years. The most memorable school integration controversy centered around the Little Rock Nine in 1957. Since that landmark event, the state school system has repeatedly been at the center of disputes with regard to educational funding and equity between class and race. Most recently, the Lake View School District filed several lawsuits (first in 1992), claiming that the "state's school-funding formula fostered discrimination based on wealth."[58] The state supreme court agreed with the school district (first in 2002) and mandated that the state resolve the funding inequity. Although the state developed new funding formulas in 2004 and 2005, and the Arkansas Supreme Court ruled in May 2007 that the state had met its duties, educational equity remains a problem. In parallel, Alabama voters, in 2004, "rejected by a slim margin an amendment to the state constitution that would have nullified a segregation-era amendment declaring that Alabama's children have no constitutional right to an education at public expense."[59] Education, race, and income are, nonetheless, intimately linked, thus, any vote regarding

Rural Pie Shop. In addition to the prevalence of home modifications in the rural South, other adaptations illustrate a mix of resourcefulness, imagination, and whimsy.

education automatically affects the other two. All affect access to suitable housing.

GENDER AND RACE   Race and, to a slightly smaller extent, gender are tied directly to income and poverty rates and are important predictors of housing vulnerability throughout the life cycle. In 2006, median household income varied across all ethnic groups: white households earned $52,375, while black households earned $32,372 and Hispanic households earned $38,747.[60] More middle- and older-adult women (forty to sixty years of age and sixty to eighty years of age) spend a year or more in poverty than those between the ages of twenty and forty.[61] The poverty rates for the same age groups are higher among African Americans. For example, 33.41 percent of late-adult black women with a twelfth-grade education or higher live in poverty while the rate for late-adult white women with the same education level is half that (16.84 percent).[62] The poverty rates for the same age group also differs for men and women: later-adulthood white males with twelve or more years of educational experience a rate of 13.64 percent, while the poverty rate for black males with the same education is 34.04 percent. Frequently, a household will overcome poverty for a period of time, only to experience job loss, illness, or divorce that forces them into poverty again. Once a person experiences poverty, it is likely that it will occur again rather than being an isolated event.[63]

The relationship of gender and poverty and, therefore, vulnerability to housing deficit is more pronounced when considering the growing number of grandparents who are serving as primary caregivers. Of those children living with two grandparents present in the home, 27 percent are poor. Nearly two-thirds of the grandmother-only households are living in poverty.[64] The grandparent households may be particularly vulnerable as grandparents may no longer qualify for elder housing since the number and the ages of the additional residents disqualifies them.

The South is home to the highest percentage of single-mother households (7.7 percent of households); Mississippi, Louisiana, Georgia, and South Carolina lead the country in single-mother households. Arkansas is fourteenth. Taken as a whole, the South does parallel national averages in the number of married-couple households, but, viewed more locally, sixteen of seventeen counties in Arkansas and Mississippi that border the Mississippi River possess married-couple households at a much lower rate than the rest of the nation.[65] This trend will likely continue as most of these counties are also experiencing population declines. What are the implications? The need for more affordable, smaller, more efficient housing becomes much greater, as housing costs—rent/mortgage, utilities, maintenance, and extra expenses—are less likely to be shared. Single-person and single-parent households dole out a much greater percentage of income to cover housing costs.

The relationship between gender and housing vulnerability is also noted in the lack of income equity. In 2005, median earnings show a 22.6 percent discrepancy between men and women across the United States, $42,210 and $32,649, respectively. In Arkansas, the gap was slightly more at 25.2 percent, where men earned $35,144 and women earned $26,277. Nationally, discrepancies can also be observed between races, although the gap between men's and women's incomes is less. Black males' median earnings were $35,480, while black women earned 88.2 percent of their male counterparts. For Hispanics of all races, males earned $27,490, while females earned 90 percent of their male counterparts. While the Equal Pay Act of 1963 equalized pay scales of men and women responsible for the *same* work within the *same* company, significant differences result from men and women working in different companies. Employees working in firms employing 76 to 90 percent male workers were paid 40 percent more than like-businesses where the workforce was predominantly female. Legislation to equalize pay based on job descriptions has lessened discrimination within firms, but it is the demographic differences between firms that contribute to income disparity between genders.[66]

AGE   As persons grow older, other demographic and personal characteristics change. For example, adults over the age of sixty-five are more likely to live alone, have a smaller income, live in poverty, and have a disability or chronic illness.[67] These characteristics place older adults in increased likelihood that their residence will not meet most of their physical and psychosocial needs. It is also more likely that the housing itself will be substandard.

Housing presents a variety of challenges to the aging homeowner or renter. While most older adults are homeowners (77.6 percent of persons over the age of sixty-five), the peripheral costs of homeownership are not always predictable. Increasing costs for heating and cooling impact monthly budgets and cause hardships for many households on fixed incomes. Many older adults live in structures that require significant maintenance. Aging structures in need of repair may result in a loss of value and reduce financial resources needed by these households. The home often represents financial security and may be the single biggest investment made by the household. If those financial resources are required by one household member, the remaining spouse or other family member is left with fewer resources and potentially put at risk.

The "old-old" (generally those over the age of seventy-five) are not the only demographic group at risk. Recent findings suggest that baby-boomers (those born between 1944 and 1964) will suffer as they try to manage increased healthcare costs, falling rates on investments, and a longer retirement.[68] The suggestion that boomers are not as well positioned for retirement will come as a surprise to many; however, it is the gap between those that have been able to prepare for retirement and those that have not, coupled with the rising cost of living that puts a large percentage of this cohort at risk.

Health is directly influenced by age. Age is the greatest predictor of disability and is exacerbated by the increased likelihood of chronic illness. Adults over the age of sixty-five report some classifications of physical disabilities at more than four times the rate, mental disabilities at twice the rate, and communication disabilities (e.g., vision and hearing) at four times the rate of the twenty-five to sixty-four population.[69] Although it is important to distinguish between the concept of disability and illness, older adults experience both disabilities and illness more frequently than younger adults, significantly impacting independence and quality of life.

HOMELESSNESS   The demand for affordable housing has grown constantly since the 1930s when the first housing legislation was created. The National Coalition for the Homeless identified "an increasing shortage of affordable rental property" as one reason for the increase in homelessness. Significant to the rural South, the National Alliance to End Homelessness reports that 9 percent of the homeless population is in rural areas and are homeless for the same reasons as in metropolitan settings.[70] Because income is such a significant factor in homelessness, rural settings can exacerbate potential homelessness as a result of fewer jobs, less steady income, and lower average incomes. In addition, many agricultural jobs do not qualify for unemployment compensation and the rural setting of these jobs results in a significant distance between the unemployed individual and unemployment services, leading to high travel and communication costs.[71] Although there has been positive growth in employment between 1992 and 2000, unemployment rates in nonmetropolitan areas have been slightly higher than in more metropolitan areas.[72] More important, employment growth rates were lowest in agricultural and mining counties.[73] When employment rates drop, rural areas are generally hit more severely and they are usually slower to recover than more urban areas. Generally, rural low-income families have less education than comparable urban dwellers and face a greater number of barriers to success.[74] Rural residents have lower earnings, less access to employment, less amenities and supportive services, and fewer housing choices. For the rural homeless population, relocation—to the homes of family or friends in other locales, to places that have supportive services/housing, or to areas with more affordable housing or better employment—is often the only alternative.

4. Public Perceptions

There are a wide variety of attitudes and predispositions about affordable housing and the individuals who reside there.[75] Not all of these attitudes are accurate. Neighborhood residents have concerns about the economic impact on the community, the impact of large numbers of people and large family sizes, and a misperception about who is in need of affordable housing. An examination of public perception must be compared to research findings to determine the accuracy of these beliefs. The initial economic concern centers around the belief that property values will drop and that the tax base will be eroded. This fear is not unreasonable. For most American families, a home is the greatest investment that the family will make; any threat to that investment is of immediate concern.[76] But are these fears valid?

When low-income housing is discussed, the immediate vision is that of Chicago's Cabrini-Green or St. Louis's Pruitt-Igoe. Both settings were stricken by all of the stereotypes of low-income housing and both developments were eventually torn down. High concentrations of poverty are characterized by chronic joblessness and increased welfare use.[77] Outcomes of this poverty include increased incidences of violence, crime, substance abuse, and school drop-out.[78] Certainly any area troubled with these characteristics may experience low property values.

With regard to housing values, most existing research suggests that the development of subsidized housing does not lower, and in some cases, actually increases local property values. Housing values, in contrast, seem to have a negative relationship with the size of the housing development: as the development size increases, housing values begin to decrease.[79] Economic erosion is not an inherent component of developing low-income housing in a community. As development decreases the number of abandoned buildings and creates a more vital community, economic prosperity has more often grown. Further, multifamily complexes pay a higher tax rate than single-family homes and contribute to a strong local economy.[80] A larger population means more potential customers for local businesses as well as a larger population of prospective employees. Further, increased density can reduce the cost of sprawling waterlines, roads, and other infrastructure.

Another concern is that affordable housing results in sudden growth in population size and attracts large families with many children thereby taking a toll on local infrastructure and schools. The increased density often associated with affordable housing developments offer both pros and cons for the community. Many apartments and smaller homes are inhabited by singles, families without children, and older adults. Only if housing is designed to accommodate large families is there the potential of significant population growth. At the macro level, most apartments have smaller household sizes and fewer vehicles than single-family dwellings.[81]

The impact on local schools is a significant factor when many families purchase a home. While apartments typically house smaller families, the potentially larger number of families can still result in an increase in the number of students in a particular district.[82] In general, any increase in a school district will require accommodation, thereby straining those resources.[83] Schools and the quality of education can benefit from the more stable population provided by safe low-income housing. If families move less often, a child's education improves, including fewer missed days, higher standardized test scores, and better teacher recruitment.

Finally, people benefit from affordable housing, even if only temporary. There is distinction between housing tenure (how long you live in one place) and neighborhood stability (quality, cohesion, and safety of a community).[84] A community can enjoy stability without necessarily having long tenure. Additionally, renters often meet or exceed community involvement and feelings of commitment to the neighborhood.[85] A significant number of individuals in the service and public sector workforces—in addition to older adults, immigrants, persons with disabilities, and families just establishing themselves—need safe, quality, affordable housing. Some of the occupational categories with lowest income brackets include building and grounds keepers, healthcare support personnel, food preparation employees, and farm, fish, and forestry workers.[86]

5. Neighborhood Planning, Development, and Zoning

Zoning has also played a significant role in housing density and housing form. Historically, zoning regulations have supported the development of single-family dwellings and have restricted the addition of smaller housing alternatives, such as "granny flats," garage apartments, and shared group residences.[87] The Planning Commission of the city of Fayetteville, Arkansas, for example, debated the advantages and disadvantages of these residential alternatives ("accessory dwelling units") in early 2008. Some of the commission's primary goals were to increase density, "serve families throughout their life cycle," and close the increasing gap between income and housing costs by providing more affordable options.[88] While suburbia and its emphasis on single-family dwellings and proscriptive zoning forces reliance upon cars for transportation and increase distance between home, services, community activities, and employment opportunities, accessory dwelling units allow families to provide support, while promoting independence and privacy for older adults and persons with disabilities.

Inclusionary zoning, a community mandate that requires a portion of new development to be devoted to low- or moderate-income households, is one method of providing affordable housing. This type of zoning requires either incentive or mandatory programs. Incentive programs provide fee waivers, density bonuses, and more flexible zoning as a way of encouraging affordable housing development.[89] These incentives reduce the initial overhead on projects and, theoretically, allow for reasonable profit.[90] Many municipalities have developed incentive programs with varying success. In contrast, mandatory programs have specific guidelines that state both what the developer and the municipality are to provide. Evaluation by the developer can be made well in advance of the commitment; this is important because the "worst barrier to housing production . . . is an unpredictable development atmosphere."[91]

Inclusionary zoning has both supporters and challengers. Some suggest that by having neighborhoods with "built-in" diversity, segregation can be reduced, schools become more economically and ethnically diverse, housing is provided for a wider workforce, the aging, and persons with disabilities, and neighborhood cohesion can be increased.[92] Others believe that this approach simply underscores the differences between families and can increase feelings of isolation. Inclusionary zoning regulations can be effective in urban and suburban areas where community growth provides a foundation for development. In rural areas, however, there is limited opportunity to direct development due to lax or nonexistent zoning regulations. The National Coalition for the Homeless claims that one reason homelessness is on the rise is a lack of affordable dwellings, nowhere more the case than in rural areas.

6. Space-Making Conventions

Many of the barriers that prevent persons with disabilities from fully integrating into the community are attitudinal. Public perceptions, attitudes of realtors and the building community, and the decisions made by policy makers all affect neighborhood and housing options. Conventions of construction and space making also have a significant impact. The real estate industry tends to market two generic types of single-family homes in terms of interior spatial organization: the "open floor plan" (also referred to as the "free plan") and the "traditional floor plan" (or discrete room arrangement). The open floor plan, which has become increasingly popular, because it is more adaptable and appears to have larger interior spaces, is characterized by minimal interior partitions and visual connectivity between the primary spaces of the home—such as living, dining, and kitchen spaces. The traditional plan, on the contrary, is typified by separated rooms; in this scheme each function is circumscribed by walls with small openings that serve to connect one space to the next. Both of these interior spatial schemes affect not only marketability but also usability.

Among the most significant spatial barriers to individuals with mobility impairments—especially persons who utilize wheeled mobility devices, such as wheelchairs and power chairs—is adequate space for maneuvering. Traditional home plans often lack sufficient maneuvering space in many of the primary spaces, particularly once fully furnished. The open plan is less constrained by walls and door openings (and furniture placement) and, thus, more easily accommodates space requirements for maneuvering. Some designers, developers, and residents, however, state concerns about reduced privacy in some open-plan scenarios.

Although the primary spaces are different in the way they function, the secondary spaces of both plan types, including bathing and sleeping spaces, nonetheless, pose significant challenges. As the spaces that accommodate bathing, toileting, washing, and sleeping tend to be more private and intimate, the space allocations tend to be minimal; these activities take place within circumscribed walls with lockable doors (so commonplace it seems pointless to discuss). The bath "room" and bed "room" are cultural conventions, however, not timeless, worldwide standards. Other cultures may variously accommodate bathing, toileting, washing, and sleeping in facilities other than the Westernized "bathroom." In fact, in the rural South indoor plumbing was a "luxury" throughout much of the twentieth century. The intention here is not to undo American or Southern customs in housing design but to refocus thinking on human activities of dwelling, to design housing not based on previous images of housing but to design housing based on current individual and cultural needs. To address the demographic shifts of the coming years, new design solutions will need to be created.

> The creation of any new group identity typically requires the "invention of tradition," which, according to Eric Hobsbawm, is likely to occur wherever and whenever "a rapid transformation of society weakens or destroys the social patterns for which 'old' traditions have been designed." These invented traditions often secure the emotional allegiance of the populace at large through the veneration of a particular flag, symbol, song, significant historical event, or a national hero.[93]

Housing also plays a role in substantiating cultural, economic, and technological paradigm shifts. New styles are created to represent new attitudes. New spaces are made to accommodate new functions. Likewise, new homes need to be designed to support changing mobility, perceptual, cognitive, and affective needs. As society transforms, housing must adapt.

7. Construction Conventions

It is well known, even among people not directly involved in the housing or construction industries, that various architectural materials—solid hardwood versus veneer, brick versus vinyl siding, et cetera—have different costs associated with them. With the advent of "green building," the general public has also become more cognizant of the long-term effects of selecting various materials and assemblies, such as recycle-ability, embodied energy, off-gassing, and long-term maintenance. Both the public and the single-family housing industry, though, may be less aware, or only tacitly aware, of the ergonomic ramifications of flooring surfaces, thresholds, countertops, wall surfaces, and so forth.

Like interior spatial organization, the materials and assemblies designers and builders utilize can significantly affect usability. The most problematic interior details are slippery interior flooring surfaces, poorly designed flooring seams, and inadequate lighting. Among adults age sixty-five and older, falls are the leading cause of injury-related deaths, as well as the leading cause of hospital admission. In 2000, falls among older adults resulted in $19 billion in medical costs.[94] Although the majority of this book discusses home design and community integration for older adults and persons with disabling conditions, it is also noteworthy to discuss means of preventing illness and injury. Slippery flooring in bathing and food preparation spaces can be problematic for anyone, but for older adults, people with mobility impairments, children, and people with impaired strength, balance, vision, or cognition, such surfaces can be injurious or deadly. In addition, raised thresholds or transitions, for example, the bottom plate of an exterior entry, can be equally problematic. Raised thresholds and transitions can be serious trip hazards, especially to persons who have a shuffling gait and/or who have visual impairments. Raised thresholds and transitions also impair mobility for individuals utilizing wheeled mobility devices. Yet these functional aspects are often superseded by the designer's, builder's, realtor's, or home buyer's unswerving focus on aesthetic or economic concerns. Home safety is an often-overlooked design feature.

8. Conventions in Appliance and Fixture Design

In parallel to the lack of awareness of the implications of construction detailing, consumers and the building industry, again due to a myopic focus on aesthetic and economic issues, tend to ignore functional aspects when selecting and purchasing home appliances and fixtures. In fact, color is often a more important selection criteria than usability. Appliances, however, are the most function-oriented feature of the American home; and the contemporary American home is filled with them. Architectural critic Reyner Banham once said that homes have become so full of technological gadgetry—plumbing, electricity, appliances, etc.—that a house no longer needs structure; it could be supported by all this high-tech equipment.[95]

As appliance designers have become increasingly aware of the concept of "universal design" and other ideals of user-centered design, some appliance manufacturers (GE, for example) offer UD product lines.[96] These newer appliances offer improved interfaces—more intuitive visual, tactile, and auditory cues—and improved safety features in comparison to their traditional counterparts.

Screen Door. Among all elements of home design, the "front door" possesses the most symbolic and functional importance. Negotiations of climate, security, privacy, and identity occur here.

Conclusion

Nothing is a greater barrier to change than tradition. The single-family housing industry exemplifies this. Contemporary single-family housing design and construction, for example, is rooted in conventions that are a century old, techniques that have been passed down from one generation of builders to the next since the early 1900s. Despite their pervasiveness, a majority of the structural techniques, systems of enclosure, and material assemblies currently utilized are impracticable in today's technological, social, and economic world. Designs (and designers) have been instrumental in many U.S. disasters, evidenced specifically by the levee and housing failures in New Orleans during Hurricane Katrina and by the ubiquitous "cookie cutter disasters" of American suburbia. In addition, housing policies and real estate marketing are built upon the perceived value systems and family structures of a traditional American society, rather than on the actual demographic composition and diversity of preferences that comprise American society today. As tradition plays a presumably heightened role in the South, the housing industry is more resistant in this region than other parts of the country to needed changes.

Moreover, construction, design, and real estate professionals continue to perpetuate practices that do not respond to the changing demographics of the United States and the South. This shortsightedness is further confounded by the lack of building codes and regulations in single-family housing. Concomitantly, the persons that most benefit from inclusive design are those least likely to have knowledge, finances, and availability of well-designed homes. Without argument, knowledgeable individuals with financial resources are those most likely to have the most housing options available to them. The American Dream, once characterized by freedom from social hierarchies, is now encumbered by economic status; and that which represents the fulfillment of the Dream, the detached single-family home in the suburbs, is equally tangled by an array of sociological factors. Even in its earliest forms, suburbia did not fulfill its promises. Levittown was quite homogeneous in terms of race, class, marital status, and age. This "homogeneity violates the American Dream of a balanced community where people of diverse ages, classes, races, and religions live together."[97]

The physical contexts in which individuals and families live are complex and highly varied, particularly in the South. Choosing the location of one's residence is important. The ability to live in a community where one can share a language, religion, and social values is central to the continuance of cultures and identities. Relocation for the simple purpose of employment or housing alone fails to satisfy many of the requirements for gaining a sense of home. Remaining in a residence that limits independence and participation or that puts self and family at risk also fails to fulfill the concept of home. Housing, healthcare, and food security are in jeopardy; for many Arkansans, these basic needs are threatened every month. Improving education, employment opportunity, public transportation, and other services are necessary to a comprehensive solution, yet the challenge of changing policies and practices in the tradition-laden South cannot be overstated.

Redrawing the Line

5

Redefining Disability

**JENNIFER WEBB, BRENT T. WILLIAMS,
KORYDON H. SMITH, AND NANCY G. MILLER**

Disability is a part of life. And some of us are gonna have it
young, and some of us are gonna have it older.

—"SPECIAL" ED ROBERTS, *When Billy Broke
His Head . . . And Other Tales of Wonder*

In 1962, Ed Roberts entered the University of California, Berkley
against the protests of university and state officials who claimed
he could not be successful either in school or, later, in the workplace. Living on the third floor of the university hospital, Roberts
and eleven other classmates with severe disabilities, self-named
the Rolling Quads, fought to overcome an inaccessible campus
and community, attitudinal barriers, and stereotypes. "Special Ed"
remembered one dean on the university campus, who stated:
"We've tried cripples before and it didn't work."[1]

Roberts and his fellow students found themselves limited
not by their own abilities and dreams but by social convention,
misassumptions, and a restrictive physical environment. By the
students' thinking, there was little that they could not achieve;
they were fully aware of their own potentiality given adequate
and appropriate resources. The students' needs and desires were
at odds with the existing infrastructure. If a person desires intellectual stimulation and camaraderie in a college setting, segregation in hospital-like living quarters does not suffice. If a person
wishes to develop workplace skills and pursue employment, an
inaccessible public transit system is problematic. Roberts and his
classmates sought resources that would enable them to live as
independently as possible and fulfill their aspirations. The variety of challenges faced by Roberts and his classmates underscore the biggest obstacle in the discussion about and the
investigation into people and their environments: constructing

and defining the infinite number of variables and the complex relationships between them.

As observed in the 2008 Beijing Olympics, Michael Phelps was able to set multiple world records as a unique function of his personal characteristics: a particularly wide arm span, a longer torso proportional to legs, larger feet, the ability to recover quickly, and mental fortitude. Additionally, there were design and environmental factors that contributed to his performance: a high-tech swimsuit, sophisticated timing equipment, a pool deeper than required by Olympic specifications, and the support of his coaches, teammates, and family. This confluence of factors resulted in accomplishments many believed were impossible. An interesting comparison is sprinter Oscar Pistorius's fight to compete in the same Olympics; opponents argued that the prostheses known as Cheetah blades gave him an unfair advantage over fellow athletes. His failure to qualify for the South African team nullified the argument at that particular time, yet the contrast remains: design elements that assisted Phelps were sanctioned, while the elements assisting Pistorius were condemned. Any other human outcome (i.e., cognitive functioning, mobility, attitude) is equally influenced by a wide range of factors. Therefore, attempts to delineate even a single relationship are encumbered by both known and unknown factors. Relationships between and among variables must be described with specificity to be useful.[2]

Additionally, variability is found in every species on earth and all of the aforementioned characteristics of person and environment have inherent elements of variability. Some variation can be categorized for a useful purpose. Days of the year can be described as hot or cold and these categories facilitate water cooler conversation. These categories do not, however, suggest whether a jacket, coat, umbrella, or sunscreen may be necessary. The categories "hot" and "cold" do not suggest that it is windy, humid, dry, or will change drastically over the course of the day, week, or season. "Hot" and "cold" do not take into account any of the activities that would influence individual evaluation. This binary does not take into account the differences between an individual accustomed to hot, humid climates or the perceived differences between a woman experiencing menopause and an athlete with very low body fat. As mundane as a weather example may be, it exemplifies the deeply rooted perspectives that individuals maintain throughout their lives. Weather, and one's ability to tolerate and even thrive in its extremes, is the source of much bragging on the part of both Northerners and Southerners. Eugene Walter, southern personality and writer, described southern summer "not only a season, a climate, it's a dimension. Floating in it, one must be either proud or submerged."[3] Hot temperatures combined with high humidity of the South are untenable by many and are often derided by all but the natives. Difference in perspective is well illustrated in Porter Wagoner's lyrics to "Highway Headin' South," sung most notably by Dolly Parton on the 1974 album *Love Is Like a Butterfly:*

> I'm gonna rest these chillin' bones in the Southern sunshine . . .
> The earth's sub-zero wind will never touch me again.
> A Southern girl can't live on snow and ice.
> When I cross the Dixie line, I'll throw away my coat,
> And my goose-down underwear will have to go.
> I'll never live again where the weather chills you to the bone.
> I'm tired of livin' like an Eskimo.

The dichotomous example of weather is also helpful in understanding the archaic concept of disability. As has been discussed in earlier chapters, previous notions of disability continue to promote segregationist perspectives that marginalize particular individuals without promoting understanding. Classifying human functioning as "abled" or "disabled" is as useless as classifying weather as hot or cold. Further, this perspective fails to advance design solutions that maximize individual opportunity and enhance quality of life.

Ed Roberts and other students with severe disabilities at Berkeley collectively garnered information and resources: a list of accessible apartments, wheelchair repair technology, work opportunities, and changes in policy both on campus and across the state. They sought ways in which to manipulate their environment to benefit themselves and others and that would allow them to live not in a hospital but in the community. Central to this discussion is the goal to eliminate the person-centric notion of disability and to expand our conceptualization to the range of human functioning. With regard to race, Rogers Brubaker and Frederick Cooper argue:

> This reduction of American society into a multi-chrome mosaic of monochrome identity groups hinders rather than helps the work of understanding the past and pursuing social justice in the present.[4]

Racial identity has transformed from the simple binary of black and white, now subsumed by subgroups such as biracial and multiracial. For the 2000 U.S. census, there were sixty-three combinations of racial categories, making the multiracial population the fastest-growing population in the United States.[5] Barack Obama, lauded as the first African American president, can himself be categorized a number of different ways: white, black, biracial, multiracial, and so on. Even the Irish have claimed him as a native son.[6] Similarly, the division of human functioning at any single point of the continuum is irrelevant and further fragments society. Individuals must be seen as existing on a continuum of functioning rather than as a cluster of diagnoses. Central to the purpose of this book is the need to create environments that respond to the continuum of human variation. It is first necessary to redefine disability.

No single theory is ideal in explaining the complex human-environment relationship; however, many theories, analyzed, combined, and reconstructed allow for a description of both human and environmental variables and their potential interactions. This synthesis can be useful to diverse stakeholders. For academic researchers, individual portions of the framework can be extracted for examination and testing. For the practicing designer, contractor, or architect, the model frames design decisions in a larger context so that the impact of small decisions can begin to be realized. For the policy maker, advocate, or service provider, the framework can help to frame arguments and decision-making processes for the lay audience.

The purpose of this chapter, therefore, is to describe a framework to achieve two separate but important goals. First, discussion will synthesize the significant elements that have been discussed in detail earlier in the book—variables influencing human and environmental variability, social, cultural, and legal trends—and explore the relationships between the elements. Second, a proposed model will provide a structure for examining these elements and from which questions and answers can be derived. In the following pages, a continuum of functioning will be examined along with the concept of person-environment fit. Functioning and fit are complementary ideas that, when examined concurrently, begin to define a new range of solutions with regard to the built environment. The Model of Person-Environment Fit describes this complex, reciprocal, and dynamic relationship.

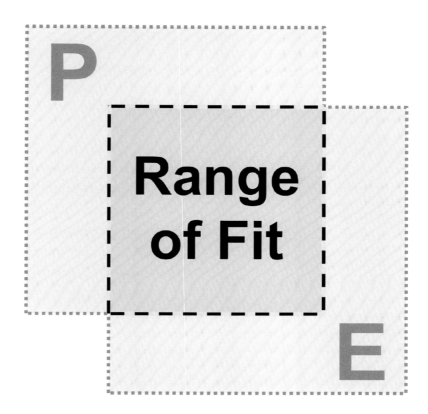

Figure 5-1. Range of Fit. The P=E Fit Model illustrates fit as the convergence of the person's and the environment's attributes.

Person-Environment Fit

The concept of fit, or the forming of a part to the whole, is a concept familiar to clothing. Consider, for a moment, the perfect pair of jeans: hip, butt, length, color, style, pockets, and cost are just a few of the most relevant factors. The search for the perfect jeans is legendary and has evolved to body scanners and "mass customization" to achieve the perfect fit.[7] Extreme? Yes, but as any five-foot, two-inch woman and any six-foot, eight-inch man can tell you, one size does not fit all.

The fit for a perfect home can be equally elusive. We use the term fit as an abbreviation for the phrase *person-environment fit* (P-E Fit), referencing the reciprocal relationship between the person and the environment.[8] P-E Fit exists on a similar continuum from complete "lack of fit" to "optimal fit" as an outcome of these interactions. The extremes, however, rarely occur. Instead, some degree of physical and psychosocial correspondence as well as incongruity is usually present.[9] It is the incongruity that triggers actions to improve fit either through behavioral adaptation or through environmental adjustment. Figure 1 illustrates the intersection between the person and the environment and the resulting fit achieved by the confluence of factors.

For the model to be an effective tool in explaining more

than the generic person-environment fit, the model's components and interactions must be defined. The person, or P, represents the unique set of characteristics inherent to that individual (Figure 5-2). Physical characteristics, sometimes described in terms of function, include biological health, sensory and motor skills, and cognitive ability; these can be objectively listed and measured quantitatively. These characteristics also provide a view of individual and population well-being using such parameters as disease, functionality, and aptitude. An abbreviated list of these characteristics include height, weight, gender, heart rate, pulmonary function, blood pressure, aural and visual acuity, tactile sensitivity, long and short-term memory, information processing ability, and the presence of disease.[10]

Additionally, the psychosocial category includes individual characteristics relative to behaviors and emotions, and how information about the world is generated, sustained, and applied. The identity developed and maintained by the individual as well as the ensuing self-concept are the foundation of this category. An abbreviated list of characteristics includes memory, perception, religious beliefs, values and mores, personality attributes, and self-efficacy.[11]

There is a positive relationship between an individual's adaptability and his or her physiological and psychosocial characteristics. For example, a great majority of individuals can traverse an airport quickly by accessing moving sidewalks. However, an individual with high levels of endurance and strength can also move easily in an airport without this amenity. Therefore, those individuals with higher levels of strength and endurance are able to adapt to a greater range of environments. Equally, most individuals can navigate an environment with the aid of a map but individuals who are able to construct cognitive maps with less experience are able to find their way more easily in novel environments.[12]

The person is fully defined, not simply through the physiological and psychosocial characteristics but through the interaction of these variables. The interactions are more significant than the groups of variables independent of one another. In Arkansas, for example, more than 7 percent of adult residents have diabetes; that percentage increased over 30 percent in an eight-year period.[13] A person who has diabetes can experience very serious, long-term consequences of the disease including heart and kidney damage, vision impairment, or damage to

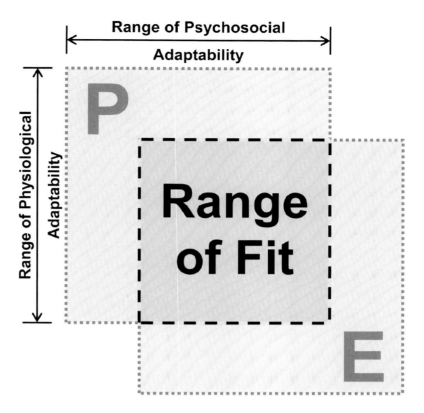

Figure 5-2. Physiological and Psychosocial Domains of the Person. The second step in the creation of the Range of Fit Model illustrates the physiological and psychosocial domains of a person.

nerves or vascular system. If this individual values good health, he or she will be more motivated to control diet, exercise regularly, and take medications. If health and well-being is not a priority, the disease outcomes can be severe. Additionally, the poor health resulting from diabetes can limit, by reducing the range of functioning, the individual's adaptability.

These interactions can be further illustrated through a more specific example. Imagine a man in his forties living in a small town in rural northeastern Arkansas. Following an outstanding high school football career, he received a degree in education from a local state college when most of his peers pursued employment in food service, agriculture or manufacturing. Returning home, he married and now has two children, teaches at the local high school and coaches football. He enjoys a good bit of prestige as a local boy done well and serves on numerous committees in his job, his church, and his community. He is a leader in his community. His sports interests have continued through his life and he continues a rigorous exercise routine and engages in a variety of sporting activities on a regular basis. Even his hobbies, hunting and fishing, require physical activity.

The family home, high on a hillside, requires careful

maneuvering in a four-wheel drive vehicle, especially during bad weather. The long flight of stairs up to the deck is viewed as a place for holiday decorations. The community is small with limited employment outside of forestry and agriculture. Healthcare and social services are limited due to the rural setting. While there is a family physician and local pharmacy, residents drive two hours to Little Rock or Memphis for special shopping, medical care, and large purchases.

His physical fitness enables him to drive to and from home and work, walk up and down the many stairs inherent in a hilly terrain, including access to his classroom and to the football field. His education has allowed him to secure employment that commands status in the community. The family doctor has adequately provided care for minor accidents related to his active lifestyle. His physical aptitude was the foundation of his earlier successes and now continues to contribute to his self-identity and role in the community.

When the environment exerts pressure on the individual that falls within the person's range of functioning, the adaptive range is considered positive. Generally, this adaptive range would mean that the individual finds the environment to be challenging in a positive way because the skills and abilities are being used. When the pressure falls outside of the person's range of functioning, adaptation may be negative. Skills and abilities may atrophy through lack of use or the person may stop trying if the demands seem too harsh.[14] For example, even a short walk to the mailbox may be avoided if the pavement is uneven and the individual has a shuffling gait as a result of Parkinson's Disease.

This example illustrates the range of fit when the person has substantial adaptability both physically and psychosocially (Figure 5-3). A physically inaccessible environment has not limited his success and perhaps may have even contributed to his current role. The environment offers a number of challenges and this man may feel tested by the environment and enjoy his triumphs over the barriers. The lack of public transport, few employment opportunities, and limited social services and medical care have not had an impact on his quality of life. In this instance, his personal characteristics have allowed him to live and even to thrive in this environment.

Similarly, the environment, or E, can be divided into two spheres: the physical environment and the cultural environment

Range of Psychosocial Adaptability

Range of Physiological Adaptability

P

Range of Fit

E

Range of Physical Adaptability

Range of Cultural Adaptability

Figure 5-3. Domains of Personal Adaptation. This diagram illustrates how range of fit is maintained as a function of an individual's psychosocial and physiological adaptability.

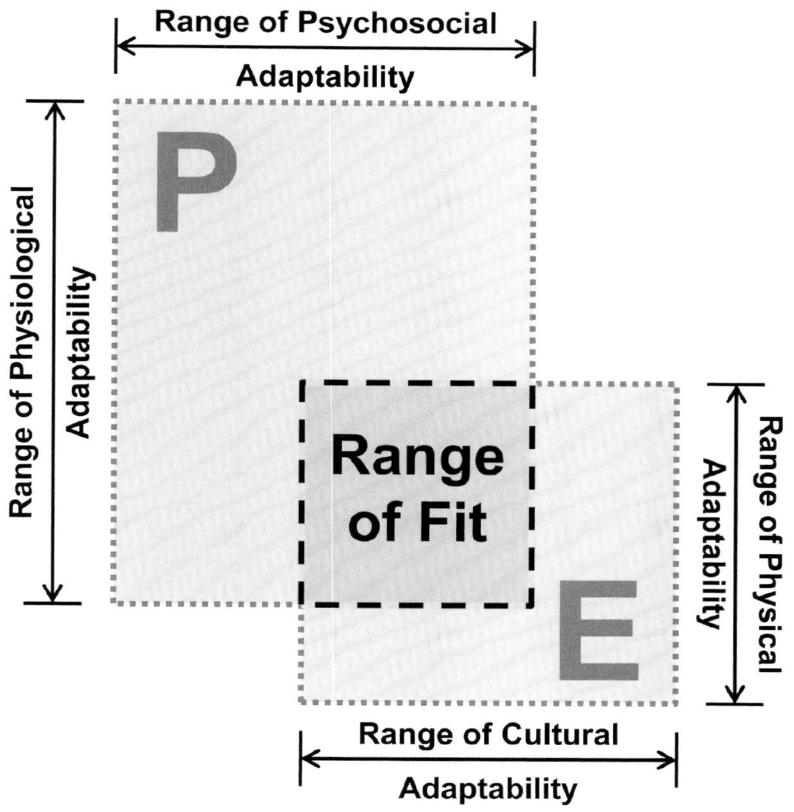

(Figure 5-4). Both natural and constructed environments comprise the physical realm.[15] Topography, climate, flora, and fauna are part of the natural environment. The constructed environment includes all that people construct, from a temporary shelter used for camping to the farms, homes, and cities that constitute the contemporary genre, as well as infrastructures, such as water, power, and transportation systems.

Equally diverse is the cultural environment that includes the symbolic structures that are shared between group members. The cultural environment is created by the society and is comprised of shared values, mores, and rules of behavior.[16] The cultural environment not only directs or limits human activity but is also evidenced through artifacts such as music, art, and literature. Social roles, sanctioned by the culture, are significant to the development of identity. Cultural environments, similar to physical environments, exist on many scales[17] and include family, community, and in contexts such as political environments and international organizations. Infrastructures, influenced by cultural values, exist in education and training, social service programs, and the provision of healthcare.[18]

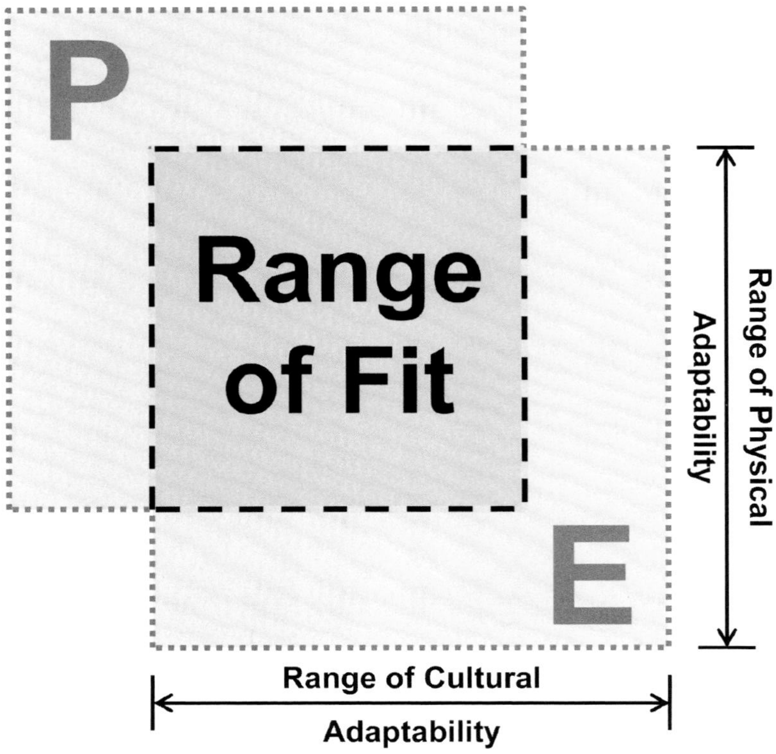

Figure 5-4. Physical and Cultural Domains of the Environment. The third step in the creation of the Range of Fit Model illustrates the physical and cultural domains of the environment.

As with people, environments are not defined solely by the broad classifications of variables but by their interactions. This interaction is illustrated by the example of the University of California, Berkeley campus. In 1962, Ed Roberts found a single person, Dr. Henry Bruyn, who facilitated his use of the campus hospital as a dormitory. Combined with the financial resources to pay personal attendants, Ed began changing the attitudes of campus administrators, faculty members, and students. In six years, the hospital come dormitory became a formalized program and the city of Berkeley committed $50,000 a year to provide curb cuts around the city. The students facilitated physical changes in the environment (i.e., an accessible campus and community) by changing values in the cultural environment.[19]

Another, more specific, example can illustrate these interactions. Imagine a woman in her early twenties living in Atlanta, Georgia. She is African American and has a large, close-knit family and circle of friends. She lives with her husband in a home near friends and family. The church is a cornerstone of her life, providing both social and emotional support. She received a diploma from a noted technical high school and has skills applicable to quality-control positions in the manufacturing industry. She has cerebral palsy and depends on a power chair. The chair is both heavy and large, requiring a good deal of space for maneuvering, ample sidewalks, curb cuts, and lifts.

Atlanta is the largest urban setting in the southeastern United States. The actions of Concrete Change pushed visitability standards forward and new housing is required to have an accessible entrance, wide doorways, and a bathroom with basic accessibility features. The city has mass transit that includes a bus system, each bus complete with chair lifts, as well as a train system where stations and trains are accessible. There is a variety of commerce that includes healthcare, higher education, corporate enterprises, and manufacturing. The urban population is diverse and there are a variety of advocacy groups and many services available to Atlanta's residents. The African American community provides social, emotional, and informal support to its members through church and cultural affiliations.

This woman and her family found a variety of housing that fulfilled their needs. There is a bus stop connecting to the train station just a block from their home. The reliable public transit allows her to commute independently to her manufacturing job some distance away as well as to access healthcare and other services. This setting also allows her to complete many personal errands in her neighborhood. The variety of enterprises in the region has allowed her to find a job that is well suited to her skills and that provides benefits such as health insurance. The church community provides volunteers to assist with small home repairs and maintenance and on most any given evening there is some activity in which community residents can participate.

This particular example illustrates how an individual with limitations in mobility is able to live independently because of her environment (Figure 5-5). This woman's health status has resulted not only in reduced mobility but also requires assistance with many activities of daily living such as bathing, dressing, and meal preparation. Without transportation, employment, and access to services it would be very difficult for her and her family. The density of her urban neighborhood allows her to fulfill most of her needs in a small geographic area and has allowed her to develop many personal relationships. The culture of her family is inclusive and supportive. When this is coupled with a community rich in resources (i.e., family and inclusive community, notable city

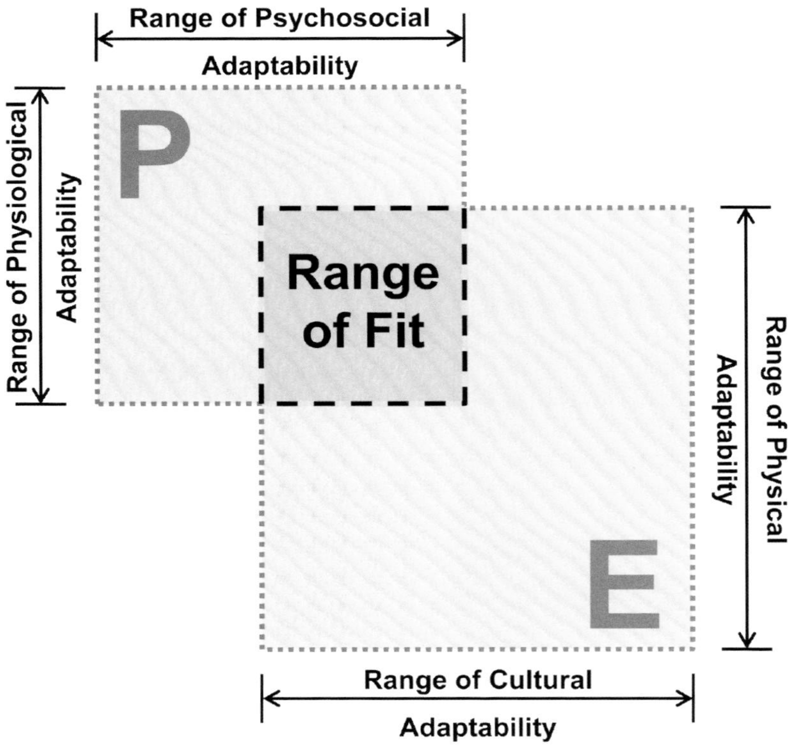

Figure 5-5. Domains of Environmental Adaptation. This diagram illustrates how range of fit is maintained as a function of an environment's physical and cultural adaptability.

infrastructure, variety of services, education, and employment), this individual is able to participate in her community and enjoy a high quality of life. Her person-environmental fit is the culmination of personal attributes, constrained by the influence of cerebral palsy, but expanded by a diverse, supportive physical and cultural environment.

Specific examples aid understanding of complex interactions between multiple variables. It is important, however, to place these examples in the larger context. For personal factors, both physiological and psychosocial, there is a range of responses that encompasses the entire population. The speed with which one completes the 100-meter sprint can vary from the world recordholder who requires just a few seconds to the individual who needs hours or days to complete the same distance. Just as important as the total range of variability between people is the variability experienced by each individual. While the sprinter runs faster than anyone else in a particular race, there is a range of time associated with day-to-day performance. A poor night's sleep, a mental distraction, or a temporary change in health status can alter performance. Each person has his or her own range of functioning that falls within the population domain.

Environments possess similar ranges of diversity with regard to particular attributes. Temperatures can soar in desert areas but drop far below zero near the poles. Terrain can be flat or mountainous. Services to enable independent living (e.g., job training, health professionals, housing advocates) may be diverse in urban areas but may be nonexistent in a rural setting. Some regions value and protect the environment, celebrate the arts, or champion sports teams. There may be liberal or conservative ideologies that are prevalent in particular settings. Like individuals within the population, each context possesses a dynamic set of characteristics that exists within the larger environmental sphere.

As with the significantly more mundane example of the weather, human functioning can be measured in discrete units on a variety of scales. Functioning varies, therefore, between individuals in minute degrees. There is also difference in which particular factors are most relevant for each individual. Characteristics associated with cognitive functioning may be significant in employment type and performance but not relevant in the relationships developed socially. Decreased visual acuity may prevent one from playing baseball but may not influence one's ability to work effectively with others, to perform housekeeping tasks, or to parent children. Variation in either psychosocial or physiological adaptability limits the range of fit with the environment, although the specific variables at play will vary from person to person.

This variability can be influenced by any number of factors that are in flux on a regular basis. Wellness and health status vary significantly even over small time frames. Some illnesses can be influenced by temperature or time of day such as arthritis. Other chronic illnesses can be long lasting or recurrent and influence human functioning on a highly variable schedule. For some individuals, a particular level of functioning can be relatively static with small increments of change over long periods of time. For others, a change in functioning could be both sudden and extreme. Judy Heumann is credited with the term "temporarily able bodied,"[20] a concept suggesting that no person is or will be without a disabling condition at some point in his or her future. These temporary conditions include the aftereffects of the flu, chemotherapy, stroke, or a car accident. Within the aforementioned context, someone with a short-term reduction in ability is not considered disabled, while a permanent or lengthy change results in a reclassification of that individual. Despite many individual efforts, even the most careful lifestyles and health regimes do not negate the eventual changes associated with aging. For each person, these changes will happen asynchronously as a function of genetic makeup, lifestyle, and other factors.

Return to the example of the man living in northeastern Arkansas, fifteen years in the future. He is experiencing the onset of arthritis as an outcome of his athletic injuries. He is no longer able to climb the stairs to his home, his classroom, or the football field easily. The doctor believes knee replacements would help, but that means travel to one of the regional cities for the surgery and physical therapy. The discomfort has resulted in weight gain, resignation from several committees, and has left him feeling unlike himself. A single factor, changing his health status, has altered his fit within his environment and, therefore, his quality of life.

Figure 5-6 illustrates these changes in his person-environment fit. Because of the arthritis, our high school football coach has experienced an overall reduction in his physical functioning. The axis is smaller in size, thereby reducing his overall range of fit. Additionally, these physical changes have also reduced his feelings of self-worth and competency, further reducing the range of fit. The environmental barriers that were surmounted by his generally robust personal attributes are now significantly more important. The representations in Figure 5-6, therefore, are simple snapshots in time and do not adequately illustrate the possible variation that may occur over time.

If each person is unique, so too is each environment. The final design outcome is not only influenced by the sensitivities of the design team and necessary functions but also by the physical characteristics, users, and activities.[21] Physical determinants include site and climatic conditions, materials, and so on. While many buildings are often based on prototypical design standards, adjustments are necessary in varying degrees to assure a reasonable interface with each context. There are particular factors that will be more significant for some structures than for others; for example, a flat site may force vertical circulation to be a determining factor while a sloped site may allow on-grade entry from several levels. Further variations inherent on cultural contexts influence the final design outcome, as do legal building codes and similar legislation. Just as people have been encumbered with labels relative to performance, so too are buildings

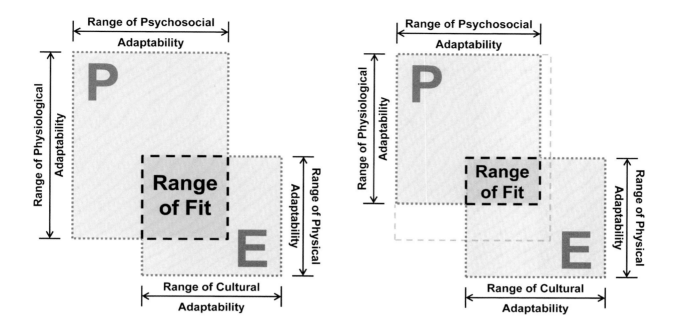

Figure 5-6. Changes in a Person's Attributes. This diagram illustrates how changes in a person's physiological and psychosocial attributes can result in decreased fit.

labeled accessible, even if the only accommodation has been a ramp for persons who use wheelchairs.

That buildings are relatively static over their life span seems obvious. However, change occurs when buildings are renovated or when usage is altered. Changes in legislation relative to accessibility as well as in building technology can have a significant impact on entrances, circulation spaces, public areas, signage, and communication systems. Even changing values in a cultural context can affect building form; the growing movement for sustainable or "green" architecture is indicative of the change values with regard to energy and water usage and resource preservation. Buildings change over the course of a day, a week, or a season as factors such as weather, position of the sun, and rainfall vary.

Environments are even more dynamic when the users and activities are considered. Most public buildings are the site of a wide range of users over the course of days or weeks. A hotel that hosts a wedding reception one weekend may serve as the conference site for a local Area Agency on Aging. The local health club may provide traditional fitness opportunities but may also have classes for cardio-recovery, childbirth, and weight management. Buildings change as the activities within change. Rural schools, for example, house students in academic endeavors during the day, but may also be the place of extracurricular activities in the afternoon, and a location for community groups during the evening. The school is a good example of the need

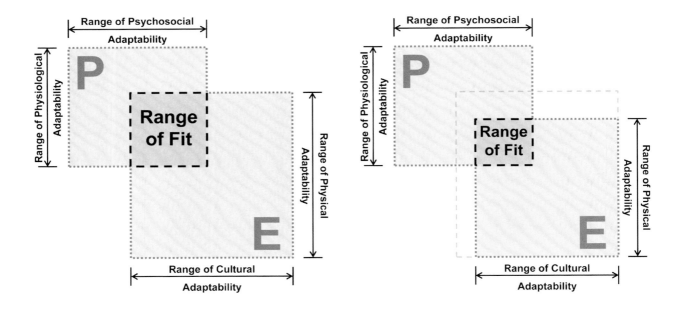

Figure 5-7. Changes in Environmental Characteristics. This diagram illustrates how changes in environmental characteristics can result in decreased fit.

for universal design. The multiple functions and the multiple user groups require a design solution that is responsive and inclusive. Just as importantly, individuals move from one space to another as they pursue their daily activities; home to transit station to workplace to café to grocery store and home again is a common sequence of daily activities.

The woman living in Atlanta has relocated to a small town outside of Atlanta due to her husband's employment. In this town, there is no public transport. Abruptly, she is no longer able to reach her doctor or other service providers without assistance. The absence of sidewalks and curb cuts means that she is unable to shop and complete other errands independently. Without reliable transportation, she has been unable to find employment that works with her family's other demands. She has become isolated as she is unable to visit friends or participate in community activities very easily. A single factor, changing public transport, has completely altered her quality of life. Figure 5-7 illustrates the changes in her person-environment fit. Because she now resides in a community without public transport, her range of fit has been significantly reduced.

These examples provide two very different, but realistic, scenarios. In both cases, the person and the environment are well suited to each other. However, relatively small changes such as a reduction in physical functioning or the loss of public

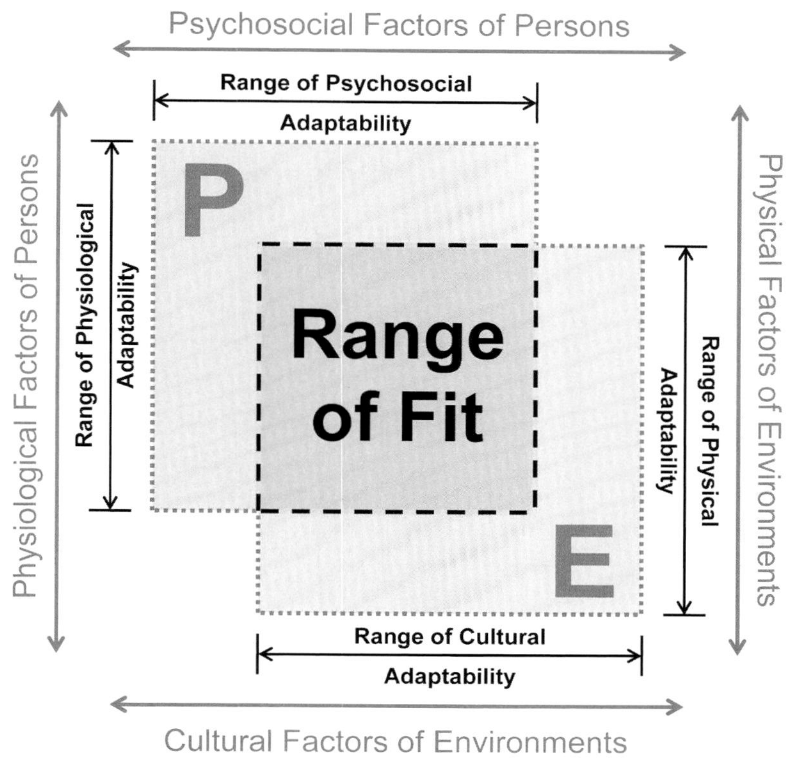

Figure 5-8. Complete P-E Fit Model. The final diagram illustrates the Person's and the Environment's unique range of attributes in the context of all possible variation in people and environments.

transport clearly illustrate the reduction in person-environment fit. In the first scenario, the woman enjoys independence and a high quality of life as a direct function of the environment: public transport, accessible housing and neighborhood, employment opportunities, a supportive cultural environment. In the second scenario, the man enjoys independence as a function of his physical aptitude, education, status, and sense of self. Change one of these variables—one element of the environment (E) or one attribute of the person (P)—and independent living is altered for both individuals.

In the model presented, the interaction between people and their environments has been illustrated. Each individual, P, has a unique set of physiological and psychosocial characteristics, while each context, E, has a responding set of physical and cultural attributes. These particular characteristics fall within the greater range of all people and all environments. The Range of Fit is the interaction between these groups of variables (Figure 5-8).

Conclusion

The proposed framework suggests that attributes of persons and their environments are circumstantial. However, it is necessary to understand that, in spite of all of these forces, fit can be transformed. These purposeful manipulations must be carefully weighed against one another to create a good person-environment fit. First, the major facets of fit—person and environment—must be understood, as they are interrelated. In addition, person-environment fit must be assessed across scales: from federal to local, policy to practice, and society to individual. As well, P-E fit must also be understood across domains: health and housing, needs and preferences, physical and psychosocial. Finally, policy makers, builders, designers, and the general public need to understand the ever-changing status of person, environment, and resultant fit.

Fit is a dynamic and complex process. The relationship between the person and the environment is not static but is contingent upon the complexities of human intentions and changing priorities of the individual's role at a particular point in time and place. Achieving greater fit does not come without associated costs both to the individual and to the larger society. Improving person-environment fit requires changes to the person, the environment, or both. Alterations to the environment require resources such as materials, labor, money, and time. While the investments can be made by the individual or family, the community can also make investments on individuals' behalf. Likewise, changes to individual health, aptitude, knowledge, and attitudes can increase the degree of fit. These efforts, like changes to the environment, require individual and/or public resources.

On many scales, improved fit may never be addressed because both individuals and communities have become immune to the impact of the environment on behavior. Many public policies, community plans, and housing designs are generated without full understanding of implications. This is particularly true in the rural South. A homeowner may be stymied by a lack of available resources, basic construction knowledge, and foresight, while professionals and service agencies may rely on incomplete or incorrect information covered up by tradition or a "that's the way we always did it" mindset. Persons with disabilities may find the costs of achieving fit greater than average. The efforts to change the environment can negatively influence emotional health and physical or mental fatigue. Resulting behavioral changes may not always be positive for the individual. Overcoming barriers by altering one's behavior can be maladaptive due to reduced participation, avoidance of particular locations or activities, or simply lowered expectations at the individual's expense. In some cases, fit with the built environment may not be achievable through environmental change alone.

It is critical to the proposed framework that fit is achieved through the interface between the person and the environment at all scales. While the weaknesses of the medical model were addressed earlier, the role of the individual and his or her unique range of functioning must be considered. The significant difference in this reciprocal relationship is that the person is not viewed as broken but as part of the solution. If the costs of improving person-environment fit are completely examined, it becomes clear that for some individuals, at some point in their life span, a medical intervention—pharmaceutical, surgical, psychological, or physical therapies—may be the most efficacious method of improving functioning. Most important, these medical interventions can, at times, be the least invasive, least stigmatizing, and/or least costly of available options.

People are not static beings. Human functioning can change on a moment-by-moment basis due to environmental factors, such as weather or location, as well as human factors, such as activity or illness. Equally important, preferences and needs change as life circumstances and roles change. Individuals must balance, on an ongoing basis, priorities and resources with needs and preferences. As a college student, Ed Roberts wanted to "go out and drink a little," while as a parent, this priority more than likely shifted to playground access later in his life. In parallel, drawing upon limited resources, Johnny Cash and the members of his first band wore black shirts as a way of unifying their appearance. Later, Cash persisted in wearing black attire: "everything else aside . . . it just felt right. I wore black because I liked it." Fit, ultimately, simply feels right and good.

Redefining Home

KORYDON H. SMITH

I have a friend. She rents. She needs to move. She relies on a walker. Last week we looked at many new rental[s]. It was disheartening. The lack of design principles and construction in my town serve to inconvenience, deter, or exclude her. Good decent people are being denied choices right where they have lived all their lives.

—CARROLL STEEN, *resident, Cabot, Arkansas*

Eleanor Smith, founder of the Atlanta-based Concrete Change, knows firsthand the importance of housing design. As a leading advocate of the "visit-ability" movement, Smith has seen the negative impacts that traditional housing design has on persons with disabilities: "I have known people who had to crawl on the floor in their own house to get to the bathroom."[1] What makes this so exasperating is not simply the laborious indignity of crawling to the bathroom but being forced to do so in one's "own house." This description, moreover, exemplifies the thousands of persons with disabilities in the United States and around the world whose "experiences are, potentially, at odds with the (ideal) conceptions of the home as a haven."[2] Instead, like a victim of domestic violence, home is hell.

A paradox emerges, as individuals and families are confronted with the question, "do we stay here and continue to be subjected to abuse or do we leave in search of a better home, but risk homelessness?" As most rural Southerners place a great deal of emotional value in their homes—the region, the locale, the place, and the residence—and also have little social or economic capital to venture elsewhere, many residents choose to reside in their own homes despite inefficacies. The current housing stock in the South does not support independent living for a growing number of Southerners, due to inadequate kitchen and bathroom facilities, ill-planned spatial organization, inadequate entry design, and nonintegrated environmental and communications systems. As both public policy and the housing industry have been slow to respond, there is still a large reliance on institutional settings for housing older adults and persons with disabilities. This option will grow increasingly unsustainable in the coming years. Institutional living is not only more costly than independent living, but is also less desirable to the majority of Americans.

Additionally, retrofitting has been the long-standing practice in design and construction for meeting the changing physical and psychosocial needs of a household. Regarding disability specifically, installing home modifications, such as equipping a home with various assistive technologies, has become an increasingly standard practice. Assistive technologies in the home have been shown to provide some cost benefit; making small-scale home modifications so that a person can live more independently is cheaper than institutional living.[3] The use of assistive technologies may be unavoidable in the context of certain disabling conditions, but many assistive technologies often illustrate deficiencies in housing and community design. Moreover, assistive technologies have had little impact on the broad population and have often been stigmatizing, unsightly, and, at times, unsafe.

The emergence of "de-institutionalization" four decades ago shifted the focus and resources from state institutions to community-based programs. This was based on the Kennedy-era precept that independent living increased the quality of life for persons with disabilities and decreased government spending. But substantial criticism of the de-institutionalization policies of the 1960s has emerged and cannot be ignored. Some of this criticism even identifies de-institutionalization as the primary cause of homelessness in the United States,[4] again, illustrating the abysmal choice between homelessness and internment. Despite legislation and judicial actions from 1963 (Community Mental Health Centers Act) through the end of the millennium (the *Olmstead Decision* of 1999), thousands of U.S. residents have remained dependent upon state and federal resources. Part of the reason is due to the immense research and funding focus on healthcare and relatively diminutive attention given to quality affordable housing, aside from the assistive technology and home modifications approach, that fosters inde-

Ad-hoc Ramp. Typically, improvised modifications are neither functionally nor aesthetically integrated with the overall home design.

pendence. Community design and community support systems are also deficient, because the spotlight is on the person not the context. A greater balance needs to be achieved in person-environment fit—the reciprocal relationship between the physical and cognitive body and the physical and social environment.

The "universal design" approach may be one such method for addressing the South's housing dilemma. Universal design has gained momentum in both the design professions and the government. Universal design is an architectural-, urban-, and product-design movement that grew out of the civil and disability rights movements as a transformation of the concepts of "accessibility" or "barrier-free design." The "accessible" design method that

Accessible Table. Public spaces, such as restaurants, often utilize a specialized rather than universal design approach to include persons with disabilities.

the potential for inclusive design philosophies to improve quality of life and increase independence, meet the legal mandates of the ADA, and/or provide a cost-effective alternative to institutionalization. Unlike the recent surge in the "green building" movement, however, UD still remains largely unknown among the general public, despite national efforts such as the National Endowment for the Arts' sponsored Universal Design Identity (UDiD) Project.[18] Some of the informal discussions resulting from this initiative have resulted in a push for more assertive, intuitive nomenclature.

Throughout much of the remainder of this chapter the phrase "inclusive design" will be used instead of "universal design" for two primary reasons. First, it is viewed that "universal design," as a descriptor, is problematic. The term "universal" in no way implies notions of human-centered design (i.e., ergonomics) and, more problematically, is misinterpreted by some designers to refer variously to issues of context, environmentalism, or mass production. Second, as disability and poverty have strong statistical correlations, it appears necessary to synthesize the two aforementioned notions of inclusive design—cost-effectiveness and ergonomic function—in housing design. This initiates a more critical discussion of the role that universal design has played, how it might be modified, and the role that inclusive-design thinking might play in future housing in rural America.

Universal Design: Three Popular Criticisms

Throughout the past two decades, UD has gained increasing support. UD has, however, also faced significant resistance and critique. Predominantly due to specialization, three major criticisms of UD have arisen in the past decade. These critiques are not evident in the literature on UD, nor are they found more broadly in professional or scholarly housing policy or design publications. The devaluation of and resistance to UD is, nonetheless, apparent in more informal discourses in the design and construction industries and in academia. The informality of these criticisms makes them difficult to articulate and discuss, but their enculturation in academic, professional, and popular settings necessitates their inclusion in this discussion. For example, "when universal design is disparaged despite the compelling arguments for the concept, the real problem may be a lack of will to be inclusive, or more insidiously, the profit motive masquerading as an effort to protect the public."[19] The purpose of revealing these criticisms is not to undo the cumulative efforts that have been made by disability rights scholars and advocates but to shed light on the cultural barriers that remain and suggest how these impediments might be navigated or removed.

Criticism 1: Specialization and the Need for Integration

Among the greatest challenges any designer faces is describing, to a nondesigner, what designers do. Design education and practice is unique, not for its specialization, but for its synthetic, integrative nature. Designers draw upon knowledge from many other fields—art, mathematics, philosophy, physics, sociology, and so on—and the act of designing is about synthesizing these diverse and contradictory disciplines. This may be best summed up in the adage: "engineers learn more and more about less and less until they know everything about nothing, while designers learn less and less about more and more until they know nothing about everything." But this is changing.

The design disciplines—urban design, landscape architecture, interior design, architecture, and industrial design—have become increasingly autonomous and specialized, each with its own educational and professional cultures, design principles and regulations, and value structures. There has also been an explosion in the number of subdisciplines and areas of expertise within each field. Although specialization (and the depth of expertise and knowledge that it produces) may be necessary, arguably the hardening of the lines that separate these disciplines undermines the essential characteristics of design: interdisciplinary and integrative. This is especially problematic in housing design, debatably the most complex design endeavor. As discussed throughout this book, the factors affecting housing design and construction are diverse and interrelated. Economic, technological, environmental, and sociological issues all influence housing decisions, while the ideologies that emerge from each of these areas are not without consequence on one another. For example, the notion of "value engineering" emerged from the economic domain, "rapid prototyping" came out of the technological arena, "green building" surfaced from the environmental sphere, and "universal design" emerged from the sociological realm. The increased reliance on specialization has thwarted the synthesis of these issues. Universal design, therefore, has remained at the periphery, but is, nevertheless, impacted by these other concepts.

Advancements in assistive technology have begun to influence standard practices of housing design and construction—most notably in environmental systems technology—but other aspects of user-centered design, including UD, have found difficulty integrating into mainstream design and construction practices. Much like "green building" practices, universal design has fallen prey to specialization and the disciplinary isolation that comes with it. Both movements, green building and universal design, have become autonomous design practices and methodologies, though green building has gained momentum in recent years. This increasingly specialized mode of operation does not recognize the inherently integrative nature of design and construction. Greater effort is required that re-contextualizes universal design within the broad milieu of housing design: environmental technologies, community planning, structural systems, social issues, business and finance, ergonomics, construction, et cetera.

Universal design has recently been incorporated into the U.S. Department of Housing and Urban Development's literature on best practices for housing, while the state of Kentucky has incorporated UD into its housing policies, and the Arkansas Development Finance Authority (ADFA), the leading housing funder in the state, completed a similar process in 2008. State and federal housing bodies have begun to recognize the social and economic benefits of adopting "inclusive" housing standards. Kentucky was among the first states with comprehensive housing standards, which incorporated issues of affordability, energy efficiency, best practices in construction, and universal design. It is imminent that other states do the same. Yet, there is no systematic means in place for evaluating these comprehensive, inter-twined standards. A mechanism for evaluating inclusive housing practices across states and regions (and across subdisciplines) is needed. Part of the problem is that little empirical research has been done in the United States on the interrelationship between person-centered design, environmentally-centered design, and so forth. For example, what aspects of "green building" most impact "universal design" and vice versa?

The National Science Foundation (NSF), in collaboration with the Department of Housing and Urban Development, has sponsored several research and development initiatives relative to "whole-house" design with the Partnership for Advancing Technologies in Housing (PATH) program. The foundation's attempt is to integrate various aspects of housing research, such as environmental systems research, construction research, and research in enclosure systems. The PATH initiative is laudable in its attempt to develop more holistic research, design, and construction practices in housing. Most notably absent, however, is an exploration in human factors such as thermal comfort, ergonomics and anthropometrics, and environmental preferences. Furthermore, the housing industry of the rural South tends to change more slowly. If the findings and recommendations of hard-science-based research, like that fostered by the NSF, are to have impact in the South, sociological analysis, including an understanding of the culture of the housing construction and real estate industries, will need to become an integral component. The mechanisms for educating home builders are ad hoc and vary immensely from locale to locale.

For instance, the National Association of Home Builders (NAHB) maintains a large number of educational programs for its members. Moreover, NAHB offers more than fifteen "designation programs," where members can gain specialized training and certification, such as "Certified Aging-in-Place Specialist" (CAPS) or "Certified Green Professional" (CGP). Each designation program contains a series of courses that must be completed in order to obtain certification; continuing education credits are required to maintain certification, helping to establish the best-educated housing industry the nation has ever seen. These courses are conducted both nationally and locally through NAHB's eight hundred stratified state and local associations, such as the Arkansas Home Builders Association (statewide) and the HBA of Greater Little Rock (local). This stratified organization is advantageous in that it increases the sense of belonging to a local "club" rather than an impersonal national organization and it allows greater flexibility. The kind and quality of educational programs likely fluctuate across regions, and participation varies as well.

The specialized knowledge of home remodelers with CAPS designation, for example, could be immensely useful to older adults seeking home modifications. Presumably, because of the increased rate of disability and a larger older adult population, the CAPS designees in the South would be in high demand. In many cases this appears to be true. As of July 2008, many Southern states had a robust cohort of CAPS designees:

- Florida: 92
- Georgia: 70
- Virginia: 58
- North Carolina: 45
- Alabama: 43
- Tennessee: 31
- Kentucky: 27
- Louisiana: 23
- South Carolina: 12

Yet the states with the greatest needs—Arkansas, West Virginia, and Mississippi—possessed only 4, 2, and 1 certified aging-in-place specialists, respectively.[20] The building industry needs to do a better job of marketing the skills of its members to both consumers and legislators. Unfortunately, few residents have been made aware of these local experts. In addition, state and local home-builders associations need to facilitate the alignment of state needs and human resources. Arkansas's chapter of home builders has around twenty-five hundred members, but Arkansas law does not require home builders to be members of NAHB, nor is there any statewide mission to increase the number of CAPS designees. Increasing the effectiveness of existing programs could make great strides toward fulfilling housing needs.

Advocates of the enabler movements also share responsibility for the delayed incorporation of UD in housing, as advocates and scholars of UD have not actively integrated the previous (and notably innovative) research from other areas in housing, such as "smart" building systems and "green" building systems. The most significant shortfall remains the lack of integration of these innovations as well as a proposed method for developing and disseminating prototypical housing solutions.

In addition to the increasing trend toward specialization and a reduced emphasis on the comprehensive nature of housing design, three related issues have exacerbated the marginalization of universal design. First, there is a slow, but discernible, drift toward itemized regulations, what has casually been referred to as "code creep." A survey of U.S. building codes from the 1940s (the start of the first major housing boom) through 2006 reveals an overwhelming increase in regulations. Coupled with the fear of litigation, "code creep" has resulted in a greater prevalence and utilization of specialized consultants: structural, environmental, and accessibility experts, among others. Turf wars often arise. Second, there is a lack of coordination and dialogue among the various interest groups involved in housing—developers, consumers, home builders, environmentalists, et cetera. The lack of synchronization includes both the physical production of housing and the ethereal production of housing codes. There is an apparent mutual resentment among designers, builders, code officials, and consumers. The deriding often goes something like this: "developers are only in it for the money"; "architects just want to make things pretty"; and "builders just want to do what they've always done." More positive, collaborative relationships need to be fostered. Issues regarding inclusive design, sustainability, and other related issues need to be part of the dialogue. Finally, each facet of the housing industry, as well as each construction trade, uses a great deal of jargon. Does the average consumer know what pig tails, P traps, sill plates, or water bonds are? Or the difference between base molding and shoe molding? Or the advantages and disadvantages of a multi-pole GFCI breaker versus a GFCI outlet? Or the benefits of SIP construction? Or when type M copper is required versus recommended versus unnecessary? Similar to a surgeon communicating to a patient, it is essential that specialized knowledge in housing design and construction be translated into a vernacular language, so that consumers can make educated choices.

Another contributing factor to the isolation of UD is due to its relative newness, lack of public awareness, and skepticism from within the industry. As well, there is far less oversight— governmental, professional, and regulatory—over the design and construction of single-family housing than multifamily housing, especially regarding accessibility codes. This is

Trailer with Ramp and Stair. The lack of integrated design is most often illustrated in the modifications made to manufactured housing.

evidenced by a comparison of the *International Building Code* (IBC) and the *International Residential Code* (IRC). The IBC, which contains "Chapter 11: Accessibility," governs multifamily housing;[21] the IRC, the primary regulatory text for one- and two-family dwellings, contains no chapter on accessibility.[22] What has largely influenced the design of single-family housing has been cultural tradition, conventions of construction, personal taste, and local economics. Many current cultural and building conventions undermine the basic concepts of UD, as discussed in chapter 4. Conventions often result (though usually unintentionally) in the exclusion of various users. For instance, tall entrance thresholds can be trip hazards for persons with visual impairments or older adults, or may not allow for someone using a wheeled mobility device to enter. While some design and building professionals have voiced difficulty in either fully understanding or complying with certain codes, contrarily, advocacy groups have argued for additions to and/or more stringency in various architectural standards. Thus, the codification of ergonomics has remained anecdotal, though some more extensive anthropometric studies have recently emerged.[23]

Codes have also been encumbered by tensions between various interest groups.

Arguably there has been too much focus on code authoring and too little emphasis on educating design and construction professionals on the scientific and ethical underpinnings of codes. This may be the greatest impediment to the widespread acceptance and utilization of universal design. With such focus on the codes themselves, the principles that induced accessibility/usability have been veiled. In addition, enforcement of codes has remained inconsistent. Compliance with access codes is primarily the responsibility of designers and builders, while legal action is the predominant means of recourse for noncompliance. This chapter contends that both advocates and critics of inclusive design need to become more aware of the underpinnings that brought forth accessibility codes. This chapter also puts forth the need for inclusive design to be evaluated within the context of other aspects that influence housing design and construction.

If inclusive design ideals are to have greater impact on housing in the South, advocates of the enabler movements need to recognize the trend toward specialization and develop ways to re-integrate user-centered design into mainstream housing practices. This would likely include (1) a change in nomenclature, coupled with (2) educating the constituents of housing—policy makers, developers, designers, builders, and consumers—about the benefits of more inclusive design and construction practices, followed by (3) an analysis of the factors that shape housing practices—economic, technological, environmental, and sociological factors—and their effects upon one another. Housing affects everyone. The factors that affect housing should be part of a common, widespread discourse. This may be facilitated through a wide array of constituents, including professional organizations, such the American Institute of Architects and the National Association of Home Builders; governmental agencies, such as the U.S. Department of Housing and Urban Development and U.S. Department of Agriculture (USDA) Rural Development; research entities, such as the National Science Foundation and the Rehabilitation Services Administration; consumer advocacy groups, such as AARP and ADAPT; and grassroots organizations, such as Concrete Change and local chambers of commerce.

Criticism 2: Universality and the Need for Diversity

Karsten Harries, in "The Dream of the Complete Building," alludes to the fact that many Modernist (and neo-Modern) architects have imaged architecture as an "aesthetic object"—modeled round the history of art—as merely an object to be viewed, as something separate from the participation of the observer. Harries states that "such insistence on the integrity and unity of the work of art demands of the spectator that he keep his distance from it: Don't touch! The complete work of art leaves nothing for us to do."[24] Contemporary real estate marketing, in parallel, relies heavily on imagery, illustrated in the carefully cropped photographs of idyllic homes that fill the pages of free monthly real estate magazines and the real estate section of local newspapers. The goal is to market the image of the American Dream, as "the dream house [is] . . . the representation of American hopes for the good life."[25]

The primary critique of the architectural Modernist movement stems from the seemingly utopian beliefs pursued by the Modernists. Modernists, such as Le Corbusier and Walter Gropius, believed that architecture could resolve social problems, that high-style and industrialization could remedy public ills. The emergence of the International Style took this further, as adherents to the movement believed that a worldwide aesthetic sensibility and social construct would proliferate. Modernism was very much a reaction against what was viewed as the Bourgeois, overly decorated architecture of the nineteenth century and the neoclassical works of the twentieth century. Many Modern architects believed that the industrial revolution and the machine age would lead to the mass production of architecture, especially in middle-class housing, which would result in higher-quality design that would reach a larger population. The well-known American architect Frank Lloyd Wright, for example, advanced this conviction through his Broad-acre City scheme and prototypical Usonian House.

The Modernists' collective belief in the "architectural machine" did not have as socially wide an impact as they hoped. Paradoxically, Modernist architecture (LeCorbusier's Maison Dom-ino, for example) was intended for the populace (i.e., universal), but prospered primarily among elite clientele (e.g., Villa Stein at Garches). As a result, Modernism was denounced both for its utopian failings and for dismissing contextual concerns.

Typical Modern House. Modern architects, from Frank Lloyd Wright to Le Corbusier, envisioned well-designed, affordable housing for a wider range of the population through a Modern aesthetic.

Critics blamed the Modernists for the demise of Western cities and for the perpetuation of a "placeless" architecture.

Throughout the past twenty-five years, the importance of context (or "place") has been affirmed by architects and architectural theorists, such as Christian Norburg-Shulz, Juhani Pallasmaa, and others, often collectively referred to as "regionalists," in addition to "contextualists" such as Tom Schumacher. Contemporary design discourses have placed immense value in issues of site and context. Many architectural designers, educators, and critics, therefore, bristle at the term "universal" when coupled with housing design, as "universal" implies "regardless of context." This is, however, a misreading of the phrase "universal design" as it was intended by Mace. To those affiliated with UD, the phrase most simply translates as "user-centered"; it focuses on making products and buildings more usable by a larger population. UD is an issue of function rather than of context (though UD is not without contextual implications). The distaste of the phrase "universal design" as described above, in addition to its ambiguity, may be one reason that some have adopted the phrase "inclusive design."

Along with the ideals of the "regionalists" and "contextualists" has come a more general preoccupation with design specificity. There is an apparent push toward "site-specific" design and "user-specific" design. In a critical commentary on the Maison Bordeaux (designed by Rem Koolhaas/OMA) published in *Harvard Design Magazine* in 1998, Wouter Vantsiphout states that the world of architectural design has seen an increasing "concentration on making hyper-specific buildings."[26] This has both positive and negative effects relative to inclusive design and accessibility. Similar debates have surfaced regarding assistive technologies.

On the positive side, "hyper-specific" designs, including assistive technologies, have the capacity to more closely meet the specialized needs of a given user. The Maison Bordeaux (France) is an exemplar, as the interior and exterior spatial organizations of the building are designed as prosthetic extensions of the owner (a man with paraplegia). The tradeoffs, however, for such user-specific designs may be multiple, including (1) the increased cost that often comes with custom/specialized design, (2) the inflexibility of use by other occupants (also resulting in a decrease in marketability to potential subsequent owners), and (3) the increased likelihood of stigma associated with the home. Each of these issues may not be the case for the Maison Bordeaux, but are often prevalent in the specialized, ad-hoc remedies that tend to emerge in the rural, impoverished South. Nevertheless, it becomes critical to view both sides of the "universal" versus "hyper-specific" design debate.

Closely coupled with this debate is a newly emerging discourse on diversity. This debate is two-fold. First, throughout recent years there has been an increasing sensitivity to issues of racial, gender, religious, and economic diversity. What impact does this diversity have on housing design? For example, the fastest-growing racial group in Arkansas and the United States is the Hispanic/Latino population. Immigration reform has been a political hot-button throughout the first decade of the twenty-first century, but few seem to be asking the question: How will this demographic shift affect the housing industry? Second, proponents of the "green building" and other environmental movements, as well as advocates of "new urbanism," have promoted the importance of environmental diversity. "Environmental diversity," here, refers to both diversity in the ecology of the *natural environment* and diversity in *urban* and *community design* (i.e., mixed-use neighborhoods). Like the "regionalists," proponents of environmental diversity gaze a skeptical eye on "universal design." Some rather unexpected arguments against universal design have emerged. Here is one example.

As cases of childhood and adult obesity have become increasingly prevalent in the United States, physicians and health advocates have focused on the need for physical activity. Former

Arkansas governor Mike Huckabee, an ordained Southern Baptist minister and a 2008 Republican presidential candidate, made health a central platform during his tenure as governor. This advanced the work of the Governor's Council on Fitness (begun by Bill Clinton in 1992) and built Act 1220 (2003), which required the ongoing measurement of body-mass indices in schoolchildren. Huckabee himself participated in the endeavor to reduce obesity in Arkansas, losing more than one hundred pounds from 2003 to 2004. In a bizarre twist on combating obesity, as well as a twist on the logical guidance of physicians on the importance of exercise, some have cited the "obesity epidemic" as a counterpoint to universal design. The position is that while it appears that the general U.S. population is in need of a more-challenging, not less-challenging, physical environment, UD limits environmental diversity and challenges. Children's playgrounds, for example, are designed to be safe, though physically and intellectually stimulating. It could be argued that the adult environment should be equally stimulating, that physical and mental challenges should not be relegated to the gym or the classroom, but should exist more broadly in the environment that we experience on a daily basis. The counter argument—that of disability rights advocates—is that environmental challenges should be by choice; when "challenge" is unilaterally and arbitrarily imposed, user choice is curtailed: the very definition of injustice.

If disability advocates and promoters of inclusive design are to combat a seemingly endless string of red-herring arguments, again, they need to clarify the missions and nomenclature associated with the movement. In addition, supporters of inclusive design, especially those involved in housing design, need to demonstrate how both user-centered design principles and ideals of site-specific design and environmental diversity can coexist and be mutually beneficial. This may occur in various ways. The U.S. Green Building Council, for example, by formalizing a set of standards (the Leadership in Energy and Environmental Design or LEED Standards), rapidly advanced both the publicity and validity of the green building movement. Leaders in the realm of inclusive design could follow suit, and it may be advantageous to find dovetails with LEED and other existing standards. An extensive database of case studies and model homes could also be developed, paralleled by a public marketing campaign to both dispel myths and advocate the benefits of inclusive housing design. Collectively, efforts like these could help consumers and the housing industry see inclusive design as central to achieving a sense of "home."

Criticism 3: Lack of "Style"

"Style" is important in the South. Regardless of race, gender, socioeconomic standing, or location, the importance of "style" is universal. That is not to say that stylistic predilections are shared, but simply that people think about, talk about, and make stylistic choices every day. The entire Miss America line of contestants—not just Miss Arkansas, Miss Alabama, Miss Georgia, and Miss North Carolina—illustrates this. "The modern Southern belle has, of course, long been the Pageant ideal . . . so that—even in those years when a Southerner does not win—the likely winner is still probably patterned after that type." She is "vivacious, sparkle-eyed, full of fun, [and] capable of laughing at herself," epitomized by "poise and personality beneath the outward physical attractiveness."[27] Housing in the South is also characterized by these dual traits: poise and attractiveness, reinforcing the importance of both "form" and "function" in housing (and in Miss America contestants). In addition, like the image of the beauty queen, the housing styles of the South are evident throughout rural America: the Greek Revival of the "big house," the reserved "shotgun house," the robust "Federal Style," the pragmatic "dog trot," the flamboyant "Victorians," and, the most ubiquitous of all, the "shabby-chic" of the mobile home. The two common conditions of all types and styles are that all types are found in all American states and all types are marketed heavily based on style.

The renowned urban designer Michael Sorkin, like many designers and educators who have entered the UD discourse, described a personal experience of coping with a disability in an unaccommodating environment in the April 2004 issue of *Architectural Record*. More specifically, Sorkin describes the difficulties in navigating New York City on crutches. Sorkin's commentary focuses on functional rather than aesthetic performance of the built world.[28] Historically, however, architectural criticism has more often been preoccupied with aesthetic critique than with performance appraisal. Indeed, the history of architecture is typically divided into stylistic movements: *Art Nouveau, Gothic Revival, Art Deco/Moderne,* or *Modern.* Conversely, the principles of UD result from functional, human-centered aspects of architectural design, not compositional or stylistic proclivities. Consequently,

Iconic Southern House. Vestiges of the antebellum South continue to influence contemporary home design.

Home as Prosthetic Device. Personal characteristics, such as disability, require homes to assume the role of prosthesis.

UD has faced difficulty in becoming a mainstream discourse in both academia and the profession.

Like "green building," the universal design movement has suffered from its *astylistic* character; the concepts of UD can occur through nearly any stylistic language. Stylistic movements have been central if not synonymous with the history of architecture (and housing design). Architecture as well as furniture design, interior design, landscape architecture, and art are known according to distinct "periods" and the aesthetic proclivities and antipathies associated with them. As the enabler movement is rooted in functional rather than formalistic concerns, it has faced resistance from a style-minded discipline and society. In addition, in the minds of many design educators and practitioners, universal design is strongly associated with "accessibility." For many designers, "accessibility" connotes the ad-hoc, clinical aesthetic of a hospital room, complete with stainless-steel fixtures and grab bars, far from the poise, personality, and attractiveness of the beauty queen. Although UD seeks to overturn this type of design practice, its historical association with "design for persons with disabilities" upends its truer intent.

UD, therefore, is seen as having a two-fold lack of style: *astylistic,* in one sense, and hospital-like and without subtlety in another. The origin of both dilemmas, however, may be rooted in a more direct source. The nomenclature—"universal design" —is sufficiently lacking in clarity and what it connotes is widely open to interpretation. Whereas "abstract expressionism," "Victorian," or even "green building" conjure certain types of images in popular and scholarly minds, "universal design," especially to someone hearing the term for the first time, evokes both everything and nothing. Maybe this is simply an issue of temporality, of the relative newness of the term, for the term "Modern" is no more descriptive, but is understood because of its century-long existence in the public vernacular. The push for a more descriptive term may be advantageous, but could also further fragment the movement.

Nomenclature is an even more sensitive issue in the South. Terms like "equity," "integration," and "inclusion" carry immense weight and skepticism and implicitly refer to race. As such, phrases like "inclusive" and "universal" may carry unintended interpretations and consequences. Although racial segregation is still prevalent throughout various areas of the United States, it seems apparent that disability discrimination is the most patent prejudice in America, evidenced by the lack of adequately designed housing that meets both the physical and psychosocial needs of a large segment of the population. Inclusive design, if poorly marketed, could face unnecessary resistance, especially in places like Arkansas, where the building industry is slow to incorporate new design ideas and construction techniques. This has much been the fate of "green building" in the South.

There is another interesting parallel. Though many home buyers may not be versed in the jargon or technicalities of plumbing, electrical wiring, structural design, or other building trades, most know to ask certain questions or look for certain features. Granite countertops and undermount sinks exemplify that list and epitomize the buyer's tendency toward design elements that bring together high form and high function. The form versus function dichotomy is not simply a design issue, however. Disability is often conceptualized in the same way. "Disability presents itself to 'normal' people through two modalities—function and appearance."[29] Disability may be visibly present (i.e., someone may "look disabled"); disability may limit someone's capacity to complete a task (i.e., someone may "be disabled"), though no outward appearance of disability may be present; or these two factors—form and function—like in design, may be conjoined. Changing the popular concepts of disability and design, therefore, become more challenging because of their shared conceptualization.

As debatable as it may be, the facets of the enabler movement may best be advanced by breaking the ties with their historical roots. It is possible that inclusive design needs to be bisected from the disability rights and accessibility movements and positioned more broadly relative to ergonomics, anthropometrics, and user-centered design, as these areas of design have a longer, more deeply rooted history. Moreover, as long as inclusive design is seen as an extension of the disability rights movement, inclusive design will be seen as specialized. The intention is to increase the breadth of housing design issues, expanding beyond the concept of "design for disability." The proposition of breaking UD from its historical origins necessitates an alternate theorization of both the concept of home and of good design.

Universal Design and Housing: An Alternate Theorization

The citation of the phrase "universal design" by numerous state and federal agencies has caused questions about the intent, scope, and enforceability of UD. Moreover, the appropriation of this phrase calls into question the possibility of developing a formalized "Universal Design Building Code." Many scholars, consultants, and experts in the field of UD claim that UD is simply a way of thinking about design and cannot (should not) be codified. In essence, true *universal* design cannot be achieved. Designs can always be improved; and design cannot accommodate the physical and psychosocial needs of all individuals. Again, drawing on the previous parallels to green building, 100 percent sustainability cannot be achieved either; it can only be approached and sought after. Nevertheless, a formal codification of UD would give the movement legal authority and further substantiate the movement. In either case, this debate is central because the move toward or the resistance to codification radically affects the ideological underpinnings and future evolution of the movement.

The general history of UD has been outlined before, including parallels between race discrimination and disability discrimination,[30] the emergence of the "enabler" concept,[31] and the pragmatic significance of UD.[32] There are several historical and theoretical discourses on UD, however, that are noticeably absent. These neglected discourses center on the possible, though overlooked, roles of housing. Moreover, these hidden discourses could be essential to the transformation of both UD and housing. These topics include, but are not limited to (1) the notion of home as a prosthetic device, (2) the notion of home as a health device, and (3) the notion of home as an identity device. In addition to providing a larger theoretical context for UD, these issues begin to redefine the meaning and expand the roles of home.

Notion 1: Home as a Prosthetic Device

Historically, the human body has been viewed as the enabling or disabling factor in performing activities of daily living, but this has changed. As discussed in chapters 1 and 5, many designers, rehabilitation professionals, and persons with disabilities have recognized the role that the built environment plays. This has been the predominant thesis of the movement toward inclusive design. Housing is increasingly being viewed as a kind of prosthesis for activities of daily living.

As a means to recoup some functioning and remedy some cosmetic concerns of injured soldiers, prosthetic technology saw its greatest advancement following the two world wars,[33] while material and medical advancements throughout the last quarter of the twentieth century resulted in better functioning and more "realistic" prostheses.[34] Historically and popularly, prostheses have been both a part of and relatively similar in size to the human body. But prostheses have changed in both size and meaning. In the context of two examples—LeCorbusier's Villa Savoye (1931) and Rem Koolhaas's Maison Bordeaux (1998)[35]—both described as "machines for living in,"[36] prostheses are no longer limited by the scale of the human body. Houses themselves have become prosthetic devices. Designed for a client with paraplegia and his family, the Maison Bordeaux is an extension of him, complete with large moving parts and spaces. The house takes the place of the wheelchair. The body and the building, like the body and the wheelchair, become nearly inseparable. Although the Maison Bordeaux is an extreme example, Western housing in general has become more prosthetic. This has become the case for numerous features in housing not merely elements that facilitate mobility—such as modern appliances, new telecommunication systems, and the emergence of "smart" building technologies. These "changes in technologies (particularly new communications devices) are having direct and powerful effects on space and identity."[37] The rural South, for example, is now more connected than ever to the outside world, due to the Internet and satellite television. Small gray rooftop dishes are as omnipresent in the rural South as the pickup truck, integral to the culture, the main source of communication and entertainment, and front-and-center in the visual landscape.

The proliferation of telecommunications devices, the apparent increase in Americans' interests in do-it-yourself (DIY) home renovation projects, and the increasing prevalence of assistive technologies in the home have had tremendous impacts on the meaning and role of home.[38] Although seemingly science fiction, it is foreseeable that housing could play a greater assistive role as the population ages. As housing takes on greater assistive responsibility, Americans may come to expect housing that provides not only privacy and security but also "prosthetic functions." For example, modern medical and telecommunications technologies are being synthesized as a means to remotely administer medication, provide medical consultation and check-ups, prepare meals, or provide opportunities for socialization. Homes are becoming one-stop shops. Many of these advanced technologies are costly, but costs of these in-home services appear to be more affordable than equivalent institutional services, more desirable to the clients they serve, and less reliant on human resources.

It is uncertain, though, how changes in practices, and parallel changes in public perception, will affect housing and lifestyle in the South. The South is often seen as culturally conservative and resistant to change regarding such issues. Nevertheless, the ubiquitous and unassuming prevalence of rural DIY projects—porches added to trailer-homes, ramps added to entries—and the consumption of satellite TV could themselves serve as examples of the widespread acceptance and incorporation of "prosthetic sensibilities" in the South. This is similar to the way a previous generation of Southerners (and rural Northerners) "harnessed and humanized" the high technology of the time—

CB radio—as both a practical tool of truckers warning one another of a "smokey" ahead as well as a recreational gadget and social network for folks near the "home twenty."[39]

The home, therefore, serves as a means of achieving things that could not otherwise be done. The home is a mechanism of communication; it is an instrument for enabling self-sufficiency; it is an apparatus of warmth and safety. The home is an extension and augmentation of a person's identity and functioning, the very definition of "prosthesis."

Notion 2: Home as a Health Device

Throughout history, housing has been closely associated with social values. In addition to economic and climatic issues, housing is largely shaped by cultural mores, rituals, and preferences. Less often considered is how social perceptions and behaviors of health—exercise, eating, et cetera—affect housing design, and how housing design, reciprocally, impacts health and ability.[40]

Many renowned architects of the first half of the twentieth century believed Modern architecture could provide a remedy for the social ills of the time. Adolf Loos, for example, earnestly believed that people who frivolously "daubed" architecture with ornament to be "criminals" or "degenerates" and that removing the ornamental frills from architecture would result in higher social order.[41] Architects of the Modern era positioned individual and social health at the center of their concerns in housing and community design.[42] As a result, there was an international upsurge in the construction of open-air schools at the beginning of the twentieth century, the opening of dozens of sanatoria during the same time period, the emergence and proliferation of the YMCA and YWCA at the end of the nineteenth century, and the conventionalization of providing exercise rooms/facilities as part of upper-income housing throughout the first half of the twentieth century. "Modern architecture was . . . understood as a kind of medical equipment, a mechanism for protecting and enhancing the body."[43]

Throughout the middle of the nineteenth century, it was believed that disease was caused by "foul, stagnant air" and that "the best way of preventing disease was to make sure that there was constant ventilation everywhere."[44] As such, open-air hospitals and homes sprung up. Later, as scientific studies by Louis Pasteur and others exposed the root cause of disease to be "germs," ventilation was viewed as problematic. Controlling the influx of external contaminants became central; homes and hospitals were then designed to be hermetically sealed. During the mid-twentieth century, discourses emerged about "sick building syndrome," the resultant problem with buildings sealed too tightly, and the negative health effects of airtight homes and buildings. Similarly, natural light and ventilation have reemerged as central concerns in contemporary hospital and housing designs because of proven physical and mental health benefits.

Most recently designers have become conscious of the health effects that construction methods and materials may have on occupants. For instance, multiple chemical sensitivity, a disease that results in allergic-like reactions to various chemical substances found in buildings, is more commonly understood among the current generation of design professionals than in previous eras. This awareness regarding the health risks of chemical exposure in homes, though, does not necessarily ensure safety, as evidenced by the high levels of formaldehyde found by both the EPA and the CDC in the trailers provided by FEMA following Hurricane Katrina. In general, it is understood that housing design can positively or negatively affect physical health. A smaller but growing body of research also illustrates that home design influences psychological well-being. Depression and outdoor activity, for example, are reciprocally linked. Depression decreases the likelihood of going outside, while decreased outdoor activity can lead to increased levels of depression.[45] Housing design and community planning can facilitate or hinder access to outdoor activities. Similarly, housing design can facilitate or hinder access to daylight and views. Seasonal Affective Disorder (SAD), the clinical name for what is colloquially described as the "winter blues," is linked to the decreased daylight hours of winter. SAD, however, is not a "Northerner's disease"; SAD can occur anywhere. Most intriguing, SAD can be exacerbated by poor housing design.[46] So, the foil-covered windows, a means to block out the heat of the summer, typical in many rural Southern trailers, could have very real physical and psychological side-effects. This is paralleled by Johnny Cash's description of his tour bus:

> I love my bus . . . We call it Unit One. It really is my house, too. When I make it off another plane and through another airport, the sight of that big black MCI waiting by the curb sends waves of relief through me. Aah—safety, familiarity, solitude. Peace at last. My cocoon . . . I sit at a table with

Home as Health Device. Personal needs also require homes to assume the role of a healthcare environment.

bench seats on both sides, like a diner booth, with my newspaper or book . . . Curtains on the windows let me keep out the world or watch it pass.[47]

The importance of negotiating relationships to the outside world is also evident in Cash's description of his mobile camper:

I'll tell you about my camper. I called it Jesse, after Jesse James, because I was an outlaw and it had to be one, too. I imagined my Jesse to be a free, rebellious spirit, living to ramble in the back of beyond and carry me and him away from people and their needs and their laws. I painted his windows black so I could sleep in him during daylight.[48]

These examples illustrate the role that living environments play in mental health. The mainstream discourse of UD, which places great onus on the design of buildings for facilitating maximum functioning of the user, is analogous to Modernist convictions in "healthy design." Not only can people be healthy or unhealthy but homes can also be healthy or unhealthy. Homes can make us happy or sad; homes can be happy or sad. As the rural saying goes, "a happy home is a healthy home."

Notion 3: Home as an Identity Device

Discussions in chapter 2 clearly make the case that a person's home is a significant part of his or her identity: a house is a "mirror of self."[49] As such, Notions 1 and 2 just discussed are not without potential risks. There may be dilemmas associated with the "house as prosthesis" concept. Rob Imrie states that "for wheelchair users . . . the wheelchair is a paradoxical object." The wheelchair signifies to others the impaired bodily state of the individual; simultaneously it is the mechanism for mobility, independence, and freedom.[50] Similarly, the "prosthetic house," as an extension of the identity of the owner, is a mechanism of both freedom and potential discrimination. An ad-hoc ramp might facilitate physical access, but might impair social acceptance.

As illustrated in chapter 2, there is an immense complexity that surrounds housing. "Home" means different things to different people. No other architectural type is as profoundly and simultaneously personal and social as housing. As a result, there have been numerous attempts from many sides to either deregulate or further regulate the housing industry. The proposed Inclusive Home Design Act, as discussed in chapter 3, is a prime example. Most important, a home is the primary spatial and aesthetic negotiator between the individual (or family) and the society; a home is the chief mediator between individual identity and social identity. There is an apparent kinship between inclusive design and the home's role as an arbiter.

Human functioning, as defined in chapter 5, is not categorical; rather, the range of human abilities exists along a dynamic continuum. Functionality in housing design is no different. While accessible design often results in categorical design solutions and human segregation, inclusive design seeks solutions that work along the continuum of human needs. Personal identity, therefore, is defined primarily by the person not by the built environment. This is not to say that environments do not influence personal identity; they clearly do. Cash reflected, "I still sound like a combination of southwestern Arkansas, where my parents grew up, and northeastern Arkansas, where I myself was raised. It's rubbed off a bit because [I've] been to town, but it's still there." Choice, however, is the central issue: possessing the option to stay home or move homes, to change personas or keep the one you have. The greatest freedom is to have both, as Cash put it, to be "part gypsy, part homebody," living "according to a rhythm alien to most people but natural to me."[51]

Home as Identity Device. Individual preferences result in homes assuming the role of personalized billboards.

Accessibility focuses on the simple pragmatics of accommodating entry and use, but possesses no forethought regarding the aesthetic and psychosocial aspects of design. Inclusive design, on the other hand, strives for seamlessness.

Conclusion

These three notions—home as prosthetic device, home as identity device, and home as health device—though not exhaustive, seek to expand the popular and practical meaning and roles of home. This expanded definition is intended to shift housing practices toward the actualities of the South and the United States. In addition, the three aforementioned notions of home seek to provide a more holistic understanding of UD and its place in design history. UD, like other subdisciplines of design, is neither effectual nor sustainable without recognition of the parallel factors that influence housing and community design and construction. UD principles must be contextualized within the various aspects of design: aesthetic issues, environmental issues, economic issues, pragmatic and technological issues, and social/cultural issues. As well, ergonomics and user-centered design must be understood relative to the history of the disability rights movement, but are in danger if reliant on this historical connection.

Exclusivity and segregation have maintained a long, transformational history in the South. Discrimination and inequality have occurred relative to religion, race, gender, and disability. Disability appears to be the most recent among them. As such, disability advocacy is still in its early stages. The enabler movement did not gain a name until the 1980s, with the emergence of universal design, and did not gain major recognition as a mode of thinking and practicing housing design until the 1990s. UD faces dissolution if it is unable to become integrated into mainstream housing practices. Nomenclature, specialization, and education are three obstacles.

Leveraging existing legislation and social value placed in independent living may be one tack. Arguably, the federal government has maintained an interest in de-institutionalization primarily for fiscal reasons. Institutionalization is expensive for federal and state governments; independent living is not. The federal government, however, continues to spend more and more on healthcare and proportionately less and less on housing. Currently, the government funds healthcare at a nearly 15:1 ratio in comparison to housing.[52] More specifically, in 2006, 71.4 percent of Medicaid's long-term care expenditures went to nursing facilities; 38.6 percent went toward community-based living. In 2006, compared to 1999, Arkansas was one of only seven states that increased the percentage spent on nursing facilities.[53]

The healthcare industry maintains a (pardon the pun) healthy cohort of federal lobbyists whose efforts to retain current conventions cannot be dismissed. This emphasis on the status quo is aided by the housing industry's loyalty to tradition. In any case, before persons with disabilities can take responsibility for maintaining independence, adaptable and cost-effective housing must be developed and both the general public and state housing authorities must establish more inclusive housing options. Otherwise, what is likely to occur is the emergence of communities of "accessible" housing, which are nothing more than pseudo-institutional enclaves. Disability enclaves are no more sustainable than the current retrofit paradigm. And neither option fulfills the American Dream or its most important aspect, the home.

7

Redefining Equality

**KORYDON H. SMITH, DARELL W. FIELDS,
JENNIFER WEBB, AND BRENT T. WILLIAMS**

"The universal can be perceived only in the particular, while the particular can be thought only in reference to the universal." The problematic reciprocity of the universal and particular speaks to architectural thinking and making. Though the architect's practical task is always specific to its circumstances, architecture as a discipline theorizes such tasks in general terms.

—CAROL BURNS, *"On Site: Architectural Preoccupations,"* quoting
Ernst Cassirer, The Philosophy of Symbolic Forms

One of the major subtexts to Tony Dunbar's *Our Land Too* is commonality between impoverished rural white Appalachians and impoverished rural black Southerners:

> No two regions have figured more prominently in the growth of America . . . If ever this country laid foundations, they must be found in these areas. If anywhere we can hope to find a past real enough to learn from and a clear representation of attitudes that were and are central to the American system, it is in the mountains and the Deep South.[1]

Dunbar goes on to describe and compare the industrial and social shifts that have resulted in widespread poverty in these areas, but does so with a sensitivity that these are "real places . . . the home of real people." As Robert Coles states, in the introduction to Dunbar's book:

> Up those hollows and creeks live people who are proud . . .
> It *is* their land; their ancestors came to this country, as did the slaves, a long, long time ago, and they every day give to the American land all the passion and concern they can muster . . .
> They know the land's needs; know its virtues and limitations
> . . . The poor of [Appalachia and the Deep South], regardless of race, also love the land; love the pinewoods; love the promising

sunrises and flaming sunsets; love the wideness of the country-side, the elbowroom . . .[2]

Discourses on racial divisions and tensions are often pre-requisite to discussions about the South. Dunbar's and Cole's commentaries, however, shift this myth, illustrating the common experiences, "regardless of race," of rural Southerners. At the same time, both men recognize the importance of individuality ("elbowroom") and local sensibilities (the "virtues and limitations" of the land). The "universal" and the "specific" are both present. Both are evident in the shared regional and divergent local dialects and customs. Hidden beneath diversity is a great deal of similarity; concealed in the generalized stereotypes is a great deal of distinction.

"Diversity" and "equality" are apparent antonyms, yet both are valued in today's political and social climate and in contemporary design discourses. Diversity has recently become a hot topic and highly valued characteristic within businesses, institutions of higher education, and community planning. It is claimed and fairly well proven that ethic, racial, religious, gender, age, and educational diversity make a business more adaptable and better geared for participation in the global economy. Similarly, in urban design and community planning, there is a trend back toward "mixed-use" neighborhood planning and away from the strict zoning laws segregating commercial and residential areas prevalent throughout the twentieth century.

Conversely, fostering equality has been championed for decades, most notably exemplified by the civil and disability rights movement. It seems logical, however, that achieving equality is made more complex as diversity increases. Reconciling the *inevitably of diversity* and the *obligation of equality* is no small feat. The question remains as to how civil equality can be achieved as American society becomes more diverse. How can housing both (a) meet the variety of needs and preferences of a society and (b) ensure equity among the various groups that comprise that society?

From a broad view, Arkansas is often stereotyped as rural, poor, and unrefined. In a closer look at each region of the state, many of these stereotypes are upheld; some are not. An even finer view reveals a great deal of economic, educational, racial, topographic, and climatic diversity within the state. The following question, therefore, emerges: Can equity be achieved in spite

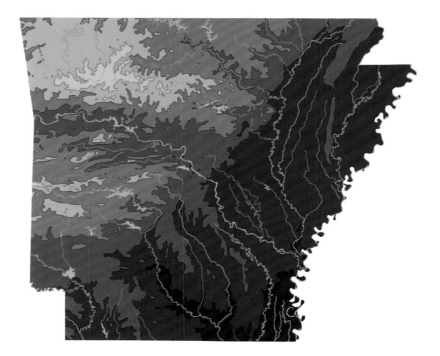

Topographic Map of Arkansas.

of the disparities; can equitable housing and neighborhoods be developed despite local economic and sociological imbalances? This question reiterates issues that arose in previous chapters regarding the duplicitous role of the "home"—both large and small scale, both public and private in nature—and the paradox of inclusive design. Among the most common questions people ask of inclusive design is "what does it look like . . . what are the features of inclusive design?" There is no single answer. Indeed, it is the absence of identifiers that makes it inclusive. Unlike other architectural movements—for example, aesthetic movements such as Art Nouveau—which are identifiable by certain stylistic features, inclusive design contains no visual identifiers. Inclusive design seeks integration and continuity, as opposed to the ad-hoc signifiers of "accessible design." This becomes, however, one of the barriers to the dissemination and advancement of inclusive design. It is most readily understood through physical experience, not through imagery; its design features are not exclamatory. One major challenge in communicating aspects of inclusive design is making the invisible visible.

For example, the framing technique used in one of the single-family prototypes discussed in this chapter includes an area of the floor between the first and second levels (the floor between two stacked closets) that is removable, allowing for the future installation of a residential elevator without structural modifications. This feature is truly hidden, only made visible when and if an elevator is to be installed. Another major challenge—paradox—of this chapter is to design a prototype that is both replicable (standardized) and site-specific (customized). The goal of this chapter, therefore, is to develop single- and multifamily prototypes that both illustrate the principles of inclusive design and demonstrate how they might be applied in particular contexts.

This chapter contains five major parts. The first part, primarily textual, provides an overview of the diverse geologic, environmental, cultural, and economic characteristics that comprise Arkansas. The second part, both textual and graphic, discusses the development of a set of design criteria and a general pattern of single-family prototypes: the Arkansas Proto-House. Through a series of diagrams, the third part identifies the major site factors that influence housing design, such as orientation to the street, bearing relative to the sun, and direction and degree of slope of a given plot of land. Through architectural drawings and models, the forth part demonstrates how the generic Proto-House can be modified to meet a given set of site factors. In this part of the chapter, three specific site locations were selected, each in a different geographic region of the state, and it is illustrated how the Proto-House might be transformed and deployed in a particular situation. Finally, the fifth part of the chapter, again through architectural drawings and models, shows how these principles can be applied to multifamily housing design, demonstrated by a duplex prototype: the LE House. The overarching goal is to find a common ground between diversity and equality.

Diversity and Arkansas

Historically, political boundaries—between countries, states, and locales—were often coincident with geologic, topographic, or other natural features (e.g., rivers, mountains, etc.). Cultural migration, advancements in military and transportation technologies, and developments in commerce, however, have diminished the magnitude of these natural features. Many newly established political jurisdictions—especially local jurisdictions—tend to operate independent of identifiable geographic figures and boundaries. The Great Mississippi Flood of 1927, for instance, shifted the flow pattern of the river, resulting in discrepancies between the state boundaries of Arkansas and Mississippi relative to the river. There are now oddities where parts of Arkansas (or parts of Mississippi) are "on the other side of the river."

Many states throughout the country are defined by shifts in geological or landscape patterns—the borders between Ohio, West Virginia, and Kentucky, for example. Yet other borders are merely circumstantial, geometric superimpositions upon an otherwise unmarked landscape, as seen in many western states, such as Colorado, Wyoming, and Utah. Arkansas, not unlike Tennessee, North Carolina, and others, possesses both naturally defined borders (such as the Mississippi River to the east) and surveyed borders (such as the northern border between Arkansas and Missouri). The Land Ordinance Act of 1785 and the Jeffersonian Grid established one-square-mile plots of land, which were superimposed on the existing natural features of the West and the Midwest. What resulted, as evident in a states map of the United States, was a hybrid condition, where both the Jeffersonian Grid and natural features work in tandem to define the political boundaries of most states.

Although the circumscription of these borders defines a political and legal territory, the sociological, economic, climatic, and topographic characteristics are not homogeneous throughout any state. Differences between urban and rural, flat and mountainous, temperate and extreme exist within any given political or legal boundary. So, although Arkansas maintains the highest poverty rate and third highest rate of disability in the country, poverty and disability are not evenly distributed throughout the state. Neither is employment nor access to health services; nor public education; nor access to suitable housing.

The eastern part of the state—"The Delta" (part of the Mississippi Alluvial Plain)—maintains a much greater prevalence of poverty and disability than much of the rest of the state, is predominantly agricultural, and is flat and prone to flood. These characteristics typify the region, but the Delta is not wholly so. The northwestern part of the state (part of the Ozark Plateau), in comparison, has both pockets of economic vibrancy and impoverishment. While Washington and Benton counties (northwest Arkansas) are among the ten fastest-growing economies in the country and home to the largest company in the world (Wal-Mart), Newton and Searcy counties, respectively, have 20.4 percent[3] and 23.8 percent[4] of individuals below poverty level. Northwest Arkansas also possesses diverse economic sources— education, retail and business, agriculture and livestock, as well as

Ozark Plateau

Gulf Coastal Plain

Mississippi Alluvial Plain

Regions of Arkansas.

healthcare services—and is geologically unique to the United States, as the Boston and Ozark Mountains are erosion, rather than uplift, mountains. The third major geographic region of Arkansas, the southwest part of the state (the West Gulf Coastal Plain), is predominantly rural and wooded, maintains poverty and disability rates higher than the national average, and relies on manufacturing for much of its employment.

Given the sociological, economic, environmental, and technological diversity previously described, it is difficult to imagine the design of a singular prototype that accommodates these variations. Nonetheless, as previous chapters have illustrated, an economy of means (some degree of standardization) is essential to providing high-quality, affordable housing. Pure customization is not viable. This chapter puts forth a pattern of single- and multifamily prototypes to explore this paradox—the need for more standardized housing design and construction and the necessity for variation. Each prototype seeks to create both a physical and a psychological "sense of home" as outlined by previous chapters. The prototypes seek to create a sense of home, of individuality, as well as adequately address local site constraints and achieve a sense of community. It is both a cultural and highly individualized task to, in the words of Johnny Cash, create "a place that moved into my heart immediately, a place where I knew I could belong."[5]

Design Criteria and Patterning of the AR Proto-House

Many factors influence the decisions people make about buying/renting a home, including location, cost, family structures and needs, and aesthetics. While the housing industry and popular culture tend to place emphasis on the fourth item— "looks"—the first three play a greater role in selecting a residence (e.g., proximity to work, school, and/or family), especially among less-affluent rural Southerners. While parts 3 and 4 explore issues regarding location, this section of the chapter investigates the role that cost and family size/structure play in housing, in addition to overarching principles of design and construction.

First, design criteria were developed by analyzing Arkansas's diverse geologic, environmental, cultural, and economic characteristics, as well as an understanding of the interrelationship of poverty and disability in the South. Eleven major principles, under the auspices of two overarching concepts resulted:

1. Maximize Adaptability:
    a. minimize interior load-bearing walls
    b. construct continuous structural surfaces in bathrooms/kitchens
    c. utilize easily adapted cabinetry, fixtures, and furniture
    d. utilize open-space planning/minimize space used exclusively as circulation
    e. ensure ease of mobility, operability, perceptibility, and security for diverse users

2. Maximize Efficiency:
    a. utilize modular construction
    b. cluster utilities together
    c. size structural members for material efficiency
    d. size HVAC systems for energy efficiency
    e. site building for energy efficiency
    f. utilize durable, low-maintenance materials and assemblies

Second, these design criteria led to the general design of the Arkansas (AR) Proto-House through a patterning of nine single-family types. This taxonomy included three major types: (1) a one-story family, (2) a one-story efficiency, and (3) a two-story family. Each major type included a range of three subtypes, including one "family option" and two "live/work options." The family options center on sleeping and family gathering spaces, while the live-work option includes a home office—for an accounting, consulting, or Internet business, for example— accessible from the main porch entry and able to be closed off to the rest of the home. In addition, each subtype is designed to be easily transformed into another subtype. For example, "Type 2A: 2BR Efficiency" can easily be modified to become "Type 2B: 1BR Live/Work A." This is achieved by replacing the bedroom window to the porch with a door. It is intended that, during the initial construction of the home, the bedroom window to the porch is framed like a door to facilitate future adaptation (another example of a "hidden" feature). The common features in all major types and subtypes include the following: (a) a fully accessible ground floor, including access to living, eating, food preparation, bathing and toileting, and sleeping spaces, (b) a fully accessible porch that provides exterior living space and mediates between the public exterior and private interior of the home, (c)

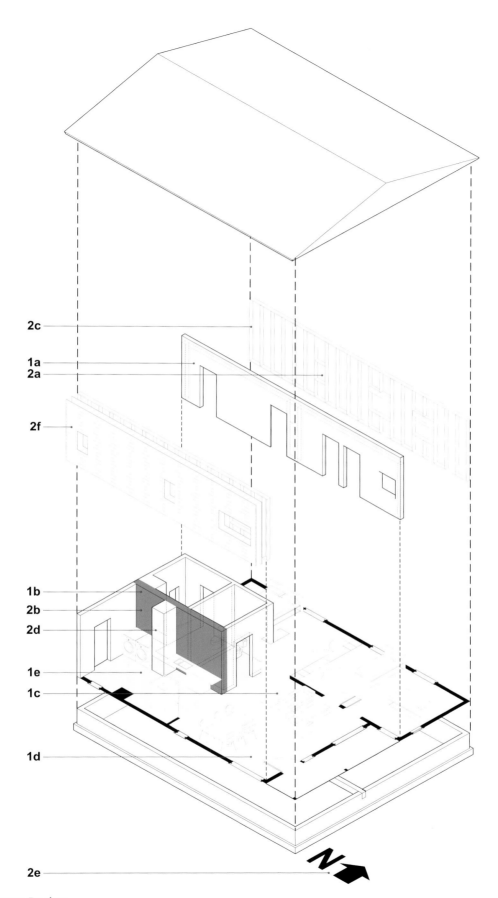

2c

1a
2a

2f

1b
2b
2d

1e

1c

1d

2e

N

AR Proto-House Design
Principles: Exploded
Axonometric Drawing.

Utility Core

Shared Spaces

Personal/Bedroom Spaces

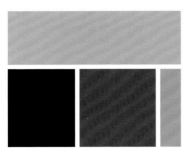

TYPE 1:
Single Family

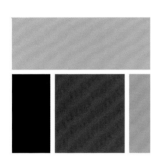

TYPE 2:
Single Family

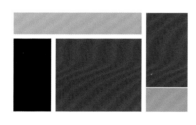

TYPE 3:
Single Family

AR Proto-House Taxonomy of
Types: Diagrams and Plans.

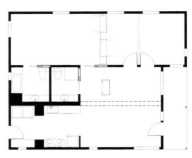

TYPE 1A:
3 BR Family

TYPE 2A:
2 BR Efficiency

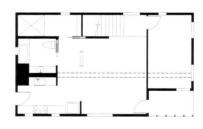

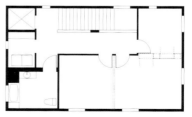

TYPE 3A:
4 BR Family

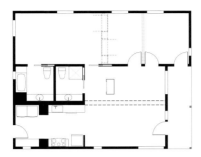

TYPE 1B:
2 BR Live/Work A

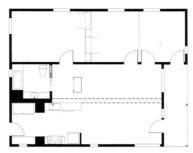

TYPE 1C:
2 BR Live/Work B

TYPE 2B:
1 BR Live/Work A

TYPE 2C:
1 BR Live/Work B

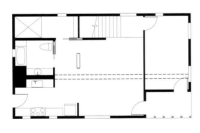

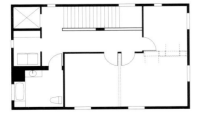

TYPE 3B:
3 BR Live/Work

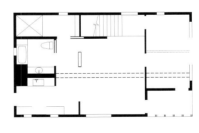

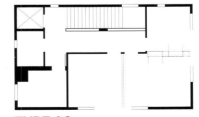

TYPE 3C:
4 BR Live/Work

173

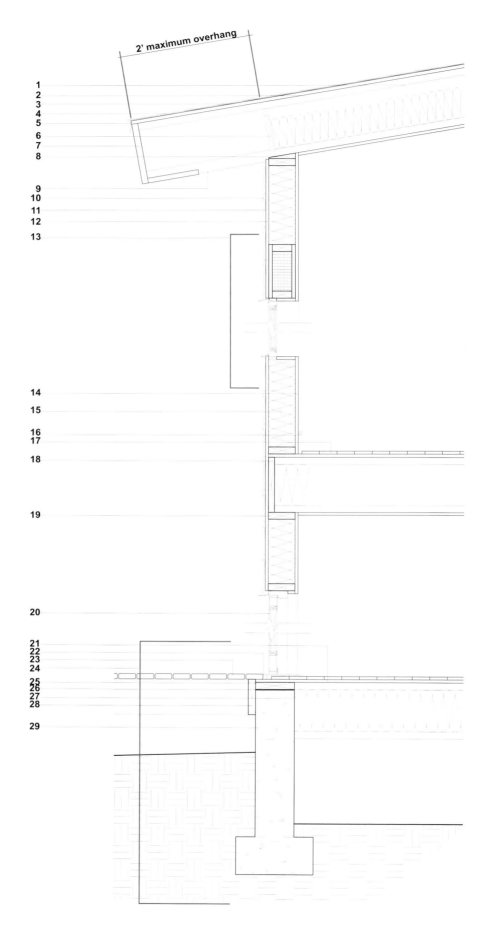

2' maximum overhang

1
2
3
4
5
6
7
8

9
10
11
12
13

14
15
16
17
18

19

20

21
22
23
24
25
26
27
28

29

AR Proto-House Typical
Wall Section.

174

13.1

24.1
24.1a
24.1b
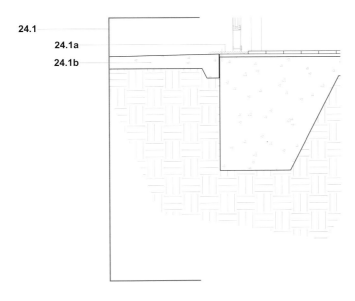

1. rafter ventilation
2. engineered wood I-joist commensurate with manufacturer's specifications
3. roof sheathing
4. roof cladding
5. drip edge
6. joist cross bracing
7. facia board
8. mitered top plate
9. soffit vent
10. exterior wall cladding
11. vapor barrier
12. wall sheathing
13. window assembly w/ insulated load-bearing header: prefabricated or site assembled
13.1. window assembly w/ non load-bearing header with 2"x6" nominal (typ)
14. interior wall surface
15. batt insulation (typ)
16. baseboard
17. finish flooring
18. rim board
19. 2"x6" nominal (typ)
20. door assembly
21. subfloor
22. half-saddle commercial threshold
23. 1"x4" nominal decking
24. crawlspace + deck assembly
24.1. slab on grade + slab assembly
24.1a. half-saddle commerical threshold
24.1b. poured-in-place slab (2% slope)
25. 2"x8" nominal sill plate
26. styrofoam sill seal
27. joist hanger
28. moisture resistant 2"x8" nominal ledger
29. reinforced, poured-in-place or masonry block foundation walls commensurate w/ soil conditions, etc.

AR Proto-House Typical
Wall Section.

interior circulation that enables movement for diverse occupants or visitors, and (d) fixtures (e.g., door hardware, sink fixtures, etc.) which are easily operable by diverse occupants/visitors. The underlying principles, organization, and structure of the various AR Proto-Houses is the same, facilitating a more efficient approach to urban, suburban, and rural housing developments, while the subtle differences and transformability of the types allows for diverse family structures and accommodates disparate topographic, sociological, and climatic contexts.

Site Factors

Decisions in housing design and construction are affected by four major factors: (1) economic factors, (2) sociological factors, (3) technological factors, and (4) environmental factors. Economic factors include costs of materials and labor, interest rates, shipping and transportation costs, as well as heating and cooling costs. Sociological factors might consist of aesthetic preferences, traditions and rituals, local and national laws and codes, as well as family structure. The skill of local laborers, local conventions in construction, the expertise of available design professionals, and/or innovations in material assemblies might be some technological factors affecting design and construction. Environmental factors might include climate and weather, topography, availability of infrastructure, lot size, and orientation to the sun. Clients, designers, developers, and builders/tradespeople negotiate a vast number of factors in the design and construction of housing. The same is true in the purchase or rental of existing housing, as rental/purchase price, maintenance and utility costs, aesthetics, location, and size influence the buyer's/renter's judgments. All of these factors include micro-, meso-, and macro-scale issues that are often interrelated. The hierarchy of these issues may change greatly from one project to the next, as clients, sites, and material costs change.

Although other factors, such as material costs, greatly influence housing design, construction, and purchasing decisions, four primary factors associated with any given site tend to exert the greatest influence on single-family housing design. These site factors include topography, orientation to the street, bearing (orientation to the sun), and parking. The hierarchy of these issues may change greatly from one project to the next, as clients, sites, material costs, and other factors change.

The tendency in many single-family developments and tract housing is to eliminate or ignore these features by flattening topography, ignoring the cardinal directions, and dogmatically repeating the housing across the landscape, resulting in increased site costs, increased heating/cooling costs, and decreased neighbor interactions and participation in the community. The generic AR Proto-House, on the other hand, was modified by these four factors. The approach, threshold space (e.g., porch), and interior organization of each prototype was transformed to create a better fit and increased usability. The major design challenges and strategies employed are demonstrated in each localized case study discussed below.

Deploying the AR Proto-House

This section of the chapter proceeds by illustrating how the aforementioned taxonomy of types might accommodate diverse sites (e.g., flat, sloping, flood-prone, etc.) and diverse household structures (e.g., single-parent families, extended families, traditional families, etc.), while maintaining a certain degree of universality. More specifically, one exemplar was designed for each of the three regions of Arkansas: the Ozark Plateau, the West Gulf Coastal Plain, and the Mississippi Alluvial Plain, demonstrating how the general prototypes might be deployed within a given context. In each of these regions, specific lots were identified in three cities—Fayetteville, Hot Springs, and Arkansas City—to serve as case studies as to how the prototypes might accommodate and be modified by the particularities of a given situation. These lots were chosen primarily for the design challenges that they presented and served to test how efficiently the AR Proto-House could be transformed.

Site specificity is important, as, according to John Shelton Reed,

> Southerners seem to have retained a greater degree than other Americans a localistic orientation—an attachment to their place and their people. Although there are some cracks in this pattern, localism can be expected to color the outlook of many Southerners for some time to come.[6]

In addition, each of these case studies—the Ozark Prototype, the Ouachita Prototype, and the Delta Prototype—demonstrated circumstances that were prevalent not only in that given region but also throughout Arkansas and the South. As such, each resulting prototype is more typological than regional; each prototype maintains the possibility to be deployed within similar circumstances in an alternate region. Although the prototype designs focused on the house proper, relationships to the surrounding infrastructure, natural landscape, and community were essential.

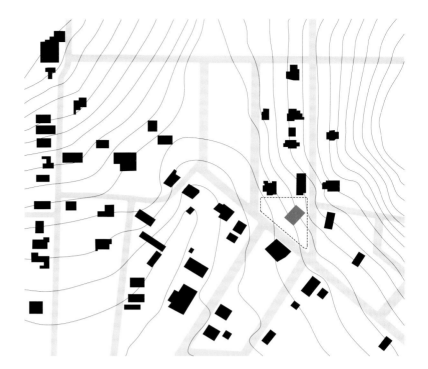

Context of the Ozark Prototype.

OZARK PROTOTYPE

The first site selected was in Fayetteville, a diverse college town in the Ozark region of the state. The site possessed numerous challenges. The site had a triangular lot with two adjoining streets, was steeply sloping, and sat on the border between commercial and residential zoning. Type 1A (Family) and Type 1B (Live/Work) were utilized to create a stacked duplex. Duplex housing is prevalent in the area, but typically possesses two major shortcomings. First, the duplex housing that occurs in northwest Arkansas is often conceived as two independent houses "merged at the hip," not as an integrated whole. Second, parking, approach, and privacy between the units is seldom well resolved. The Ozark case study, though, is conceived as a whole unit, and, from the street, looks like one large single-family home. This strategy enables the residence to appear more substantial and helps to combat the "not in my back yard" attitude often confronted in affordable housing. In addition, the Ozark prototype has two "fronts"; the lower level faces a prominent main street, while the upper level faces a side street. The lower-level, live-work unit utilizes an on-site parking strategy, whereas the upper-level, family unit takes advantage of on-street parking. The live-work unit faces the commercial zone and the family unit faces the residential zone. Most importantly, both units are accessible at grade; both units contain kitchens, bathrooms, and living spaces that accommodate the needs of a wide range of families/individuals; and both units are designed to maximize material and environmental efficiencies.

Aerial Perspective of the Ozark
Prototype (Facing North).

Ozark Prototype Site Plan.

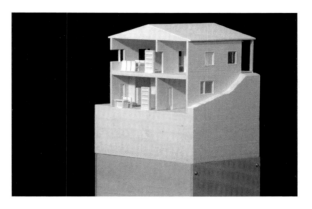

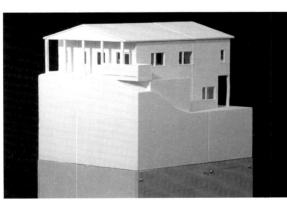

Photographs of a Model of the
Ozark Prototype.

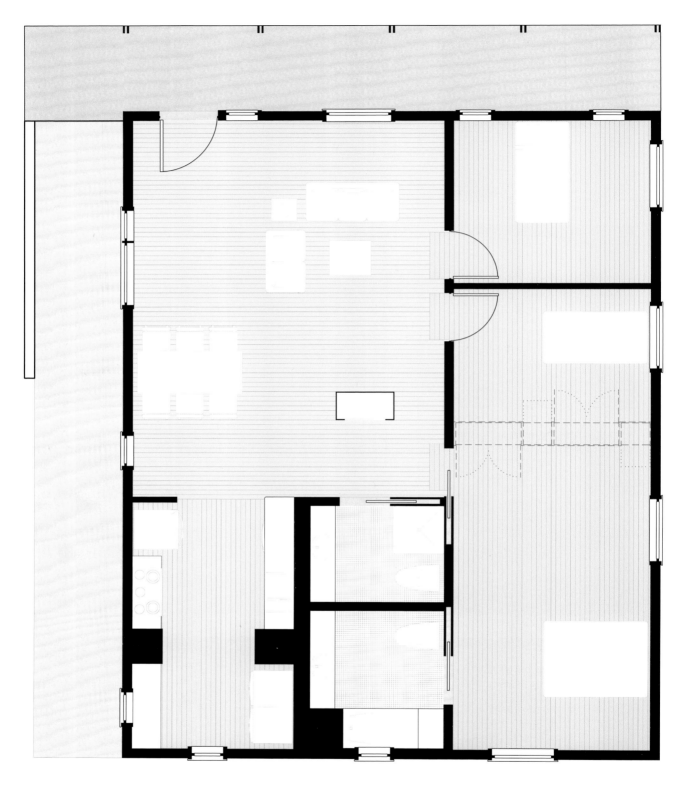

Upper-level Plan of the
Ozark Prototype.

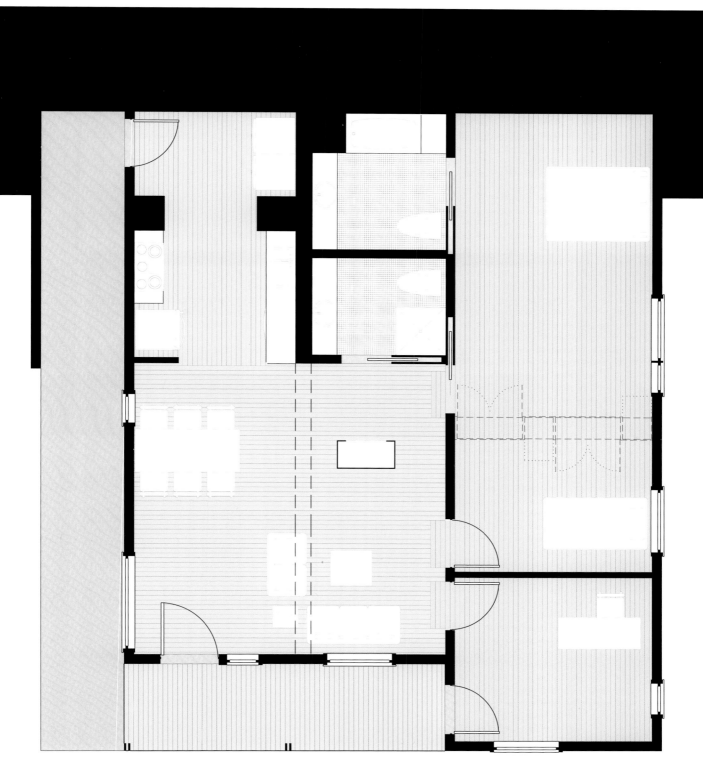

Lower-level Plan of the Ozark
Prototype.

Site Section of the
Ozark Prototype.

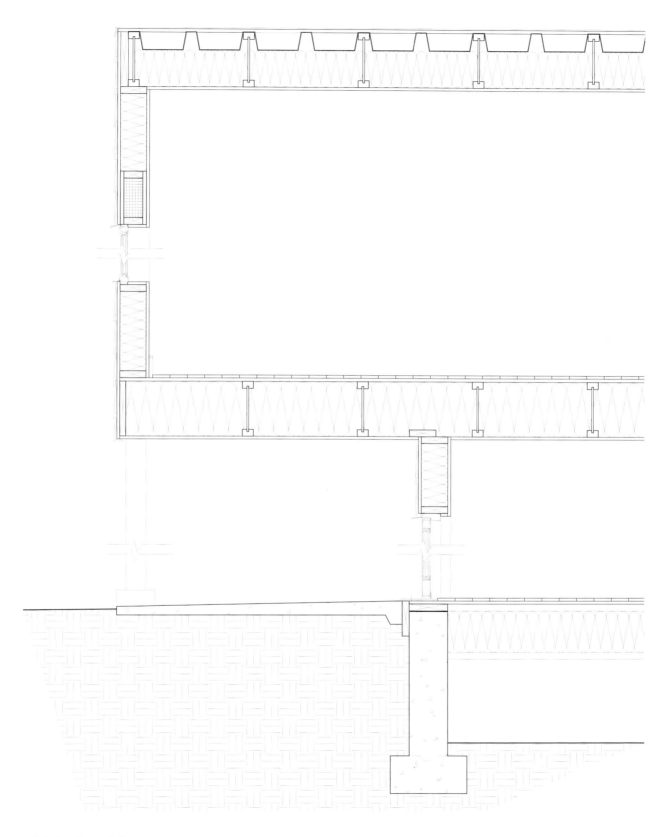

Wall Section of the
Ozark Prototype.

Context of the
Ouachita Prototype.

OUACHITA PROTOTYPE

The second site selected was in Hot Springs, a retreat town in the Ouachita region of the state. The site was steeply sloping, sat amid an older residential neighborhood on a very narrow lot, had no access on the primary public street due to a six-foot-high retaining wall between the sidewalk and the property line, and could only be accessed by a narrow dead-end alley. Homes typically marketed as "accessible" or "elder-friendly" are often one level. Due to the narrowness of the lot, a single level was not possible, only the Type 3A (Family) unit, a two-story residence, could be used. Most two-story homes follow a fairly standard organization, where the lower (ground) level contains the more public functions of living, dining, and food preparation, while the upper level houses sleeping and bathing spaces. The Ouachita prototype is a transformation of this standard typology.

As the Ouachita prototype is accessed by a rear alley on the high side of the property, the first and second levels are inverted in comparison to the norm. The top level is accessed at grade and contains living, dining, and food preparation spaces, in addition to one bedroom and one full bathroom. The lower level contains three additional bedrooms and another full bathroom. This house may not be defined as "universal," but is "inclusive" to most families. While disability rates are incredibly high in Arkansas, families that possess two or more people with mobility impairments are relatively rare. This home, because of the design of the fully function-

Aerial Perspective of the Ouachita Prototype (Facing Northeast).

ing ground level, therefore, accommodates the needs of most families. In addition, the stair is wider than a conventional stair and is a "straight-run." This design better enables assistance in ascending/descending or the future installation of a lift. The structural framing is also designed to easily accommodate the future installation of a residential elevator if the homeowner so chooses. Despite the small footprint, the open-plan, cathedral ceiling, and large glazing allow the interior to seem spacious. The Ouachita prototype also possesses a wrap-around porch that provides exterior living space, entry, and a "front face" to the public street.

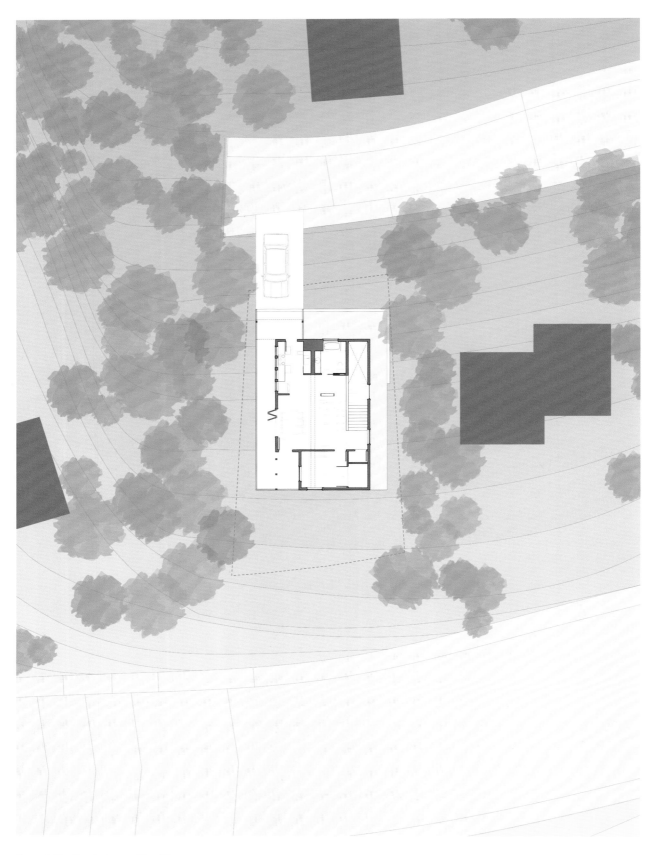

Ouachita Prototype Site Plan.

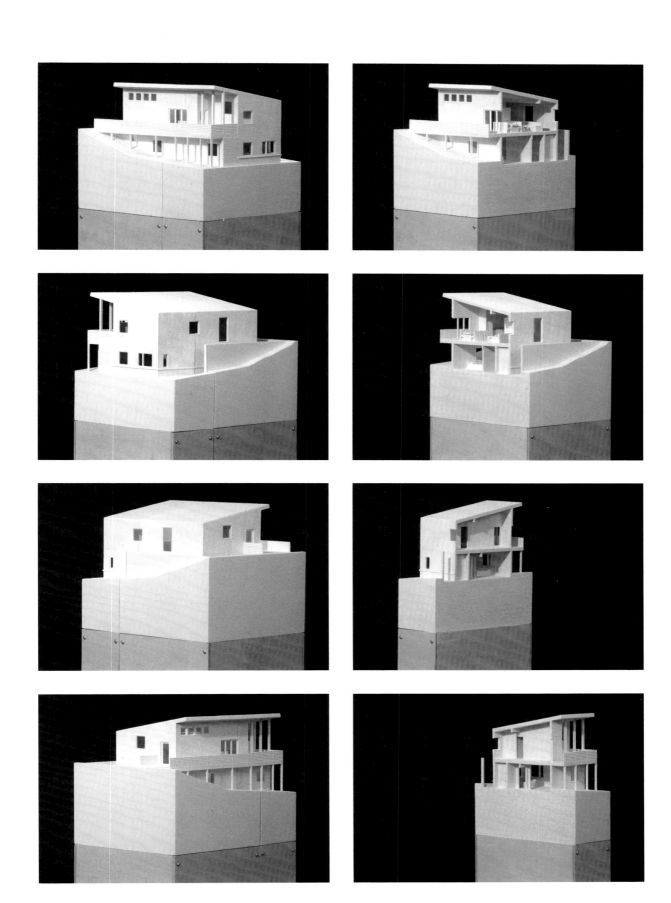

Photographs of a Model of the
Ouachita Prototype.

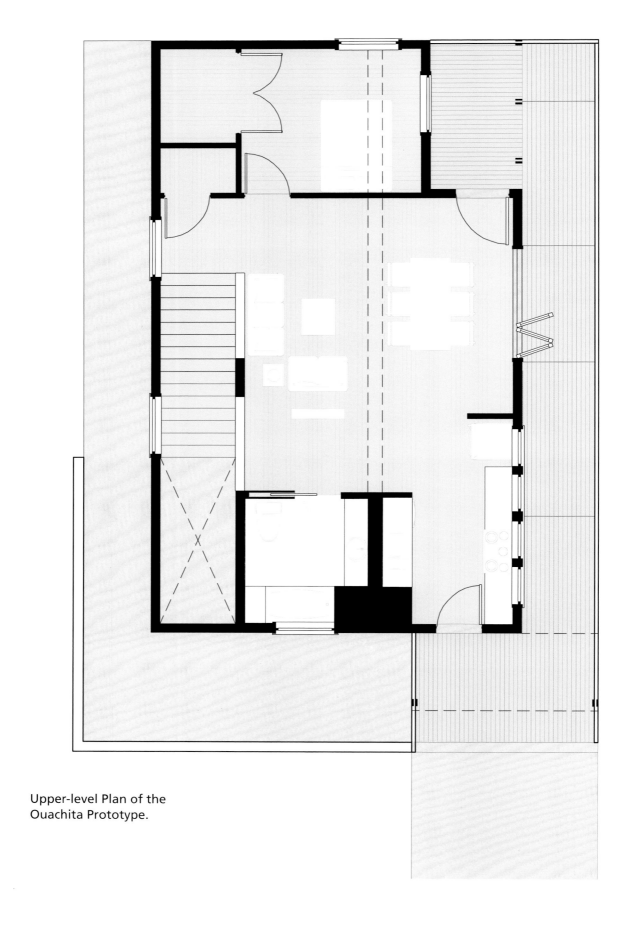

Upper-level Plan of the
Ouachita Prototype.

190

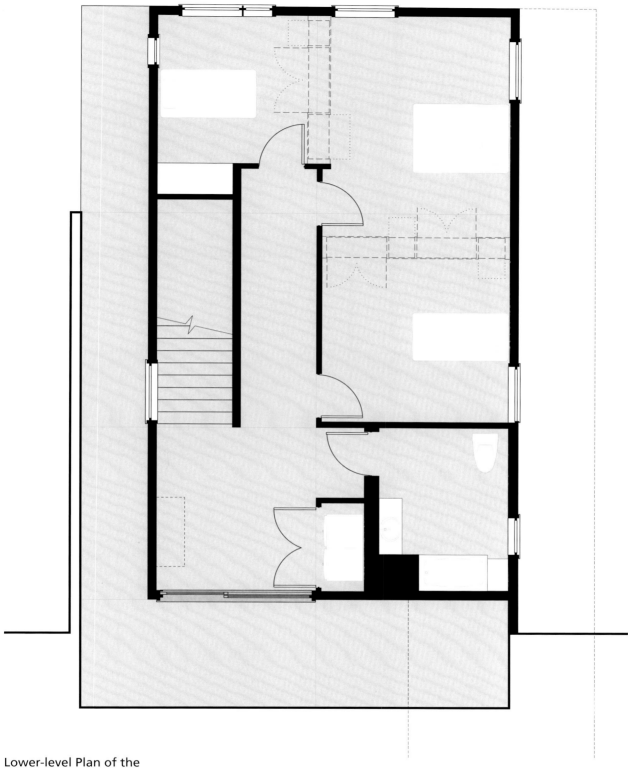

Lower-level Plan of the
Ouachita Prototype.

Site Section of the Ouachita
Prototype.

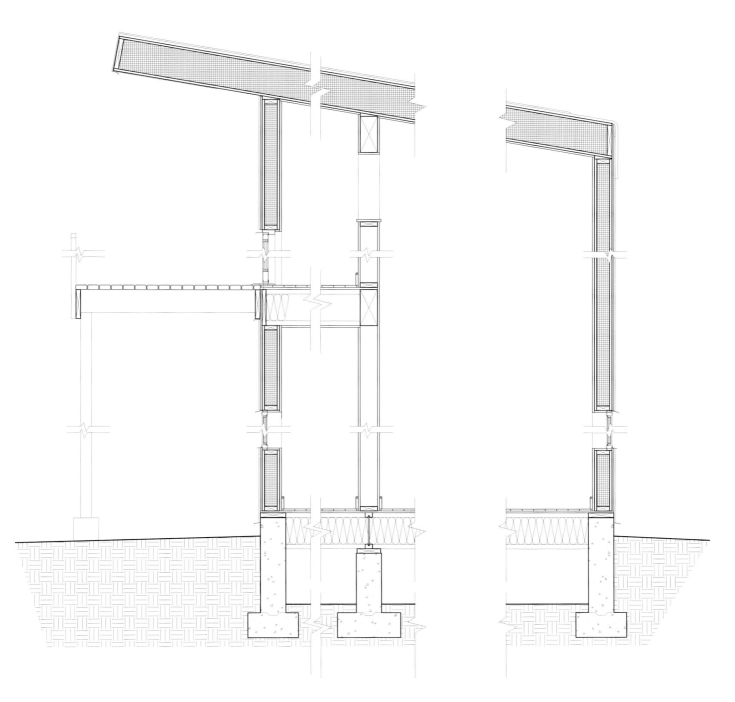

Wall Section of the
Ouachita Prototype.

Context of the Delta Prototype.

DELTA PROTOTYPE

The third site selected was in Arkansas City, a historic Mississippi River port town in the Alluvial Plain. The site was incredibly flat, prone to flood, hot and humid, and existed on a fairly visible corner lot. Steeply sloping sites are often considered to be the most challenging for accessibility and the least desirable to many developers. This may be a bit of an oversight, however, as slopes can be used advantageously, like those of the Ozark and Ouachita prototypes. The biggest challenge to inclusive housing design in the Delta—aside from the strained economy—is the flatness of the landscape and its propensity to flood. This requires that homes be raised several feet above grade. So, how can entry and exit be accommodated efficiently without steps? In some cases, the surrounding land can be graded to slope up to the house. Typically, however, this is prohibitively expensive. What often results are the ad-hoc ramp solutions represented throughout this book.

Due to these factors and the prevalence of single-parent and single-resident households and high rates of poverty in the Delta, the Type 2A (Efficiency) was chosen. The home was raised three feet above the surrounding land and a porch was provided. The porch was designed such that it wraps around the corner of the home and transforms into an integrated ramp. From the street, only the porch is legible. The porch also provides exterior living space and protection from the sun. The open floor plan facilitates ventilation and allows the interior to seem more spacious. The home is accessible from a rear parking area, from which an ambulatory occupant (or visitor) can ascend the ramp/porch to the main living space or move directly into the kitchen (with an armload of groceries, for instance) via a small set of steps.

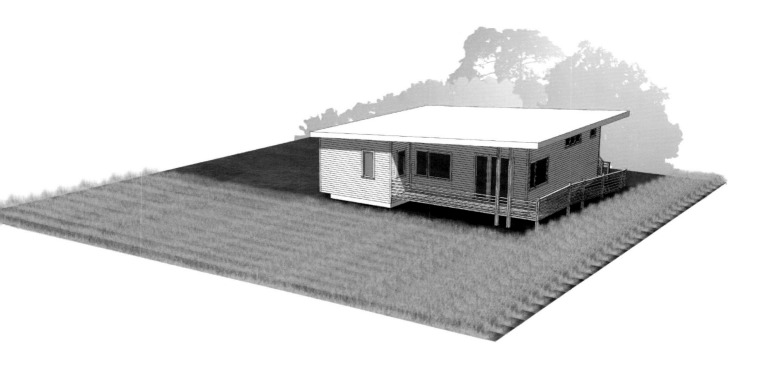

Aerial Perspective of the Delta
Prototype (Facing North).

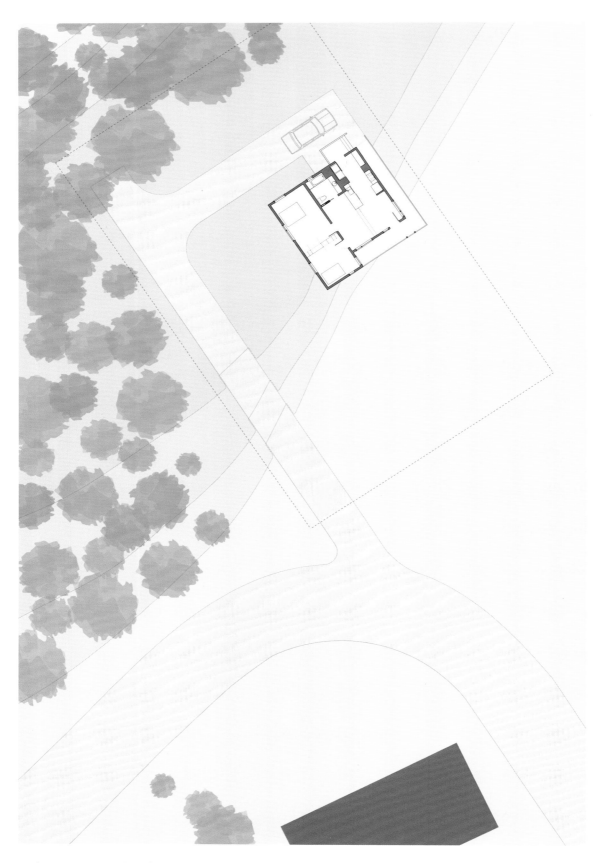

Delta Prototype Site Plan.

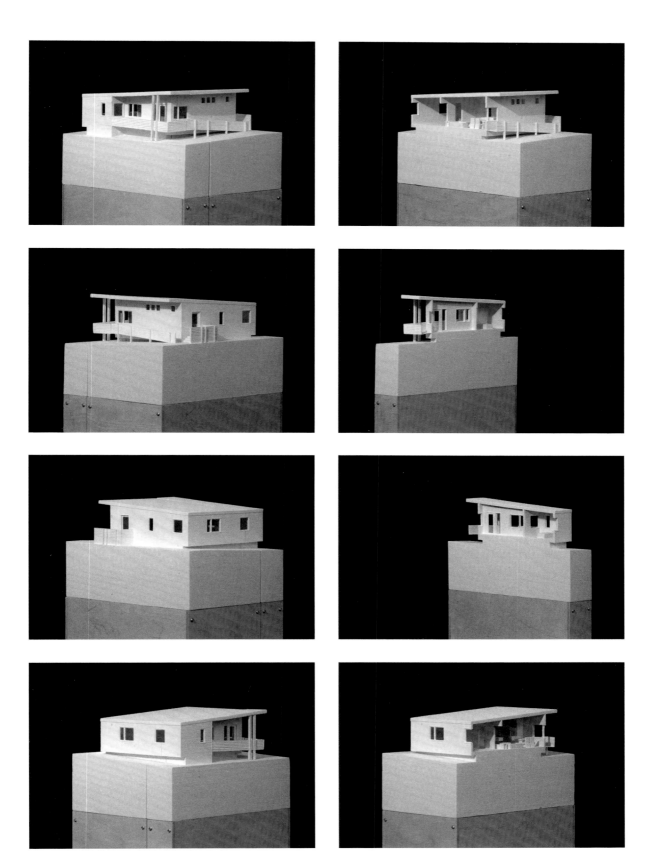

Photographs of a Model of the
Delta Prototype.

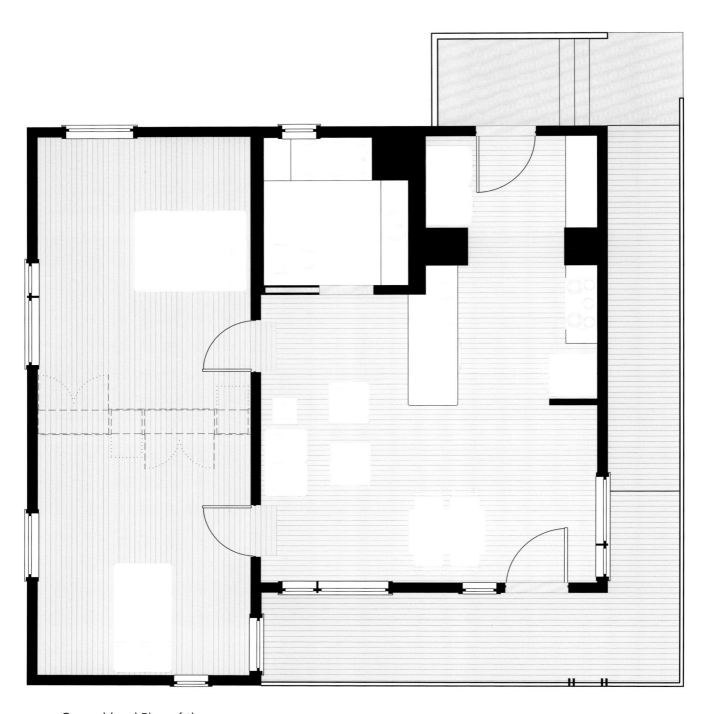

Ground-level Plan of the
Delta Prototype.

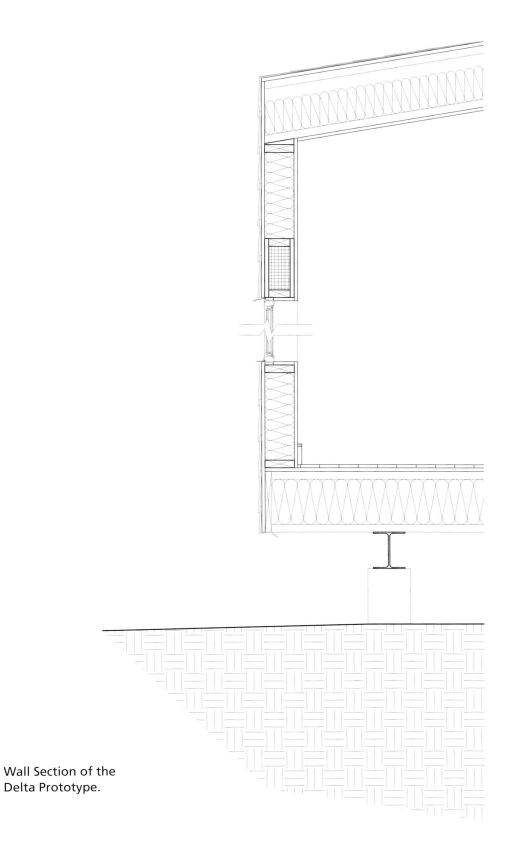

Wall Section of the
Delta Prototype.

Interior Perspective
of the LE House.

LE HOUSE, MULTIFAMILY PROTOTYPE

In parallel with the single-family prototypes, the proposed multi-family prototype seeks to demonstrate a fundamental set of principles for designing and constructing higher functioning, affordable housing. This prototype—the Limited Edition (LE) Product House—utilizes contemporary prefabrication techniques and modular design, while accommodating an array of stylistic preferences, family structures, and site conditions.[7]

The LE House conforms to performance standards governing the manufactured housing industry and demonstrates the technical and aesthetic potential of modular construction.
The industry currently produces model homes aspiring to the generic "American" suburb aesthetic (e.g., pitched roofs, textured interior ceilings, vinyl "wood" siding, etc.). As a result, a truly innovative method of construction appears in the form of a typical suburban home. The LE project's design goal is to distinguish the production process from aesthetic dependencies and propose a new aesthetic/production model fully compatible with industry standards. Because the LE Product House is based on a technological concept rather than a predetermined style, the aesthetic/spatial range of the house is virtually unlimited and can easily avoid the negative connotations associated with modular construction.

The net result of the LE House's technological and spatial characteristics is a home produced at a lower cost, as well as greater structural integrity and greater spatial flexibility, all of which are critical in the design and habitation of inclusive housing. For example, while maintaining the existing dimensions and relationships of a typical structural module, the house was "split" to accommodate two different occupancies: a ground-floor studio apartment and a two-story large-family unit. In addition, the interior partitioning of the ground floor module of the two-story unit was treated as a somewhat independent condition, with its own entry, kitchenette, bath, and study/bedroom. The upper floor of the two-story unit

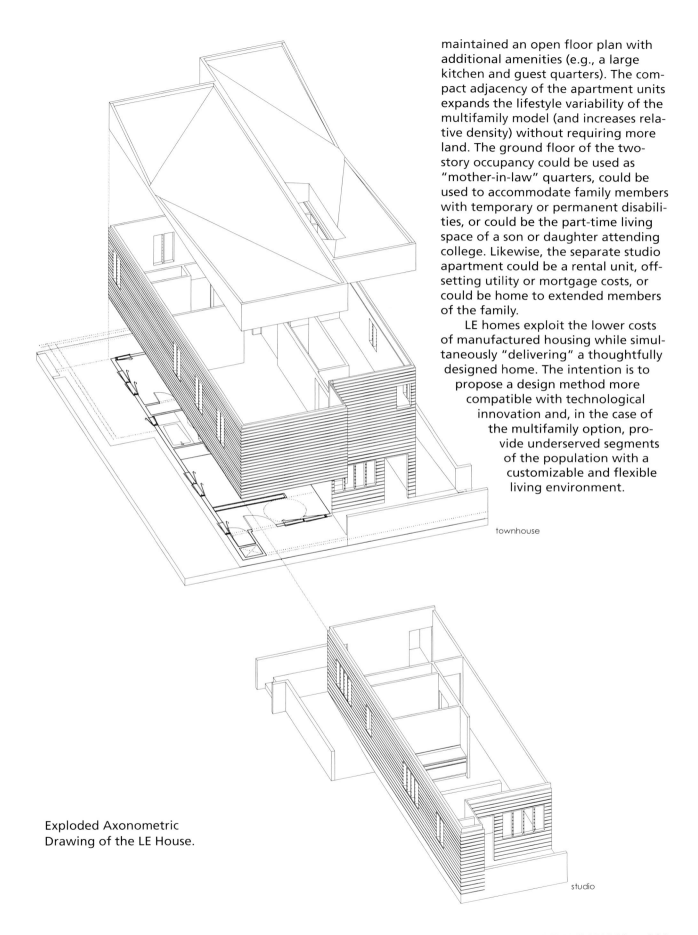

maintained an open floor plan with additional amenities (e.g., a large kitchen and guest quarters). The compact adjacency of the apartment units expands the lifestyle variability of the multifamily model (and increases relative density) without requiring more land. The ground floor of the two-story occupancy could be used as "mother-in-law" quarters, could be used to accommodate family members with temporary or permanent disabilities, or could be the part-time living space of a son or daughter attending college. Likewise, the separate studio apartment could be a rental unit, offsetting utility or mortgage costs, or could be home to extended members of the family.

LE homes exploit the lower costs of manufactured housing while simultaneously "delivering" a thoughtfully designed home. The intention is to propose a design method more compatible with technological innovation and, in the case of the multifamily option, provide underserved segments of the population with a customizable and flexible living environment.

townhouse

Exploded Axonometric
Drawing of the LE House.

studio

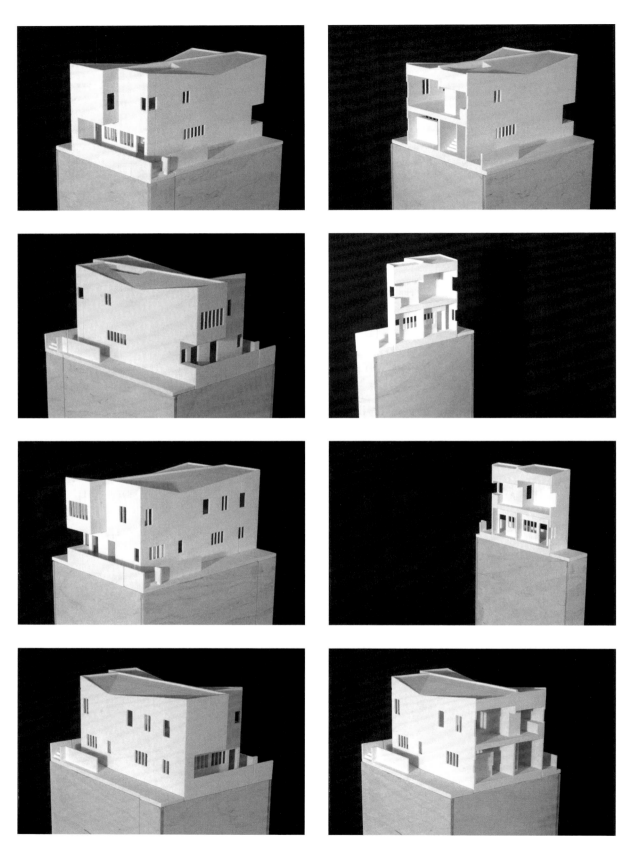

Photographs of a Model
of the LE House.

202

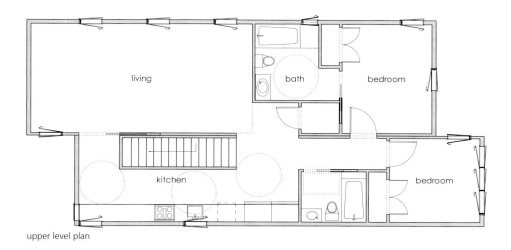

upper level plan

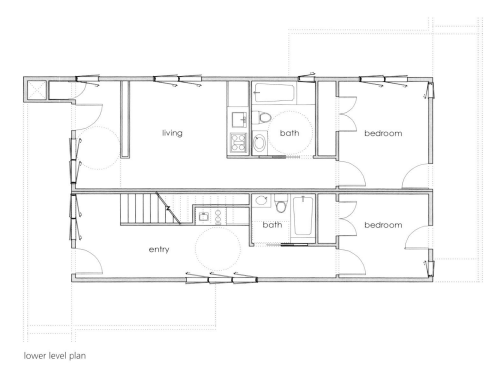

lower level plan

Lower and Upper Levels
of the LE House.

Conclusion

As housing production has slowed, healthcare costs have risen, and demographics make massive shifts, America confronts a tremendous question: How can housing (a) meet the variety of needs and preferences of the society, (b) ensure equity among the various groups that comprise that society, and (c) be created at low costs and high quality? Nowhere is this question more pertinent, timely, and challenging than in the South, a region characterized by strong contrasts in economic, racial, geographic, educational, and health statuses (not to mention the political mythology of the "segregated South"). In essence, Southerners are as diverse, if not more so, than any other subculture in the United States. This diversity is intensified as one looks deeper at the complex and often-contradictory definition of "Southern culture." This definition was a popular topic among regional sociologists and geographers throughout the latter part of the twentieth century and has long been debated. Does the South have its own unique identity or is this a mythic stereotyping of the region? Are characteristics associated with the South unique or do other areas of the country possess "Southern" traits?

Researchers have examined factors stereotypically associated with the South: religious and political beliefs, attitudes toward guns and violence, family and social values, food, et cetera. Many findings countered previous assumptions about Southern culture. Several studies, for example, illustrated that "Southern identity" is deeper and more prevalent among more-affluent, higher-educated Southerners.[8] This is in contrast to poor Southerners who, as research has shown, are much more in tune with their "poorness" than their "Southerness."[9] In either case, housing plays a central role in developing a sense of identity, place, and culture.

Arkansas, however, is an unlikely place to look for lessons in good design. In fact, it may be the last place Americans look for counsel about anything. Arkansas is more likely to be the punch line of any number of "trailer trash" jokes than an exemplar of good housing practices. But, as the English professor Fred Hobson states, "The South always makes good reading. It features the virtues and vices, writ large, of the nation as a whole."[10] The AR Proto-House and the LE House are attempts to address the varied economic, sociological, environmental, and technological conditions of the South. These residences tackle the challenge of developing prototypes that are both replicable and culture and site specific.

The Arkansas Proto-House is an exploration in meeting the

physical and psychosocial housing needs of the state, and an analogue for solving parallel concerns across the South and all of the United States. For example, one of the greatest challenges to attainable housing in areas experiencing economic and housing booms (e.g., northwest Arkansas) is the rapid rise in land values. Increased land costs push affordable housing to the outskirts of town, increasing the distance inhabitants must travel to access employment, education, healthcare, and amenities. The Ozark version of the AR Proto-House takes advantage of a site that is typically considered "un-buildable" due to slope and zoning—a site that is centrally located, yet vacant. Each example illustrates how a "standardized" prototype can be deployed in a "custom" setting. The AR Proto-House seeks to work within the diverse social and physical contexts of the South without pandering to stereotypes. Its design features are not exclamatory; this is a central value of universal design, or, quite simply, good design.

In any case, there is necessity for diverse housing options; it is difficult to imagine a singular prototype that accommodates all family structures, physical and psychosocial needs, and other factors. Nonetheless, an economy of means, realized through standardization, is essential to providing quality, affordable housing; pure customization is not viable. Truly "custom" housing, like custom automobiles, is often exclusive to persons and families of lofty economic means. The aforementioned single-family and multifamily prototypes seek to provide "customization" for a much broader population. These prototypes are intended as exemplars of how to reconcile and achieve both diversity and equality in Southern housing. This is achieved by coupling contemporary manufacturing technologies with the ideals of universal design, sustainability, and site-specific design.

What results is a greater degree of fit at all scales—individual, familial, communal, and regional. First, the prototypes nurture personal identity by fostering independence, privacy, and choice. Second, the housing models also accommodate differences between and changes within families. Third, the ability to participate in the community—through work, recreation, education, and social interaction—is promoted through the prototypes' designs. Finally, the AR Proto-House and the LE House fit within specific regional contexts, taking into account topographic, climatic, economic, and cultural distinctions. Providing greater physical and psychosocial fit at all scales improves quality, increases attainability, and fosters adaptability.

Array of Fenestration Types
in Manufactured Homes.

Redefining Policy and Practice

BRENT T. WILLIAMS, KORYDON H. SMITH, AND JENNIFER WEBB

Congress acknowledged that society's accumulated myths and fears about disability and disease are as handicapping as are the physical limitations that flow from actual impairment.

—WILLIAM J. BRENNAN JR., *associate justice of the Supreme Court of the United States*[1]

The interrelationships between health and housing are not tacitly obvious, yet their reciprocity is substantial. As previously stated, one of the primary purposes of this book is to illustrate the synergistic relationship between these fields, that housing design affects physical and psychosocial well-being, while personal health influences needs and preferences in housing. The policies and practices that underlie the health and housing industries, however, still remain predominantly autonomous and struggle for broad societal impact. More than a decade ago, Johnny Cash observed,

> Apart from the Vietnam War being over, I don't see much reason to change my position today. The old are still neglected, the poor are still poor, the young are still dying before their time, and we're not making any moves to make things right. There's still plenty of darkness to carry off.[2]

Consistent with the "Man in Black's" sometimes austere perspective, this critique of health and housing policy is still made today by advocates of such diverse perspectives as AARP and ADAPT.

The U.S. Government's role in housing policy dates primarily from two critical points in the nation's history. First, at approximately the turn of the present century, tenement reform laws set the precedent that local governments would set standards and be the primary regulators of housing safety. Second, during the New Deal Era of the 1930s, the public housing program and banking reform established the precedent for a federal role in homeownership generally and in providing housing subsidies to poor residents in particular.[3] From the New Deal Era through the 1970s, U.S. housing policies were based on the belief that solutions to the nation's housing problems required the direct assistance of the federal government. Through policy pledges that guaranteed every American decent housing (e.g., Housing Act of 1949), and by federal policies that stabilized the banking industry, thus giving lenders incentives to make long-term loans to home buyers, the federal government played an ever-expanding role in housing issues. As Washington provided subsidies to local public housing authorities and private developers for low- and moderate-income housing, politicians, lenders, property owners, and real estate agents largely agreed on the basic premise that the federal government had key responsibilities and a central role to play in housing policy.

Regarding governmental structures, housing and health-related agencies emerged separately and have continued to remain autonomous in the legislation and practices that underlie them. Housing is principally in the purview of the Department of Housing and Urban Development, whereas health policy and funding is chiefly administered by the Department of Health and Human Services. "Because the current systems of health and housing services were conceived in isolation, so remain their respective funding sources, performance standards and regulatory bodies."[4] Due to various social and political changes, these independent agencies have held disparate, if not conflicting, agendas and practices.

In the business realm, housing and health practices have also remained separate due to the specialized knowledge necessary to operate in each field, though synergies between health and housing have recently emerged. As such, the goals of this chapter are to assess current policies and practices and to provide recommendations for change. The summative purpose is to illustrate how individual quality of life may be improved and government fiscal efficacy may be enhanced.

Overview of Housing Policies and Practices

The intention of this chapter is not to delve deeply into the fine points of housing legislation. Nevertheless, legislation influences both policies and practices and even at times establishes administrative agencies. The U.S. Access Board, created by the

Rehabilitation Act of 1973, is one example. The immediate purpose here is to provide the reader with a general understanding of the most significant pieces of legislation that influence housing for people with disabilities and low-income families, the programs associated with these legislative acts, and the agencies who supervise these programs.

As housing programs change often, and for purposes of clarity, not all programs are discussed. In addition, more than other chapters, this chapter places equal focus on disability-related and income-related housing programs. The reason for an increased focus on income is two-fold. First, the bulk of the discourse on housing policy centers on income-related programs. This makes sense, as the bulk of the legislation, funding, and policies related to housing center on economic status not disability status. Second, income and disability are intimately related statistics. There are strong correlations between disability status and economic status. "Low-income," "affordable," and "attainable" housing programs, geared toward lower-income individuals and families, also serve a large number people with disabilities. Both disability-related and economically related programs may serve individuals and families who have both lower incomes and disabilities. Appendix 4 provides an overview of housing legislation, programs, agencies, and funding. Many of these programs serve dual or multiple roles.

Fair Housing is the component of the 1968 Civil Rights Act that has been the slowest to be implemented and enforced. While antisegregation laws have been advanced in education, employment, and healthcare, housing has seen fewer gains in both the federal courts and in everyday practice.[5] Fair Housing, however, is merely one piece of legislation in the more than four-decades-old legislative history of disability rights in housing, which includes the Community Mental Health Centers Act (1963), Civil Rights Act (1964), Fair Housing Act (1968), the Architectural Barriers Act (1968), the Rehabilitation Act (1973), Education for All Handicapped Children Act (1975), the Fair Housing Amendments Act (1988), the Americans with Disabilities Act (1990), the Housing for Older Persons Act (1995), Telecommunications Act (1996), Individuals with Disabilities Education Act (IDEA, 1997 and 2004). Some legislation (e.g., Fair Housing) focuses on housing directly, while other legislation (e.g., IDEA) invokes housing more indirectly, as location and quality of housing affects access to and effectiveness of education.

Regarding the Fair Housing Act, there is some debate about whether the legislation simply prohibits discrimination or whether it prohibits discrimination *and* charges proactive measures to ensure integration. The implications of a ruling in either direction, nonetheless, would be titanic. For example, a ruling in favor of the latter would likely necessitate the creation of numerous programs (and potentially agencies) charged with developing health and housing services that would support community integration, as well as the creation of ear-marked funding to support these programs. As housing services are more significantly lacking than health-related services, it is likely that significant funding would need to be directed toward the design and construction of housing. A ruling in favor of the former, however, would not require substantive changes. Funds would likely be directed toward prosecuting discrimination, while institutional living would likely remain the general practice for housing people with severe disabilities. As of 1999, the higher courts had yet to establish a clear reading on this controversy.[6]

Three significant themes should be noted. First, the bulk of federal housing legislation and programs focus on economic issues (i.e., income), and to a much lesser degree on disability-only programs. This is not without reason, as income is the greatest predictor of an individual's/family's access to housing. The bulk of disability-centric programs are related to enforcement (e.g., FHIP, FHAP, and ADAAG) rather than facilitating design and construction of inclusive housing. The lack of disability-centric legislation and programs geared toward "bricks-and-mortar" initiatives, however, fails to recognize the increased difficulty that many individuals with disabilities face in finding suitable housing, regardless of economic standing.

Second, there is a trend away from the construction of federally owned/-managed housing (i.e., public housing). Presumably, this results from the negative criticisms (e.g., ghettoizing) that public housing projects, such as Chicago's infamous Cabrini-Green, have faced, as well as the overhead in managing public housing. This trend is paralleled by an increase in block grants and a simultaneous reduction in specialized programs and "bricks-and-mortar" funding. The Native American Housing Assistance Self-Determination Act (1996), for example, eliminated a series of programs begun in 1937 with the U.S. Housing Act geared toward housing for low-income Native Americans. The Native American Housing Assistance Self-Determination Act

Mailboxes and Houses. The systematic approach to design and infrastructure limits responsiveness to individual and local conditions.

consolidated the U.S. Housing Act initiatives into a single program of block grants.

Finally, as Appendix 4 illustrates, the U.S. Department of Housing and Urban Development maintains the greatest number of housing-related programs, more than twenty; for example the Housing Choice Section 8 Voucher Program, FHA Mortgage Insurance Programs, the Public Housing Development Program, the Rural Housing and Economic Development (RHED) Program, the Supportive Housing for the Elderly Program, and the Supportive Housing for Persons with Disabilities Program. The U.S. Department of Agriculture has around ten housing-related programs (e.g., the Direct Homeownership Loan Program, the Loan Guarantee Program, the Mutual Self-Help Housing Loan Program, the Rural Housing Repair and Rehabilitation Loans and Grants Program, the Rural Rental Housing Guaranteed Loan Program, and the Rural Rental Housing Program). The U.S. Department of Health and Human Services (DHHS) administers around four (e.g., the Low Income Home Energy Assistance Program [LIHEAP], the Leveraging Incentive Program, the Residential Energy Assistance Challenge Option [REACH] Program, and the Home and Community-Based Services [HCBS] Waiver Program). Whereas HUD and the USDA provide funds for housing construction, rehabilitation, infrastructure, and rental assistance, DHHS only provides funds for maintenance, such as home modifications and utilities payment assistance. All U.S. Access Board programs are for technical assistance and enforcement. HUD, USDA, and DHHS maintain some of these types of initiatives as well.

Though not the largest budget in total dollars, the vast majority of HUD's total outlay, $616 billion, goes directly toward housing. As national priorities shifted and agencies were forced to compete for fiscal resources, many of HUD's initiatives have faced uncertain futures, as evidenced by the termination of the HOPE IV (Elderly Independence) Program in 1993. This shift in prioritization, as evidenced by a decrease in HUD's share of the federal budget, a drop of 0.2 percentage points from 1999 to 2005, makes predicting HUD's future impact difficult.

Among all of the aforementioned agencies, DHHS possesses the largest overall budget, a little over $616 billion in total allocations for 2006. In addition to having the largest total budget, DHHS has, by far, seen the greatest increase in percentage of funding and actual dollars. The DHHS percentage of the federal budget has grown 2.4 percent from 1999 to 2005, second only to the Department of Defense. Conversely only a very small percentage of DHHS's budget is geared toward housing. With a greater emphasis being placed on health and human services in the current political environment it is unlikely DHHS will see a decrease in its future allocations.

The USDA, with outlays of $93.5 billion and credit/loan activities of $26.9 billion in 2006, like HUD, has faced a decrease of 0.2 percentage points in its portion of the federal budget from 1999 to 2005. The swing of the political pendulum makes it difficult to predict how USDA expenditures will shift, especially with regard to housing. It is certain, however, that reallocations—positive, negative, or transformative—will impact the South more than any other region. States with high percentages of rural inhabitants, significant reliance on agri-business, and relatively small budgets—e.g., Arkansas, Mississippi, and Alabama—would be most affected.

Many of the aforementioned programs have plausible and efficacious outcomes. As well, many of these programs have significant flaws. For example, FHA loans and similar programs aside, less than 1 percent of the federal budget is spent on housing. A much smaller percentage of the budget goes toward housing for older adults and for persons with disabilities. As will be shown, this lack of spending on supportive housing has significant negative consequences for agencies such as DHHS who fund nursing-home care and other alternative housing schemes. Programs geared toward providing "home-health services" continue to remain focused on "health" not "home" services. Another major criticism resides in the legislation, programs, and funding associated with enforcement of equal rights. The legislation places little focus on disability discrimination; the programs rely too heavily on complaints from individuals with few self-advocacy skills; and the funding remains small. One-tenth of 1 percent of HUD's budget goes toward ensuring compliance with the Fair Housing and Fair Housing Amendments Acts, through the Fair Housing Initiatives Program (FHIP) and the Fair Housing Assistance Program (FHAP).

Transformations in Housing Policies and Practices

The overarching transformation in recent housing policies can be conceptualized in terms of a shift from federal to local oversight which began in the early 1970s, a move from federal to state and civic implementation and control.[7] The most notable

Agri-business in the Rural South. Housing in rural areas is affected by both local land use and federal funding, competing directly with agri-business for resources.

instance of this transformation is exemplified in the increase in voucher programs. With substantial research demonstrating the social and fiscal inefficacy of federally controlled public housing, policy and funding was shifted away from the provision of affordable and accessible housing and away from brick-and-mortar structures operated by federal government to voucher programs. This transformation has resulted in a single focus in solving housing issues where formerly construction, maintenance and modification, and tenant assistance had served as a multifaceted effort.[8] This focus did not represent a heightened degree of communication, collaboration, and/or service provision nor consensus among governmental entities. It merely represented a response to past criticisms and the consequent privatization of affordable and accessible housing and the relinquishing of oversight and enforcement at the federal level.

The transformation from federal leadership to state and civic control was facilitated in large part by an increase in block grants to states and cities. The replacement of categorical and ear-marked funding by block grants has afforded considerably more fiscal discretion to states and cities.[9] This discretion has resulted in less prescriptive funding requirements, which have, in turn, provided states and cities with more flexibility in addressing their specific, often idiosyncratic, housing dilemmas. Conversely, this same discretion comes with decreased federal oversight, which has served to increase disparity in both implementation and management. While affording opportunities for states and cities for innovation, this transformation has resulted in divergent regulations and practices that have been cited as the impetus behind the nation's persistent affordability and accessibility problems.[10] In many instances, by limiting the land available for and density of new development, as well as imposing impact fees and subdivision requirements that raise production costs, state and civic governments have made it difficult to build affordable housing. While many of these regulations serve other public policy purposes, they exacerbate affordability pressures, and, in the absence of specific funding mandates, these regulations are all but immune from federal oversight.

Programs once required by federal guidelines to have uniform administration across each state no longer must meet this criterion.[11] For example, states vary with respect to time limits, family caps, asset tests, and work requirements. This combination of unique state and civic programs and less stringent program administration guidelines has had a negative impact on the private sector's willingness to participate in these programs.[12] It can be argued that the Section 8 voucher program has survived the transformation of public housing because it is based on privatism. Rather than building affordable housing itself, the government guarantees subsidies for rents in the private market. This longevity, however, can, by no means, be equated with stability. Privatization comes with a price. These types of programs, typically funded through block grants, represent a heightened vulnerability since vouchers are at risk each year during the federal budget cycle.[13]

As federal and state oversight diminished Community Housing Development Organizations (CHDO's) and Community Development Corporations (CDC's) have emerged in many regions. These not-for-profits typically administer block grant programs and have been increasingly significant in the development of affordable housing. As with other block grant programs these community not-for-profits have a large degree of autonomy and fewer direct links to state and federal oversight.[14] In many states, State Units on Aging (SAUs) have become increasingly involved in housing issues. For a few of the SUAs, their emphasis on community based care systems has led to a newly evolving commitment to housing, particularly accessible housing. Because these community-based not-for-profits have limited interaction with other state and federal agencies, FHIP-funded organizations have emerged to assist individuals in filing housing-related complaints.[15]

While legislation, policy and programs at the federal level have primarily focused on antidiscrimination and the distribution of federal funds state and local municipalities have concentrated more on accessibility policies and in particular visitability. Municipalities and states across the country have already formalized and enacted visitability programs (Appendix 5). Despite their common goal of increasing the supply of accessible housing, these visitability policies vary significantly. The three distinct ways they tend to differ are in the types of dwellings to which they apply, the design elements specified, and the strategies by which they are implemented and enforced. Most existing visitability legislation, at both the state and local level, only applies to new publicly funded housing; however, some jurisdictions use alternative strategies to promote visitability in new single-family homes. For example, some municipalities and states have mandatory visitability legislation that applies to all new housing, including privately financed homes. Naperville, Illinois (2002), Pima County, Arizona (2002), and Bolingbrook, Illinois, as well as the state of Vermont (2000), for instance, have legislation that requires visitability in all new housing. This legislative initiative began in the South, when in 1992, a city ordinance in Atlanta, Georgia, mandated that all builders of new single-family, duplex, and triplex dwellings who received financial benefit from the city (such as impact fee waivers, Community Development Block Grant funds, etc.) had to meet basic access requirements, including at least one zero-step entrance and adequate interior door widths. Since then, more than fifty additional ordinances have been passed to facilitate visitability in Atlanta.

The visitability movement is exemplary of an emergent social and political drive seeking better access to private properties. The aim is to persuade local rule-making bodies to mandate that all new residential construction be designed to accommodate a broader population, such as persons using wheeled mobility devices. Proponents point out that houses are built to last for many decades, that a current or subsequent owner might be in a wheelchair or might invite persons in wheelchairs, and that persons in wheelchairs should be able to have access to the insides of homes and to needed spaces, such as restrooms. Opponents of the movement insist that the rules are an intrusion on the sovereign right of persons to do what they will with private property, provided that they do not infringe on the rights of others, such as neighbors whose view they may block, or pedestrians who must have pathway rights. They argue that only a small percentage of the population uses wheelchairs, that they personally do not know persons who use wheelchairs, and, if they did, they would make arrangements convenient to both parties. Visitability has thus emerged as a subject for discussion by public authorities in several cities, counties, and states in the United States. Many have been considering adopting visitability guidelines, statutes, and ordinances for newly built houses.

But does it matter whether the accessibility is voluntary or mandatory? From an equity perspective, it does. A law, though not always effective, ensures that all houses have almost identical features required by ordinance. With a voluntary program, accessibility features are likely to vary significantly. The voluntary program therefore offers no assurance that a home buyer can expect a particular standard set of components. Accessible features are often difficult to install after the house is constructed, so it is not entirely up to the "market" or the buyer. If all builders do not choose to put equal emphasis on accessibility, a lack of parity between regions, developments, and homes will result.

Advocates of accessibility within the industry are very important, though the role of these advocates is different between small and large builders. Among smaller builders, innovation is often driven by the personal preferences of the owner rather than by the company's business plan. While these owners are willing to take the significant risks associated with innovation, they have relatively little impact on the broader market unless their innovations are picked up by others. These innovative builders address niche markets that attract highly knowledgeable consumers willing to pay a premium for accessibility.

Since the 1930s, housing production has depended on light-frame platform construction done on the building site using dimensional lumber. Home builders typically have been small firms that produce only a few homes using their own crews or subcontractors. The success of this business model relies on knowledge of sites and local market conditions and quick response to business cycles. Advocates of innovation in home building have criticized this model as resistant to change and contributing to the industry's reputation as a "laggard." Attempts to promote innovation in housing, including the Civilian Industrial Technology Program, and Operation Breakthrough in the 1960s, failed to achieve any significant changes in home-building practices.

Innovation in home building in the United States has largely involved incremental improvements to the dominant model of onsite frame construction. A few components have been replaced with manufactured, engineered products shipped to the site (e.g., trusses replaced rafters), and larger production builders have gained efficiencies and quality control through value and process engineering, without replacing the dominant model of home building. As a result, most innovations in home building are improvements in or substitutes for existing materials and products. Many of these innovations address natural resource conservation (energy and water), persistent problems of moisture (mold and rot), or building processes that reduce costs. Examples include mold-resistant gypsum, solar water heating, insulated concrete forms, structural insulated panels, and permeable paving. Initiatives such as "green building" have had some positive effects.

In the domain of accessibility, since initial attempts in 1965, many efforts have been made to enable persons with disabilities to access buildings. The goals were to increase access to public services, work, medical care, and entertainment and sporting events. The Americans with Disabilities Act of 1990 focuses almost solely on public buildings or buildings whose cost is partially underwritten by federal funds. Nevertheless, it has been pointed out that despite these policies, many public buildings constructed toward the end of the twentieth century and later are still not fully accessible. As such, accessibility has become part of the common discourse in the design of public buildings or publicly funded buildings. Access to nonpublic domestic buildings, however, is not required by public policy or laws in most areas, and are, therefore, not accessible. Conventional housing design and construction, similarly, places little focus on accessibility issues. Thus, persons with disabilities face usability problems when conducting their domestic lives and visiting relatives and friends.

Criticisms and Recommendations

People with disabilities receiving SSI benefits fell further into poverty between 2004 and 2006. Between 2004 and 2006, the median income of people with disabilities dropped from 18.4 percent to 18.2 percent of median income, the lowest level since data has been recorded. Median income is an important housing policy indicator because most government housing programs have eligibility requirements that relate to median income. For example, all households at or below 50 percent of median income qualify for HUD public housing units, Housing Choice Vouchers, and HUD Assisted Housing with project-based Section 8 units. Households at or below 30 percent of median income are considered extremely low income under HUD guidelines and receive a priority under the Housing Choice Voucher program. With incomes at 18.2 percent of median, SSI recipients are one of the lowest income groups eligible for federal housing assistance. The data in Table 8-1 demonstrate the insufficiency of current housing programs designed to address the housing needs of the most disenfranchised of our society.[16] For many Southerners, the income received from SSI is not enough to cover housing costs. In the best cases, for persons with disabilities receiving SSI, rent takes about half of the income; in the worst case, the District of Columbia, average rent is nearly double the person's income.

Nationally, traditional rental units represent a significant percentage of the housing used by people with disabilities and people with low income, the manufactured housing industry fulfills much of the market need for these demographic groups in the South. Seventy-three of Arkansas's seventy-five counties exceed the national average for mobile home occupancy.[17] The

Table 8-1. Percent of SSI Needed to Rent a One-Bedroom Housing Unit in the South

STATE	PERCENT OF SSI	STATE	PERCENT OF SSI
Alabama	78.8%	Mississippi	78.2%
Arkansas	75.7%	North Carolina	95.1%
Delaware	87.5%	Oklahoma	45.3%
District of Columbia	188.1%	South Carolina	66.4%
Florida	118.6%	Tennessee	85.4%
Georgia	99.5%	Texas	44.3%
Kentucky	75.8%	Virginia	128.4%
Louisiana	101.5%	West Virginia	72.2%
Maryland	47.9%	National Average	132.1%

Rental Sign. The lack of choices for home buyers is mirrored by a lack of diversity of rental options in the rural South.

reliance on this housing model is illustrative of failures in policy and practice at all scales. The manufactured housing industry is not governed by the same standards as those that apply to multi-family housing or traditional single-family housing. Regulation in manufactured housing is much newer and, arguably, less stringent than other housing arenas. The population that has come to rely on manufactured housing—and all of its conventions—have entered housing that is more affordable in the short term, but is also less durable, less affordable to maintain, less efficient to heat and cool, less resistant to severe weather, less accessibly designed, and prone to decreased resale value in the long term. As considerable as these problems are, none of them outweigh the contextual problem. Residents of the South, and Arkansas in particular, face high risks of physical and economic unrest. Low educational attainment, low income, and high unemployment combined with high rates of disability require many individuals and families to juggle scarce resources.

Ironically, public perception may be the greatest barrier to change regarding housing policies and practices in the South. Though frequently overemphasized as the "rebel" trait, Southerners self-identify resistance to authority, particularly governmental authority, as part of their cultural heritage. Being told what to do and doing it the way you want is colloquially described as being "ornery," a trait that is often regarded with a begrudging sense of pride. It is this boot-strapping sense of pride, a value for learning things the "hard way," that is viewed as more authentic in Southern culture. Johnny Cash once commented on his own tendency to learn by his mistakes and his own Southern values of self-reliance and perseverance.

> So, I learn from my mistakes. It's a very painful way to learn, but without pain, the old saying is, there's no gain. I found that to be true in my life. You miss a lot of opportunities by making mistakes, but that's part of it: knowing that you're not shut out forever, and that there's a goal you still can reach.[18]

Southern suspicion of oversight, a degree of skepticism with regard to breaks in tradition, and genuine pride in overcoming obstacles can make innovation both in policy and practice difficult. Both at the macro and micro scales these traits can impede the passage of visitability laws, dissuade contractors and real estate agents from marketing accessible features, and restrain the willingness of persons with disabilities to accept "help" in the form of accessible design. In the time-honored Southern tradition, it is better to be identified as having overcome unique obstacles than having unique needs.

Persons with disabilities are often targeted as recipients of state and federal housing programs. However, individuals and families do have unique needs, increasing the requirement for diverse housing typologies and locations. Social, medical, economic, and educational provisions are intimately related to housing location and type, and must be compared against individual needs and preferences.[19] The ability to define some characteristics of persons requiring housing will not resolve the issue. Not only are there stereotypes of residents in affordable housing but homeless persons are equally misunderstood and equally in need of permanent, safe shelter. Many believe that people without permanent homes are alcoholics or drug addicts, mentally ill, or have serious character flaws. While it is true that the chronically homeless (repeated or long-term homelessness accompanied by a disability) represent 25 percent of this population, the remainder are families, youths, and other single individuals.[20] The long misunderstanding of homelessness and its causes has resulted in rifts between economic development organizations, neighborhoods, and homeless persons.

Approximately 800,000 people in this country are homeless, though their numbers and the sociocultural influences that impact their lives remain difficult to track. Rigorous research into homelessness did not begin until the late 1980s; by that time many misperceptions and myths about homelessness had become deeply engrained within U.S. culture, the most common of which was the romanticized life of a hobo, chosen and desired by those who lived it. The stark reality of homelessness is far from romantic, or desirable, and is seldom, if ever, deliberately chosen.

According to data gathered in northwest Arkansas in January 2007 within Washington and Benton counties, on any given night, approximately 1,170 adults and youths were homeless. Nearly half of these homeless were children. In follow-up research in March and April that same year, it was determined that 21 percent of the homeless in northwest Arkansas are chronically homeless and that 73 percent of the adults reported disabilities. Going against the aforementioned myths, the majority of these individuals worked an average of thirty hours a week. In northwest Arkansas, as is the case across the country, affordable housing has become more and more difficult to find. For these individuals, disability further complicated their lack of public transit systems, job skills training, and childcare. For the individuals who are homeless, affordability is a complex barrier that encompasses a broad continuum of social and fiscal variables.[21]

Similarly, there are implications in the way that designers and realtors conceptualize, build, and market housing for "special needs" populations. The focus tends to center on the economic, social, or health "problems" of the individual rather than on universal needs—eating, bathing, and so forth—and how those activities have been incorporated into the design. There is an undercurrent attitude of "if you are fucked-up, this house is for you," rather than a "this house is designed to enable residents to . . ." attitude. As such, housing in the South requires policy and practice changes.

First, housing professionals, financiers, realtors, and consumers must be educated about the need for and the benefits of inclusive design. Homes are the most complex and expensive pieces of machinery Americans encounter, yet they do not come with an operating manual. From available productions to the wide range of benefits to diverse individuals and families, knowledge can assist professionals in both providing responsive housing and in returning a fair profit. Consumers of housing must be educated to ask for design features that will enable them to live independently for the greatest portion of their lives.[22] Homes that fulfill the physical and psychosocial needs of individuals and that are financially accessible are in dire need and will be in high market demand throughout the coming decades.

Developers and builders of housing are significant to developing responsive and responsible housing. The majority of financiers and constructors, however, have not been trained in accessible design and many beliefs and construction standards linger despite popular awareness. Builders are often aware of a higher percentage of accessible design features than they implement on a project.[23] Simple design changes, such as door levers instead of doorknobs, continue to be overlooked despite nearly zero increase in construction costs compared to conventional features. Indeed, many builders see accessibility requirements as being out of proportion to the need of just a few primarily mobility-impaired persons.[24] This perspective underscores the lack of understanding about disability, disability rights, and the role of the constructed environment. On the other hand, some builders have realized that accessibility features benefit not only persons with disabilities but also the general population, and, therefore, are more marketable.[25] If the building industry adopts standards that apply to all builders, issues of parity can be sidelined. After all, accessibility arose as a concern because builders had not previously considered it as part of their normal specs.

The current conventions of the American suburban house emerged from the tremendous housing needs following WWII. Housing was designed for a then-young, middle-class, married, white population not for the aging, dwindling middle-class, single-parent, and ethnically diverse population of today. Large kitchens, for example, are no longer an essential component of the single-family home, as families have grown smaller and eating out has become more frequent. Equally, there is much less need for numerous bedrooms; in fact, with the rapid rise in single-parent households and single-occupancy widow/widower households, one- and two-bedroom efficiencies will be among the fasting-growing market demands, not large multibedroom residences. With the decline in the number of bedrooms needed, there is little necessity for corridors and reciprocally, the open-plan is more readily achieved. There needs to be greater awareness on the part of financiers, developers, builders, and designers about long-term market trends.

Less obvious design features should also be brought to the collective consciousness of the various players in housing. Traditional wood framing, for example, often results in a large amount of material waste as well as a structurally and environmentally inefficient wall system. The U.S. Green Building Council has made great strides in disseminating alternate framing techniques, such as the substitution of traditional noninsulated window headers with insulated headers, assuring the alignment of roof trusses or rafters with the wall studs, and the use of two-stud rather than three-stud corners. Unfortunately, the difference between alternative and traditional framing techniques, once the house is sided and the interior painted, are undetectable to the buyer or renter. Nonetheless, alternative building systems, such as SIP (structurally insulated panel) systems, can provide significant savings in long-term energy costs. Increased focus in the building industry should be placed on educating all constituents about their benefits. Environmental and ergonomic functioning needs to be a more centralized part of the marketing of housing.

Designers, builders, and consumers need to have increased awareness of the effects that construction details and material assemblies have on ergonomics and other functional issues. Doorway widths, threshold design, window design, flooring surfaces, and door hardware are a few key items that need to be considered. An individual with arthritis, someone in a hand cast, or someone carrying in a bag of groceries: each person will find a lever door handle easier to use than a traditional doorknob. Equally, an older adult with a shuffling gait, a babysitter pushing a stroller, and a pregnant woman in a wheelchair will be noticeably affected by the design of the threshold at the entry. All of these examples affect human functioning; and all are detectable, visible, and experiential to anyone trained to look for them. The same is true for appliance design. Oxo International, for example, with their line of ergonomically designed Good Grips kitchen gadgets, is a leading success story in the field of universal design of products. Designers, builders, realtors, and buyers/renters need to be aware of options such as these.

Second, retooling housing is not enough. Recent trends in housing policy have exacerbated segregation, which in turn has perpetuated the dearth of affordable and accessible housing. With the rise of privatization, housing policy has transformed from a proactive oversight system, which was arguably flawed and inefficient, to one that is largely complaint based. The 1988 changes to the Fair Housing Act, though significant, serve to perpetuate a complaint-driven system, where the burden and cost is placed on the individual. Current policy necessitates that individuals know that they have been discriminated against as well as the processes of discrimination law. Although privatization is frequently associated with local authority and thus increased responsiveness and flexibility, housing policy in its current block grant form focuses on generalities not on individuals or unique environments.[26]

On April 21, 1999, the U.S. Supreme Court heard *Olmstead v. L.C.* The suit had been brought by two women with developmental disabilities who were residing in a state hospital. The health professionals at the facility had agreed that the women should be served in community programs, but no slots were available for them. Supporting the state of Georgia's appeal to the Supreme Court, twenty-two states provided supporting briefs that argued, while "virtually any person can safely and appropriately be served in his or her home (or in the most integrated community setting) . . . the cost of doing so would be unduly burdensome."[27] On June 22, 1999, the Supreme Court issued its decision in *Olmstead v. L.C.,* holding that the unnecessary segregation of individuals with disabilities may constitute discrimination based on disability.

In a 6–3 opinion authored by Justice Ginsburg, the Court affirmed the Eleventh Circuit's holding that unjustified isolation of individuals with disabilities is properly regarded as discrimination based on disability. The Court held that, under Title II of the ADA, states are required to provide community-based treatment for persons with disabilities when (1) the state's treatment professionals determine that such placement is appropriate, (2) the affected persons do not oppose such treatment, and (3) the placement can be reasonably accommodated. This must also take into account the resources available to the state. The Court concluded that unjustified segregation in institutions is discrimination because it perpetuates unwarranted assumptions that people with disabilities are incapable or unworthy of participating in community life and confinement in an institution severely curtails everyday life activities, such as family relations, social contacts, work, educational advancement, and cultural enrichment. Nonetheless, the Supreme Court corroborated the need to maintain a range of facilities for the care and treatment of individuals with diverse mental disabilities.

Like many civil rights decisions, *Olmstead* has different meanings within different contexts. The decision established a broad legal standard for measuring the adequacy of publicly funded housing programs for persons with disabilities. At the same time, it is evident that *Olmstead's* intentions, which parallels those of the ADA, can be reached only through a coordinated national commitment to reforms that extend far beyond the power of courts to devise. Although U.S. courts are among the most powerful in the world in terms of their ability to intervene in broad questions of policy and to frame remedies, the center of power for transforming social mores into policy resides in the legislative process. The power of *Olmstead* to facilitate change is equally great, although not so direct.

Though housing policy has undergone a considerable transformation, one aspect has remained constant, its entrenchment within the "medical model" of disability. Current legislation continues to conceptualize people with disabilities as "broken" and thereby seeks primarily to ameliorate that which is outside the norm. Legislation based on the medical model is concerned first and foremost with "fixing" the person and not the environment. Housing policy to date continues to address the needs of the disabled rather than a broader notion of human functioning or "fit."

Numerous systemic barriers such as regulatory and fiscal restrictions, inadequate infrastructure in the areas of housing workforce, service flexibility, and information management have impeded progress; however, the failure to implement an "Olmstead Plan" can be attributed to the lack of adequate funds given by government organizations to support community-based programs. Three strategies have shown promise in facilitating compliance with *Olmstead:* (1) legislative action (e.g., policy and budgetary mechanisms for moving money around the system); (2) market-based approaches (e.g., consumer information to enable choice and create demand for affordable and accessible housing); and (3) fiscal and programmatic linkages (e.g., improving coordination between services and increasing affordable and accessible housing capacity).[28]

As with all types of developments, the construction of subsidized housing results in both benefits and costs to the community. It is important to realize, however, that the benefits are many and, with careful attention to scale, positive development can be realized.[29] Undeniably, affordable housing developments will benefit from additional planning considerations at the micro level. Additional parking, increased maintenance, and consideration of ethnic and cultural diversity can offset initial complaints about overcrowding, abuse, and misunderstanding. As urban areas implement improvement programs, the existence of homelessness in the same area undermines the appearance of prosperity. "Special needs homeless" are sometimes singled out by businesses for this reason. New policy that prioritizes effective interventions such as supportive housing in residential neighborhoods will contribute to a more effective solution.[30] There is evidence that suggests strategies must include "adequate financial supports to enable persons with disabilities . . . to earn sufficient income through employment," allowing procurement of housing, healthcare, and other basic needs.[31] The lack of housing for these individuals is rooted not only in the lack of adequate housing but also in the lack of supportive health, educational, and vocational services.[32]

In rural areas the barriers to inclusion for people with disabilities are not a crumbling or inadequate infrastructure, but the lack of infrastructure. In the absence of apparent prosperity, in an environment where "make do" and "get by" predominate, the "special needs" of persons with disabilities are often lost in the mix. Due in part to limited tax bases and limited political representation, policies and programs that could provide effective interventions are typically slower to be enacted, funded, and implemented. Whereas the funding of supports that enable persons with disabilities to live independently is the delimiting factor in urban areas, the absence of supports is the primary barrier for independence in rural areas. In the absence of supportive health, educational, and vocational services housing initiatives in rural areas are unsustainable.

Whether urban or rural, the historical clashes over housing policy in the United States have been more than a dispute over means. They also reflect wide differences over ends, the goals of government, the role of the private market, acceptable taxpayer contributions and burdens, and the responsibilities of individuals and communities. The needs of an aging population, combined with concerns about the civil rights of people with disabilities and the high public cost of nursing-home care, make the lack of accessible housing a critical issue for planners and policy makers. Although planners have traditionally focused their efforts on the built environment outside the home, the time has come for them to look more closely at the environment inside the home as well. Given the slow pace at which changes in the housing stock occur, there is urgency to act now. Increasing the supply of accessible housing will benefit not only persons who currently have disabling conditions, but also families and friends, society as a whole, and people who may develop disabling conditions in the future.

Conclusion

Housing policies and practices are entwined in dense demographic and environmental contexts, a milieu which greatly affects the implementation and outcomes of each attempt at change. It is this dynamic context that makes creating effectual housing policy so challenging. The current state of housing policies and practices reflects the difficulties of addressing divergent needs in a complex context. These difficulties have been exacerbated by the lack of coordination between governmental agencies, an inflexibility to accommodate regional differences while maintaining parity, a dearth of educational programs, and a steadfast belief in tradition. The consequences are decreased quality of life for many rural Southerners.

It is important to recognize that helping older adults and persons with disabilities lead stable and productive lives in the community is not just "the right thing to do," it is also fiscally responsible. Providing community-based housing and services cost much less than a nursing home bed, an emergency shelter, or a psychiatric hospital stay. The federal Medicaid budget continues to grow, driven primarily by the high cost of institutional housing. DHHS programs, such as "Money Follows the Person," were cre-

Aluminum Can Driveway. Improvised design is one of the most notable characteristics of rural Southern homes.

ated because officials understood that providing Medicaid services and supports in the community were a much more cost-effective approach than institutional housing. What has been missing from this policy discussion is how people will pay for the housing they need. Federal and state governments have thus far not demonstrated an awareness of this basic math, which shows that to achieve significant cost savings in programs like Medicaid, it is necessary to spend a little more money in the design and construction of accessible communities and homes.

Arguably, the primary goal of all public policy is to facilitate healthy, positive independence. Independence and self-sufficiency involves a number of issues; it is not merely economic (though financial status is primary). The capacity to move away from economic vulnerability includes more than leaving public assistance programs. Meaningful participation in the social and economic system, defined as the ability to obtain quality housing, healthcare, child care, food security, and sufficient income, must also be considered.[33] It is clear (but not a new idea) that a synthetic, holistic approach to public policy and local practices is necessary, as location, income, education, employment, and health interact to impact housing quality and security and overall quality of life.

High income equals high levels of choice. Regardless of health status, individuals and families with the highest incomes will have the greatest range of housing options available to them. In contrast, Southern residents who have lower incomes, who are living in rural areas, and who have physical, sensory, and/or cognitive impairments will have the greatest difficulty in seeking out and attaining suitable housing. This cohort is not a small segment of the population. This cohort constitutes millions of Americans, which will nearly double in size over the next two decades. How will their housing needs be met?

Unfortunately, the current housing stock is unsuitable, requiring high levels of maintenance, high heating/cooling costs, and substantive renovations to be more accessible and usable by people with diverse physical and psychosocial needs. Current housing practices, likewise, are equally problematic. There is an imbalance in the housing industry: too much focus on nonessential, nonresearched, and capricious aesthetic choices; too little focus on substantive functional issues such as ergonomics and environmental efficiency. This is coupled with the fact that most consumers (home buyers/renters) are often unaware of the design features for which they should be looking and are equally unaware of the home modifications that would benefit them or how to go about making those renovations.[34] Finally, housing policies, once effective, no longer match the current demographic makeup or cultural predilections of today's society. The bulk of current housing policies are moderate transformations of Depression Era legislation. Obviously there needs to be an overhaul, bottom to top, of the practices, programs, and policies that affect housing in Arkansas, the South, and the United States.

In general, there needs to be greater kinship and integration of the various constituents involved in housing, though it is important to recognize the preexisting context that influences housing policies and practices. No doubt, as one or more of these factors change—for example, as the population grows older—policies and practices need to respond. However, the elements of this preexisting context—including social demographics, local economic and environmental factors, conventions in housing design and construction, and public perceptions—together produce a situation that is highly complex and resistant to change. That coefficient of friction appears to be double in the South. But, as the history of "Dixie" shows, the South is also resilient. The South is the most adept region at progressing despite adversity.

Drawing the Line: Just Housing

KORYDON H. SMITH

Southerners have a genius for psychological alchemy. They know what kind of society they want, and, come what may, they usually manage to get it. If something intolerable simply cannot be changed, driven away, or shot, they will not only tolerate it but take pride in it as well.

—FLORENCE KING,
Southern Ladies and Gentlemen

Looking closely, one can see that housing, like country music, is a clear marker of the subcultures and values that make up American society. In Cash's rendition of "Southern Accents," the paradoxical relationship between Southern pride and anxious self-consciousness is clearly evident. Cash is singing about all that the Southern drawl represents—one's own way of "workin,'" "prayin,'" and "livin'"—including negative connotations: "country" and "dumb." Nevertheless, the song is imbued with resoluteness and fortitude—tenacity. And, if any one thing is a descriptor of the rural Southern ethos, it is tenacity, improvisation, and perseverance in the face of adversity. This latent quality may not only be the marker of the Southern mindset but, more broadly, may be the quintessence of the American psyche. Tenacity, however, can be duplicitous, causing people to tolerate the intolerable. This duality is visible in the innumerable assortment of home modifications and personalizations across rural America.

Housing, in its physical, material form, is both representational and authoritative. One could conduct a "forensic" analysis of housing. Examinations of the locations, boundaries, forms, materials, and spaces of existing communities can reveal the attitudes, values, and behaviors of the people who inhabit those

231

communities. The physical constructs reveal the underlying ideological constructs. Inversely, the design and construction of housing is an exertion of power. Purposeful or not, housing has resounding effects. Legislative decisions, neighborhood planning, and housing design can result in marginalization or equity, segregation or integration of various groups. The purpose of this final chapter, therefore, is to provide a thumbnail sketch of both the foundations and the recommendations we have provided throughout this book. As our goal is to positively influence housing policy, design, and construction—to promote greater quality and equality in Southern housing—we are providing this chapter especially for advocates, policy makers, and educators to incorporate and disseminate the key ideas contained herein.

Lines of Division

Seemingly invisible and arbitrary lines have been drawn for purposes of categorization and division. These include both legalistic lines—personal property, school districts, and political jurisdictions—and figural lines—poverty thresholds, racial divisions, disability status, and retirement age. These lines are drawn, and then re-drawn, to be commensurate with the ideologies of the society and/or those who "hold the pencil." These ephemeral lines are often reinforced by physical lines—gated communities, curbs, fences, stairs, and doorways—which further delineate status and power. Divisions also occur at a larger scale. If a line were cut diagonally across the state of Arkansas, running from the northwest corner to the southeast corner of the state, it would reveal an interesting parallel between physical, demographic, and economic lines. That diagonal cut would possess its highest numbers in the northwest, median numbers at its center, and lowest numbers in the southeast.

Benton County, the most northwesterly county in Arkansas, possesses the state's greatest economic growth and rise in population (27.8 percent increase in population since 2000), a median household income of $47,431 and poverty rate of 9.5 percent, and an elevation more than 1,600 feet above sea level. These numbers slope toward the median in Pulaski County, the geographic center of the state, which possesses a 1.6 percent population growth since 2000 (5.1 percent is the state average), a $40,499 median household income ($35,295 is the state average) and 14.8 percent poverty rate (15.6 percent is the state average), and elevations which approach the state mean of 650 feet above sea level. The line continues downward toward Chicot County, the most

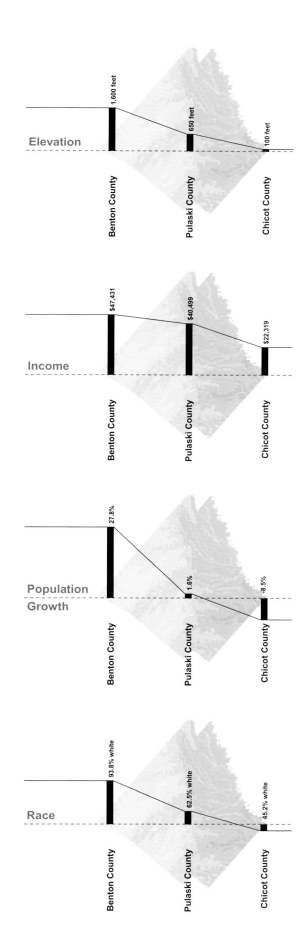

Elevation

1,600 feet — Benton County
650 feet — Pulaski County
100 feet — Chicot County

Income

$47,431 — Benton County
$40,499 — Pulaski County
$22,319 — Chicot County

Population Growth

27.8% — Benton County
1.6% — Pulaski County
-8.5% — Chicot County

Race

93.8% white — Benton County
62.5% white — Pulaski County
45.2% white — Chicot County

Lines of Division. In Arkansas, disability, racial, and economic variables are tightly intertwined. Interestingly, these factors parallel the state's topographic slope from northwest to southeast.

southeasterly county in Arkansas, where population is declining (-8.5 percent since 2000), median household income is $22,319 and poverty rate is 28.0 percent, and elevations sink below one hundred feet. The line also indicates a racial divide: Benton County is 93.8 percent white; Pulaski County is 62.5 percent white; and Chicot County is 45.2 percent white.[1] This cross-section of the state reveals that, for some strange reason, physical elevation corresponds to economic elevation. Such a deep-rooted (geological) line seems astoundingly challenging to straighten, to bring equity across its length. Although this diagonal line illustrates racial segregation and a division of wealth, disability discrimination is the most patent prejudice in housing today.

Throughout the first decade of the twenty-first century, northwest Arkansas, located just south of the U.S. Census Bureau's delineation between Midwest and South, was one of the fastest-growing economic and housing regions in the nation. As of 2000, more than one-fifth of the total number of housing units in Washington and Benton counties were constructed in the years 1995–2000, with thousands of new homes entering the market after 2000.[2] Much of this economic and housing growth was attributable to the global success of Wal-Mart, whose home office is located here. The growth of Wal-Mart is an interesting one, as "68 percent of a recent *Atlanta Journal-Constitution* poll's respondents reported that Wal-Mart was 'very' or 'somewhat important' to their definition of 'today's South.'"[3]

In addition, as northwest Arkansas has become a retirement destination of older adults seeking a more moderate climate (moving from the cold winters of the North or from the hot, humid summers of the Deep South), northwest Arkansas holds the second-highest total number of residents with disabilities in the state. Yet the majority of homes currently being constructed do not take advantage of recent research in accessibility or life-span design, affordability or energy-efficient design. The economic growth of this region is in stark contrast to regions that hold some of the highest rates of poverty in the nation. This phenomenon of the juxtaposition of deep poverty and vibrant prosperity is prevalent throughout the United States. This cross-section of Arkansas—in both its literal and allegorical forms—is a cross-section of America. Arkansas is a litmus for the future of the country.

In the century that lies ahead, dedicating so much attention to the lower right corner of the United States will be increasingly difficult to justify unless we realize that for future generations the value in studying the South's experience may actually lie not in what seems unique about it but in what seems universal.[4]

Although the fundamental, universal characteristics of the South may not be fully knowable (and may not even exist), the mythology of the South makes it worth a deeper look. As Louis E. Swanson states,

> The current crisis in the rural South involves a considerable amount of human suffering. I do not use the term "suffering" lightly. Suffering here refers to material, health, and spiritual hardships that a middle class American would find unacceptable. . . . Much of rural America is mired in a crisis which has the potential for approaching and even surpassing the relative suffering of the Great Depression. Moreover, the rural South has always persisted on the periphery of U.S. society, is worse off than most other areas of rural America.

Public health is one of the primary dilemmas of the rural South and has been for decades. As such, Arkansas is a lens to the future as baby-boomers across the nation enter retirement; and, if you can find strategies for solving the current housing dilemmas of Arkansas, you can solve the future housing dilemmas of the nation.

By 2030, the number of people in the United States that are sixty-five and older will double, which will result in a large increase in the number of persons with disabilities. Developing housing that supports the needs of this population will be crucial, especially when considering that more than 80 percent of the (noninstitutionalized) older adult population in the United States is living alone or with a spouse of similar age. As such, small-scale, universally designed living units will be significant in the future. For the South, despite the inefficiencies, this will likely come in the form of detached housing, as this type is currently the most dominant and most culturally accepted form of housing. Finding alternative—more efficient, more sustainable, more user-friendly—means of providing detached single-family housing was the focus of the prototypes included in chapter 7.

Disability is both a cause and consequence of poverty and in Arkansas people with disabilities are among the poorest of the poor. Poverty is not simply the consequence of a lack of resources. Many people with disabilities are unable to access existing resources because of who they are or where they live.

For people with disabilities this inequity is the primary cause of poverty. Poverty and disability reinforce each other in a self-perpetuating cycle, contributing to increased exclusion and vulnerability. The result is that people who are poor have limited access to quality healthcare and are at greater risk of disability, and people with disabilities have limited participation in employment and are at great risk of becoming impoverished. While bad design is not fully responsible for disability or poverty, it can certainly exacerbate the disability-poverty cycle, while good design can assuage the cycle.

Lines of Connection

Ron Mace is credited with coining the phrase "universal design" in 1985,[5] which followed on the heels of the "barrier-free design" movement of the 1970s.[6] Over the next three decades, the nomenclature of "universal design" and "accessibility," as seen by the general public, became synonymous with the design of environments and products that were usable by persons with disabilities. The equating of "accessibility" to "design features for persons with disabilities" is problematic in three areas.

First, when design features are specialized they often carry a stigma. As previously stated, "a house is a billboard"; housing often signifies the economic status, political views, ethnic background, and relative health status of the occupants. An ad-hoc ramp to the front door may increase usability for a wheelchair user, but it may also stigmatize the residence, resulting in decreased resale value, increased vulnerability to crime, and increased discrimination.

Second, specialization and customization in design are more costly in most cases than mass production. Housing design that meets the needs and preferences of the broadest population will be the most cost effective and marketable. Specialized housing will meet the needs and preferences of certain niche groups, but will come at an added cost to home buyers and tax payers.

Finally, recent legislation and Supreme Court decisions (e.g., the *Olmstead Decision* of 1999) suggest that there may be legal recourse for noncompliance with the intent of the ADA, even as it might apply to single-family housing. The city of Tucson, Arizona, serves as a clear example. In 2003 local developers filed a lawsuit against the city for its "Inclusive Home Design Ordinance" of 2002, arguing that meeting the city's stringent accessibility requirements in housing would cost developers,

The Undeveloped South. Access to resources is confounded by the absence of infrastructure.

builders, and homeowners thousands of dollars in order to comply. The developers lost the suit in the Arizona Court of Appeals in December 2003.

Class, race, gender, and religion are the most often discussed identity categories, but subcultures can be articulated in countless ways: Northern or Southern; with or without a disability; rural, suburban, or urban. These categories, however, are not fixed, nor are they idiosyncratic. Southern identity, in the stereotypical sense (the typecasts set by Jeff Foxworthy's "you know you're a redneck . . ."), is most intact in localized areas. But Foxworthy's notoriety illustrates that "redneck" is no longer synonymous with the rural South. This notion extends throughout America. The values often associated with the

South are not so much Southern, but rural, regardless of geographic location. Rural "Upstate New York" may possess more "Southern values" than urban Atlanta. As much as Northerners and Southerners like to poke fun at one another, it is a guise for a mix of self-pride and self-deprecating humor.

Likewise, the various subcultures that comprise the housing industry—policy makers, financiers, designers, builders, and occupants—seem to take great pleasure in pointing out the flaws of one another, but it is only because each group holds a different knowledge base and value structure. As a result, conflicts arise between one subgroup and another. Developers and financiers, for example, may perceive economic barriers in housing as a result of certain legislation, while potential home buyers, for instance, may not share the same aesthetic preferences as those who are designing or building. Nevertheless, the advancement of quality housing in the United States relies on the interrelationships of these parties. Each party, from policy makers to residents, is *de rigueur.*

The greatest barrier to just housing for people with disabling conditions is convention. The housing industry is sustained by convention. The industry is slow to incorporate technological change; it is slow to adapt to economic shifts; and it is incredibly slow in adapting to social changes. An aging population (and the impending needs that come with an older demographic), coupled with increased realization of economic and environmental concerns (e.g., the housing crisis and global warming), will transform housing in the United States. The South will experience these effects sooner and more deeply than other parts of the country, and thus, will need to respond more rapidly. That overarching character trait of the South—tenacity —will be called to order.

Likewise, for centuries, people with disabilities have also relied on tenacity and adaptation, utilizing extraordinary and creative means to "fit in" or simply get along. The ad-hoc design solutions that dot the rural Southern landscape illustrate this perseverance. But, despite their ubiquity, many do-it-yourself renovations carry a stigma. The ramp, like the wheelchair, "is a paradoxical object." The wheelchair is the mechanism for mobility, independence, and freedom, but simultaneously signifies to others the impaired bodily state of the individual.[7] Unlike mobility impairments, most disabling conditions are not themselves visible. Most disabling conditions are only evident in other physical artifacts but not visible on the physical person. Many visual impairments, for example, are only evident in the presence of the white cane. A long-standing debate thus ensues: the National Federation of the Blind recommends the use of full-length, noncollapsible canes over shorter collapsible canes due to added safety and functionality, while a great number of visually impaired persons, however, prefer collapsible canes because of both added convenience and the ability to "hide" this signifier. Among Southerners with disabilities, the commonality is a desire to be identified not as "handicapped" but as a valued family member, friend, parishioner, or neighbor.

Changing concepts about disability have been paralleled in recent years by changing attitudes among designers. Architects, industrial designers, urban planners, interior designers, and designers of media have become increasingly conscious of the role that design plays in the physical and psychosocial well-being of a wide range of people. The disability rights movement has catalyzed these changes and resulted in significant legislation, affecting both local and national building codes, as well as changes in the concepts of disability. Despite great strides, cultural, legislative, and physical barriers remain.

Base Lines

In the South and in Arkansas, these barriers are amplified. In the rural South: (1) there is a lower tax base, (2) there is less housing available, (3) the North to South migration pattern is increasing the cost of land and housing in the South, (4) there is less diversity and opportunity in employment and education, (5) there are fewer amenities, including health / wellness and entertainment, (6) there are fewer licensed design professionals and trained builders, (7) there are fewer continuing education opportunities for developers and builders and / or fewer members of the housing industry that actively seek out educational programs,[8] (8) there is less consumer awareness and ability to request design elements that will fulfill their needs and little organized consumer education,[9] and (9) a large percentage of the population is lower-income, older adults with disabilities.

Throughout this book, we have supplied both foundational knowledge as well as recommendations regarding housing in the South. The background and suggestions provided cut across a wide range of issues and scales. Given the complexity and interconnectedness of these issues, we have chosen to identify a "top-ten list" of summary recommendations, which fall into three broad categories: changes in ideology, changes in policy, and changes in practice. Our ten primary recommendations follow below.

Changes in Ideology

One, the concept of disability needs to be redefined. Both the American populace and the U.S. Government maintain a narrow, categorical notion of disability. Disability needs to be seen as multivalent and transformational. Disability, above all, is "normal," and must be seen as such, as part of broad spectrum of human abilities and functioning. Local and national efforts need to be made to change the public and bureaucratic view of human variability. This includes an understanding of the wide range of human physiologies and psychologies that exist today and will broaden in the future. A broad educational campaign—including a variety of media, audiences, and spokespersons—needs to be implemented. The acceptance of the redefinition of disability is the basis from which all other changes to policy and practice stem.

Two, there needs to be a redefinition of "home." Just as disability is not merely a discourse in functionality, neither is housing. In both cases—in individuals and in homes—functionality is only one part of a larger dialectic. Although physical functioning might be hierarchically primary, psychosocial needs and values are also important to quality design and quality living. For instance, Americans tend to view assistive and prosthetic technologies as purely functional subjects, but "the peculiar history of prosthetic devices reveals the extent to which [their design is] intertwined with [both] the subjective and practical needs of people."[10] The goal of prosthetic technologies is to become one with the body, to feel "natural" and integrated, and to be perceived by others as such.[11] Likewise, the goal of design is to achieve a "natural" fit between a person and her or his home. The degree to which prosthetics, assistive technologies, design features, and housing are viewed by inhabitants *and* outsiders as "natural" relies both on performance and on appearance. Efforts should be made to establish an organized public education campaign about housing design, the concept of inclusive design, and the availability of assistive technologies. Homeowners and renters need to be made aware housing features that will better suit their needs, and need to be educated about the federal, state, and local programs and agencies that are available to them. In parallel to educating consumers, programs are needed that more actively engage developers, builders, and realtors. This type of training does exist in most states, run by home-builders associations or state and local housing authorities, but often does not capture constituents who work predominantly in rural areas. Training conducted by housing authorities often relies on verbal communication and text-based handouts rather than hands-on instruction that may be more easily apprehended by tradespeople. A similar hands-on educational approach could be used for consumers and building inspectors as well. Redefining home is essential to the future well-being of Arkansas, the South, and America.

Three, the colloquial definitions of "equality" and "diversity" need to be transformed. Terms like "equity," "inclusion," and "integration" carry immense weight and skepticism in the South, and implicitly refer to race. Social justice and equality, however, is a much larger concept. In various civil rights circles, it has been said that "you can judge a nation based on how it treats its smallest minorities." Given the increasingly diverse range of ethnicities, ages, religions, and abilities that comprises the U.S. population, ensuring equality is an evermore difficult challenge. Ironically, the only way to move toward parity is through a recognition and articulation of diversity: the variety of needs and preferences of America. The South is a looking glass to the future of America because, on the surface, it appears homogeneous in its physical and social structure, but a closer look reveals the variety of splendor and flaws that make it so beautifully profound. While there may be racial, economic, and religious differences, commonality across Southern subcultures rises from the shared tenacity of its ancestry. It is crucial that popularized concepts of equality be recast.

Changes in Policy

Four, efforts need to be made to provide better health and wellness services in rural areas, and increase the overall wellness of rural Southerners. The ten states with the highest death rates are Mississippi (1,010.6 per 100,000 residents), Louisiana (994.5), Alabama (992.8), West Virginia (982.8), Tennessee (969.5), Kentucky (968.3), Oklahoma (961.0), Arkansas (939.9), Georgia (932.2), and South Carolina (925.4); all are Southern states. In the South, metropolitan counties maintain death rates between 808.9 and 925.1, while their nonmetropolitan counterparts hold increased rates (958.6 to 991.6 per 100,000 residents). The South has the highest percentage of people with fair or poor health

(11.2 percent), more than a 25 percent higher rate than the next closest region (West, 8.9 percent). Increasing participation in regular exercise will be one necessary step, as the South also has the lowest rate of involvement in leisure-time physical activity (26.2 percent).[12] Increasing the physical and mental health across all ages of Southerners is a critical means to decreasing long-term healthcare spending and increasing quality of life.

Five, housing policy is in dire need of updating. Current housing policy focuses on a demographic makeup and world-view that is five decades old. Increasing the amount and variety of suitable housing choices in rural areas needs to be addressed. There needs to be an increased emphasis on accessible, user-friendly housing, not simply on affordable housing. Current housing policies focus too greatly on the economic status of the buyer/renter and focus too little on the physical, educational, health, and psychosocial needs and preferences of the buyer/renter. It is clear that a range of housing types, occupancy types, and tenant types (ownership versus rentership) are required. Likewise, a system of monitoring and controlling housing and land costs, not unlike the federal control of the mortgage industry, might be advantageous. Such a system might help to steady rapidly rising or falling land and home costs in specific locales affected by changes in employment and migration. This would allow affordable housing to be more attainable to those who wish to become first-time home buyers and help to stabilize plummeting real estate values so that current, lower-income homeowners do not lose the equity they have established. Housing policies have to become much more flexible in responding to (if not anticipating) social, technological, economic, and environmental shifts.

Six, there needs to be greater overlap and integration of housing and health policies and practices at all scales (local to national). A great deal of controversy always surrounds allocation of public funds—how various programs, industries, regions, and so forth should be subsidized, what is each one's "fair share." Pouring public resources into rural areas, as a means to make up for the low tax base and the demographic makeup, is equally contentious. Nevertheless, as healthcare funding has increased, funding in housing has decreased over the past decade. This is a grave mistake, as investment in quality housing positively affects health, quality of life, and independence; investment in housing provides significant returns in healthcare savings. As such, increasing housing programs in areas where public health is most impaired—the rural South—should be a top priority. Federal monies directed toward housing help to reduce spending on healthcare. Housing and health sectors need to work in tandem, as they are mutually influential.

Changes in Practice

Seven, design and construction need to be rethought at the regional scale. The reason there are fewer health and entertainment amenities in rural areas is the lack of population needed to sustain them as businesses. Providing a solution to this, in many ways, is the most significant of challenges. Innovative business strategies and incentives may need to be developed. This could include (a) developing rural transportation systems that bring people to more metropolitan centers, (b) developing more mobile amenities that travel throughout rural areas (e.g., mobile health centers or mobile pharmacies), (c) providing multifunction amenities (e.g., the notion of the "live-bait / video store" discussed in the introduction), where small-scale health services and entertainment services may be provided in one general location, or (d) some combination of these or some other public or private venture. Not unlike the challenge of providing health and entertainment amenities, the lack of diversity in employment and educational opportunities in rural areas results from a lack of critical population mass. Similar strategies to those previously mentioned could be deployed here, including distance or online education and employment. Regional planning ideals and concepts must be updated.

Eight, design needs to be recast at the scale of the community and the neighborhood. Housing design is not simply about the "house." Local contexts—streets, stores, neighbors' homes, and public buildings—play a central role in people's lives. Convenient access to and participation in the various aspects of the community—spiritual, recreational, educational, and vocational activities—are what define life satisfaction. If the design and construction of infrastructure and facilities do not enable full participation, satisfaction will decrease and social and economic burdens will increase. Additionally, economic and altruistic opportunities could be created and disseminated to professional development, design, and construction organizations (e.g., the American Institute of Architects or the American Society of Interior Designers) to encourage its members to

Farmer in Rice Field. A profound tie to the land is central to the concept of *Southern* identity. It is the connection to one's own land, however, that establishes a sense of *personal* identity.

engage in community planning, housing design, or home renovation projects in rural areas. As these professionals likely possess the most expertise and creative ability, their involvement is essential. Communities and neighborhoods of the future will have to be much more integrative, envisioned as a contiguous whole, not as autonomous parts.

Nine, design and construction practices need to be changed at the scale of home design. From the entry to the bedroom, from the foundation to the roof, home design needs to be socially, economically, and environmentally sustainable. A home needs to support not only the physical necessity of shelter but also psychosocial aspects, such as identity development, autonomy, and healthy family relationships. Likewise, a home must not only address a family's current needs but also be supportive of a family's changing needs and allow for the possibilities of new households. Designers and builders of future housing will have to be educated about a wider scope of issues: social, technological, economic, environmental, and legal. The ways they conceptualize and make home will have to be transformed. Well-constructed homes last for decades, if not centuries, and, therefore, should meet the requirements not only of today but also the conditions of future generations.

Lastly, the priorities of the housing industry need to be revised. The ways homes are designed, constructed, and rented or sold do not meet the physical or psychosocial realities of

The Bottom Line

American society. The home is still a central facet of the "American Dream," and likely will be for years to come, but how the American Dream Home is characterized is problematic. Throughout history, designers have struggled over the role between form and function. During the Renaissance, architects outlined a set of formal principles for design: rules of proportion, scale, materiality, and ornamentation. During the latter part of the nineteenth century, Louis Sullivan pronounced the directorate that "form follows function." During the post-Modern era designers argued the inverse: "function follows form." Arguably, we are in an era where the value has increased for both high form and high function. The architectural philosopher Karsten Harries refers to this as "the dream of the complete building," highly resolved regarding both aesthetics and use.[13] Shifting focus away from "granite countertops" and toward issues that have greater impact—such as efficiency, sustainability, ergonomics, and safety—is an essential change that needs to be made in the way that the public and the housing industry conceives the Dream Home.

Throughout this book, we have illustrated the imminent need to redefine disability and redesign housing, and bring together the knowledge of previously autonomous fields (e.g., environmental design and rehabilitation; health and housing). We have discussed demographic trends, as well as legal and ideological shifts; and we have illustrated the economic and sociological implications of these changes. For example, it has been shown that older adults who received assistive technologies (ATs) and/or environmental interventions (EIs) in their homes, in comparison to older adults who received traditional medical care but no ATs or EIs, (a) were more likely to sustain "functional independence" for longer periods, (b) incurred less total healthcare costs (more than 50 percent less), and (c) slowed both the decline of independence and the progression toward morbidity.[14] Additionally, the costs of retrofitting (to meet a resident's changing needs, to meet the needs of a new resident, or to comply with accessibility guidelines and laws) are immense: up to 21 percent of the original construction costs.[15] Basic accessibility requirements, however, increase initial construction costs by less than one-half of 1 percent.[16] Long-term savings to local, state, and federal authorities who adopt more inclusive housing standards are immense.

Without comprehensive changes to housing policies and

practices it is clearly evident that economic, physiological, and psychosocial wellness will be compromised throughout the South. Most generally, we have illustrated the severe disjunction between current housing practices and the cultures that are affected by those practices. The economic implications are clear, but, in all honesty, we are using these unmistakable dilemmas to support more altruistic goals: just housing. The social and life-quality benefits are self-evident.

Housing is a central component of the American psyche, but its influences often remain hidden. The popular media's focus on healthcare and retirement is a myopic oversight of one of the greatest barriers to physical and fiscal quality of life: inadequate housing design. Housing design is not merely an issue of pragmatics, of doorway widths, roof pitches, HVAC systems, and grab bars. Housing design is not merely about the technical or economic act of building. Housing design possesses a much deeper responsibility. Homes demarcate identity—individual identity, collective identity, and the interface between the two. Homes provide not only shelter but also sovereignty. One of the most fundamental components of identity and sovereignty, in the South and elsewhere, is dignity. Without dignity, the positive development of a person's character cannot be achieved; true independence cannot be achieved. Housing plays an essential role in offering or revoking dignity. Creating higher-quality housing requires that cultural, technological, and economic lines be redrawn. Redrafting these contours is not simply an urgent concern in the South, though it is most visible there. The goal of redrawing these lines is to bring the physical realities of American life into alignment with the central feature of the American Dream: just housing.

The STEEL Model:
Factors Affecting Housing Design and Construction

KORYDON H. SMITH

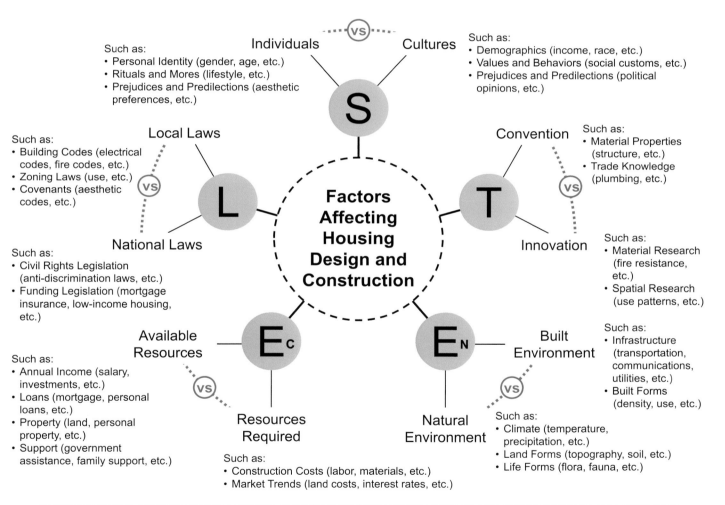

Such as:
• Personal Identity (gender, age, etc.)
• Rituals and Mores (lifestyle, etc.)
• Prejudices and Predilections (aesthetic preferences, etc.)

Such as:
• Demographics (income, race, etc.)
• Values and Behaviors (social customs, etc.)
• Prejudices and Predilections (political opinions, etc.)

Such as:
• Building Codes (electrical codes, fire codes, etc.)
• Zoning Laws (use, etc.)
• Covenants (aesthetic codes, etc.)

Such as:
• Material Properties (structure, etc.)
• Trade Knowledge (plumbing, etc.)

Such as:
• Civil Rights Legislation (anti-discrimination laws, etc.)
• Funding Legislation (mortgage insurance, low-income housing, etc.)

Such as:
• Material Research (fire resistance, etc.)
• Spatial Research (use patterns, etc.)

Such as:
• Annual Income (salary, investments, etc.)
• Loans (mortgage, personal loans, etc.)
• Property (land, personal property, etc.)
• Support (government assistance, family support, etc.)

Such as:
• Infrastructure (transportation, communications, utilities, etc.)
• Built Forms (density, use, etc.)

Such as:
• Construction Costs (labor, materials, etc.)
• Market Trends (land costs, interest rates, etc.)

Such as:
• Climate (temperature, precipitation, etc.)
• Land Forms (topography, soil, etc.)
• Life Forms (flora, fauna, etc.)

S = Sociological Factors; T = Technological Factors; En = Environmental Factors; Ec = Economic Factors; L = Legal Factors

Meaning of Home

JENNIFER WEBB

	Space	
Room or Space within a Room	Home is present in a variety of scales. The corner of a room filled with memorabilia or the country of birth. Individuals can define home as houses or apartments, regions, and states. We use our senses to gather information (sight, sound, taste, touch, smell) and these qualities contribute to our idea of a particular place. Homes at any scale can be lost for a variety of reasons. Consider the definition of sense of place.	**Homeland**
	Objects	
Personal Object	Home is established through the display of objects that contribute to personal identity. Home can also be defined as a larger place such as a neighborhood with distinct landmarks or expressions of national identity. The creation of home through the use of objects is founded on the basis of choosing the objects for display. For some individuals, objects are used to ameliorate varying levels of functioning; these objects may well not evoke the same emotive qualities mentioned previously and are not choices but are necessities.	**Landmark**
	Identity	
Autonomy or Self-Concept	One's identity is constructed through and communicated to self and others through space, objects, and activities. The identity develops over time and is protected by the individual.	**Integration or Social Identity**

Territoriality

Private

Our ability to control interactions with others is significant to feelings of autonomy and self-esteem. We seek to control our private space as well as feel safe in our home and our larger community. Manipulating the environment and behaviors facilitate desired interactions with other people. Territoriality can have negative qualities: too much privacy leads to feelings of isolation while too little privacy leads to feelings of crowding. The ability to control access to self is critical to feelings of autonomy and self-esteem.

Public

Temporality

Past

For most, home is the present. However, time can be manipulated. Homes may happen concurrently as with college students or with older adults. Perceptions of home can also be extended beyond our life span as we display heirlooms (objects) that connect us to the past and project us into the future. We extend our home (space) into the future as we envision family or others that will proceed us and will return to and use the home. There can be other temporal markers such as the onset of a disease, a change in circumstances, the improvement or decline following an illness that add a sense of rhythm to a life and to relationships.

Future

Activity

Personal

Home can be defined through activities: activities of daily living such as bathing and dressing, participating in family activities or hobbies, visiting a local grocery or vacationing in a desirable locale. Activities occur with variability in duration, predictability, and frequency. The degree to which necessary or desired activities are facilitated or supported in the environment contributes to comfort and perceived person-environment fit.

Participation

Housing Legislation, Programs, Agencies, and Funding

KORYDON H. SMITH

Green (●) indicates income-centric programs,
blue (■) indicates disability-centric programs,
and red (▲) indicates hybrid programs.

LEGISLATION	ADMINISTRATOR	FUNDING
National Housing Act (1934) **creation of Federal Housing Administration (FHA)** **FHA Mortgage Insurance Programs:**	HUD	$55 billion (2006)
■ Mortgage Insurance for Nursing Homes, Intermediate Care, Board and Care, and Assisted-living Facilities	HUD	$1.3 billion (2005)
● Mortgage Insurance for Rental and Cooperative Housing	HUD	$1 billion (2006)
■ Mortgage Insurance for Rental Housing for the Elderly	HUD	$7 million (2006)
■ Risk-sharing Program	HUD	$96 million (2006)
● Mortgage Insurance for Low/Mod Income Buyers	HUD	
U.S. Housing Act (1937) **creation of U.S. Housing Authority**		
● Housing Choice Voucher Program (Section 8)	HUD	$18.8 billion (2006)
● HOPE I (Indian Housing Homeownership)	HUD	terminated (1995)
● Public Housing Development Program	HUD	terminated (2004)
● Major Reconstruction of Obsolete Projects (MROP)	HUD	terminated (2004)
● Public Housing Capital Fund	HUD	$2.4 billion (2006)
Housing Act (1949, 1954, 1956, 1959, 1964)		
▲ Supportive Housing for the Elderly Program (Section 202)	HUD	$735 million (2006)
▲ Assisted-living Conversion Program (ALCP)	HUD	
▲ Emergency Capital Repair Program (ECRP)	HUD	
● Direct Homeownership Loan Program and Loan Guarantee Program (Section 502)	USDA	$4 billion (2006)

● Mutual Self-Help Housing Loan Program (Section 523)	USDA	$34 million (2006)
▲ Rural Housing Repair and Rehabilitation Loans and Grants Program (Section 504)	USDA	$64 million (2006)
● Multifamily Housing Rental Assistance Program (Sections 502 and 521)	USDA	$647 million (2006)
▲ Rural Rental Housing Guaranteed Loan Program (Section 538) and Rural Rental Housing Program (Section 515)	USDA	$196 million (2006)
● Rural Housing Site Loans (Section 524) USDA		
● Farm Labor Housing Program (Sections 514 and 516)	USDA	$46 million (2006)
● Housing Preservation Grant (HPG) Program (Section 533)	USDA	$11 million (2006)

Older Americans Act (1965)
creation of Administration on Aging (AoA) — DHHS

Fair Housing Act (1968, 1988)

■ Fair Housing Assistance Program (FHAP)	HUD	$26 million (2006)

Architectural Barriers Act (1968)

■ creation of Uniform Federal Accessibility Standards	DoD, HUD, GSA, USPS, DoT, and U.S. Access Board

Housing and Urban Development Act (1965, 1968, 1970, 1990)
creation of HUD (FHA becomes department within HUD)

Consolidated Farm and Rural Development Act (1972)

■ creation of Community Facilities Loans and Grants Programs	USDA	$611 million (2006)

Rehabilitation Act (1973, 1998)
creation of of U.S. Access Board

■ Electronic and Information Technology Standards	U.S. Access Board

Housing and Community Development Act (1974, 1977, 1978, 1979, 1980, 1981, 1987, 1992)

■ creation of Fair Housing Initiatives Program (FHIP)	HUD	$20 million (2006)
● Congregate Housing Services Program (CHSP)	HUD	terminated (1995)
● Community Development Block Grants (CDBG):	HUD	$4.2 billion (2006)
● Entitlement Communities Grants		
● state-administered CDBGs		
● other development initiatives		

Low-Income Home Energy Assistance Act (1981, 1998)	DHHS	$3.1 billion (2006)

▲ creation of Low Income Home Energy Assistance Program (LIHEAP)

● Leveraging Incentive Program, and Residential Energy Assistance Challenge Option (REACH) Program

---

Social Security Act (1935, 1965, 1981)

▲ creation of Home and Community-Based Services (HCBS) Waiver Program (Section 1915c)	DHHS	$22.7 billion (2005)
● Independent Living Program for youths 14–21 (ILP, Sections 470 and 477)	DHHS	$140 million (2005)

McKinney-Vento Homeless Assistance Act (1987) creation of Homeless Assistance Programs:	HUD	$1.3 billion (2006)

● Emergency Shelter Grant Program

▲ Shelter Plus Care (S+C) Program

▲ Supportive Housing Program

● Single Room Occupancy (SRO) Program

Tech Act, Assistive Technology Act, and Individuals with Disabilities Education Act (1988, 1998, 2004)

■ creation of various state programs Dept. of Ed.

Americans with Disabilities Act (1990)

■ creation of Americans with Disabilities Act Accessibility Guidelines (ADAAG)	U.S. Access Board	

Cranston-Gonzalez National Affordable Housing Act (1990, 1996

● creation of HOME Investment Partnership Program	HUD	$1.8 billion (2006)
▲ Supportive Housing for Persons with Disabilities (Section 811)	HUD	$237 million (2006)
● HOPE II (Homeownership of Multifamily Units)	HUD	terminated (1995)
● HOPE III (Homeownership of Single-Family Units)	HUD	terminated (1995)
▲ HOPE IV (Elderly Independence)	HUD	terminated (1993)
● HOPE V (Youthbuild)	HUD	terminated (1997)
▲ Housing Opportunities for Persons with AIDS (HOPWA) Program	HUD	$286 million (2006)

Telecommunications Act (1996)

■ Telecommunications Act Accessibility Guidelines	U.S. Access Board	$1 billion (2006)
● creation of telecommunications programs	USDA	$1 billion (2006)

Housing Opportunity Program Extension Act (1996)

- creation of Self-help Homeownership Opportunity (SHOP)
  Program   HUD $60 million (2006)

Native American Housing Assistance Self-Determination Act (1996)

- creation of Indian Housing Block Grants (IHBG)   HUD $624 million (2006)

American Homeownership Act (1998)

- creation of Homeownership Zones (HOZ) Program   HUD   terminated (2006)

Assets for Independence Act (1998)

- creation of Assets for Independence (AFI) Program   DHHS $25 million (2006)

Departments of Veterans Affairs and Housing and Urban Development and Independent Agencies Appropriations Acts (1993–2004)

- creation of HOPE VI (Revitalization of Severely Distressed
  Public Housing)   HUD $99 million (2006)
- Rural Housing and Economic Development (RHED) Program   HUD $17 million (2006)

Homeless Veterans Comprehensive Assistance Act (2001)

- creation of Homeless Providers Grant and Per Diem Program   VA
- Loan Guarantee Program for Multifamily Transitional Housing   VA
- ▲ VA Supported Housing Program   VA
- HUD-VASH   HUD/VA   earmarked funding
  within Section 8

Visitability Legislation in the United States, 1992–2007

BRENT T. WILLIAMS

DATE	LOCATION	TYPES OF HOMES	MANDATORY/ VOLUNTARY
1992	Atlanta, Georgia	single-family homes	mandatory
1997	Freehold Borough, New Jersey	public and private dwellings	voluntary/ developer incentives
1998	Austin, Texas	new single-family homes, duplexes, and triplexes	mandatory
1999	Irvine, California	new single-family homes	voluntary
2000	Urbana, Illinois	new single-family dwellings, duplexes, and triplexes	mandatory
2001	Visalia, California	new single-family homes	voluntary/ certificate program
2001	San Mateo County, California		consumer awareness
2001	Howard County, Maryland		consumer awareness
2002	Albuquerque, New Mexico	new single-family dwellings, duplexes, and triplexes	consumer awareness/ voluntary
2002	San Antonio, Texas	new single-family homes, duplexes, and triplexes	mandatory
2002	Onondaga County, New York	new single-family homes and duplexes	voluntary

DATE	LOCATION	TYPES OF HOMES	MANDATORY/ VOLUNTARY
2002	South Hampton, New York	new single-family homes and duplexes	voluntary/ developer incentives
2002	Naperville, Illinois	new single-family homes	mandatory
2002	Pima County, Arizona	new single-family homes	mandatory
2002	Long Beach, California	new single-family homes, duplexes, and triplexes	mandatory
2002	Iowa City, Iowa	new single-family homes, duplexes, and triplexes	mandatory
2003	Syracuse, New York	new single-family homes	voluntary
2003	Bolingbrook, Illinois	new single-family homes, duplexes, and triplexes	mandatory
2003	Escanaba, Missouri	property owners	voluntary/ consumer incentives
2003	Chicago, Illinois	20% of single-family homes and townhomes in planned developments must be "adaptable" or "visitable"	mandatory
2003	St. Louis County, Mississippi	new single-family homes, duplexes, and triplexes built with county funds	mandatory
2004	Houston, Texas		voluntary/ to developer incentives
2004	Pittsburgh, Pennsylvania	new single-family homes, duplexes, and triplexes	tax incentive
2004	St. Petersburg, Florida	new single-family homes, duplexes, and triplexes	mandatory

DATE	LOCATION	TYPES OF HOMES	MANDATORY/ VOLUNTARY
2005	Toledo, Ohio	new single-family homes, duplexes, and triplexes	mandatory
2005	Auburn, New York	new single-family homes, duplexes, and triplexes	mandatory
2005	Prescott Valley, Arizona		voluntary
2005	Scranton, Pennsylvania	new single-family homes, duplexes, and triplexes	mandatory
2005	Arvada, Colorado	new single-family homes, duplexes, and triplexes	mandatory
2006	Pittsburgh, Pennsylvania		voluntary
2007	Montgomery County, Maryland	new single-family homes and renovations to single-family attached and detached homes	voluntary
2007	Rockford, Illinois	new single-family homes, duplexes, and triplexes	mandatory

NOTES

Introduction: Just Below the Line

1. In 2003 renowned country singer Johnny Cash, a native Arkansan, posthumously released a remake of Kris Kristofferson's "Just the Other Side of Nowhere." In both Cash's and Kristofferson's versions, the song is an autobiographic account of growing up in the South, touring throughout the United States, and the pride and challenges that came with each. Arguably, the most notable difference between the two recordings is Cash's substitution of Kristofferson's "I belong" with "I'll be bound." Cash's revision holds dual meanings. For one, "bound" implies a fleeing from the North and heading home, being "bound" *for* the South. Inversely, "bound" also implies an inability to escape one's own cultural and personal histories, being "bound" *to* the South. Though the physical and metaphorical bounding lines—the lines separating this side from "the other side," the north from the south—continue to evolve, this duality is still present for many Southerners.

2. Donna Ross and Victoria Wachino, "Medicaid Categorical Eligibility Rules Are Proving a Major Obstacle to Getting Health Coverage to Impoverished Katrina Victims in Louisiana: Pending Legislation Would Address Coverage Gaps in Louisiana and Other States," Center on Budget and Policy Priorities, September 26, 2005, http://www.cbpp.org/9–26–05health.htm.

3. Marc Perry and Paul Mackun, "Population Change and Distribution: 1990–2000," *Census 2000 Brief* (Washington, DC: U.S. Census Bureau, April 2001), http://www.census.gov/prod/2001pubs/c2kbr01–2.pdf.

4. Linda Barton, "Comparing the Options," *American Demographics* 19 (1997): 48–49; and Health Policy Institute, "National Spending for Long-Term Care," *Georgetown University Long-Term Care Financing Project* (Washington, DC: Georgetown University, 2007), http://ltc.georgetown.edu/ pdfs/whopays2006.pdf.

5. Gerry Zarb and Pamela Nadash, *Cashing in on Independence: Comparing the Costs and Benefits of Cash and Services* (Derbyshire, UK: BCODP, 1994), http://www.leeds.ac.uk/disability-studies/archiveuk/Zarb/cashing%20in%20on%20indep.pdf.

6. John McNeil, *U.S. Census Brief: Disabilities Affect One-fifth of All Americans: Proportion Could Increase in Coming Decades,* CENBR/97–5 (Washington, DC: U.S. Census Bureau, December 1997), http://www.census.gov/prod/3/97pubs/cenbr975.pdf.

7. Administration on Aging, *A Profile of Older Americans: 2007* (Washington, DC: U.S. Department of Health and Human Services, 2007), http://www.-agingcarefl.org/aging/AOA-2007profile.pdf.

8. Ronald Lee and J. Skinner, "Will Aging Baby Boomers Bust the Federal Budget?," *Journal of Economic Perspectives* 13 (1999): 131. Original authors' italics.

9. Sam Ervin, "Fourteen Forecasts," *The Futurist* 34 (2000): 24.

10. U.S. Census Bureau, "Census 2000 Summary File 3, Matrix P42," http://factfinder.census.gov.

11. Judith Waldrop and Sharon Stern, *Disability Status 2000: Census 2000 Brief* (Washington, DC: U.S. Census Bureau, March 2003), http://www.census.gov/prod/2003pubs/c2kbr-17.pdf.

12. Bernadette Proctor and Joseph Dalaker, *Poverty in the United States: 2002* (Washington, DC: U.S. Government Printing Office, 2003), http://www.census.gov/prod/2003pubs/p60–222.pdf.

13. Social Security Administration, *OASDI Beneficiaries by State and Country, 2004* (Washington, DC: Social Security Administration, 2005), http://www.socialsecurity.gov/policy/docs/statcomps/oasdi_sc/2004/oasdi_sc04.pdf.

14. Lyrics from Ray Charles, "What'd I Say," *What'd I Say,* Atlantic Records, 1959.

15. James Cobb, *Redefining Southern Culture: Mind and Identity in the Modern South* (Athens: University of Georgia Press, 1999), 137, citing Roy Blount Jr.

16. John Reed, *One South: An Ethnic Approach to Regional Culture* (Baton Rouge: University of Louisiana Press, 1982), 61.

17. John Reed, *Surveying the South: Studies in Regional Sociology* (Columbia: University of Missouri Press, 1993).

18. Ibid., 98.

19. Cobb, *Redefining Southern Culture,* 141.

20. Ibid., 142.

21. James Cobb, *Away Down South: A History of Southern Identity* (New York: Oxford University Press, 2005), 332.

22. Ibid., 326.

23. Howard Zinn, *The Southern Mystique* (New York: Alfred A. Knopf, 1968), 218.

24. Cobb, *Redefining Southern Culture,* 210.

25. In his autobiography, Johnny Cash describes a Christmas special that he, along with Waylon Jennings and others, shot in Montreux, Switzerland. A reporter asked Jennings, "Why Christmas in Montreux?" According to Cash, Jennings coy "who, me?" response was: "Well, that's where Jesus was born, isn't it?" See Johnny Cash, *Cash: The Autobiography (*New York: HarperCollins, 1997), 281.

26. W. E. B. DuBois, *The Souls of Black Folk* (Boston: Bedford Books, 1997), 34, first published in 1903.

1. Defining Disability

1. "Dignity and Disability: Rolling with the Punches," *Atlanta News Daily.* At http://www.atlanta-news-daily.com/lifestyle/dignity/ (accessed June 30, 2008).

2. Johnny Cash, *Cash: The Autobiography* (New York: HarperCollins, 1997), 49–50.

3. Ibid.

4. K. Salter et al., "Issues for Selection of Outcome Measures in Stroke Rehabilitation: ICF Participation," *Disability Rehabilitation* 27 (2005): 507–528.

5. Barbara Altman, "Disability Definitions, Models, Classification Schemes, and Applications," in *Handbook of Disability Studies,* ed. Gary Albrecht et al. (Thousand Oaks, CA: Sage Publications, 2001), 97–122.

6. Talcott Parsons, "The Sick Role and Role of the Physician Reconsidered," *Milbank Memorial Fund Quarterly* 53 (1975): 257–278.

7. David Pfeiffer, "The Conceptualization of Disability: Exploring Theories and Expanding Methodologies: Where We Are and Where We Need to Go," in *The Series Research in Social Science and Disability,* ed. Sharon Barnartt and Barbara Altman (New York: Elsevier Science, 2001), 29–52.

8. Roy Amundson, "Against Normal Function," *Studies in History and Philosophy of Biological and Biomedical Sciences* 31 (2000): 33–53.

9. Michael Oliver, *Understanding Disability: From Theory to Practice* (Basingstoke: Macmillan, 1996), 22.

10. Harlan Hahn, "Academic Debates and Political Advocacy: The U.S. Disability Movement," in *Disability Studies Today,* ed. Colin Barnes and Len Barton (Cambridge: Polity Press, 2002), 162–189.

11. Saad Nagi, "Disability Concepts Revisited: Implications for Prevention," in *Disability in America: Toward a National Agenda for Prevention,* ed. Andrew Pope and Alvin Tarlov (Washington, DC: National Academy Press, 1991), 309–327.

12. Ibid.

13. Ibid.

14. Lois Verbrugge and Alan Jette, "The Disablement Process," *Social Science and Medicine,* 38 (1994): 1–14.

15. Nagi, "Disability Concepts Revisited," 309–327.

16. World Health Organization, *International Classification of Impairments, Disabilities, and Handicaps: A Manual of Classification Relating to the Consequences of Disease* (Geneva, Switzerland: World Health Organization, 1980).

17. World Health Organization, *International Classification of Functioning, Disability and Health: IQ* (Geneva, Switzerland: World Health Organization, 2001).

18. George Bainton, *The Art of Authorship: Literary Reminiscences, Methods of Work, and Advice to Young Beginners: Personally Contributed by Leading Authors of the Day* (New York: D. Appleton and Company, 1891), 87–88, quoting the submission by Mark Twain (Samuel Langhorne Clemens).

19. World Health Organization, *International Classification,* 33.

20. Ian Bradford, "The Adaption Process," in *Housing Options for Disabled People,* ed. Ruth Bull (London: Jessica Kingsley, 1988), 78–113.

21. Deborah Marks, "Dimensions of Oppression: Theorising the Embodied Subject," *Disability and Society* 145 (1999): 611–626.

22. Laura Gitlin, "Why Older People Accept or Reject Assistive Technology," *Generations: Journal of the American Society of Ageing* 19 (1995): 41–46.

23. Cash, *Cash,* 49.

2. Defining Home

1. Jimmy Carter, *An Hour before Daylight: Memoirs of a Rural Boyhood* (New York: Simon & Schuster, 2001), 14, 21.

2. Habitat for Humanity, "Jimmy Carter and Habitat for Humanity," Habitat for Humanity Homepage, http://www.habitat.org/how/carter/aspx.

3. Amos Rappaport, "A Critical Look at the Concept 'Home,'" in *The Home: Words, Interpretations, Meanings and Environments,* ed. David Benjamin and David Stea (Aldershot: Avebury, 1995), 25–52.

4. Among terms that have both overlap as well as multiple meanings there is shelter, house, home, and dwelling. The popular Web site Wikipedia terms the process of distinguishing the multiple meanings of a single term "disambiguation." Wikipedia. 2008. "Word

sense disambiguation." http://www.Wikipedia.org/wiki/disambiguation.

5. Joseph Rykwert, "House and Home," *Social Research* 58 (1991): 51–62; and Rappaport, "A Critical Look," 25–52.

6. There are many writings about the meaning of home as well as collections of literature reviews. The selection influencing this chapter include Judith Sixsmith, "The Meaning of Home: An Exploratory Study of Environmental Experience," *Journal of Environmental Psychology* 6 (1986): 281–298; Sandy Smith, "The Essential Qualities of a Home," *Journal of Environmental Psychology* 14 (1994): 31–46; Shelley Mallett, "Understanding Home: A Critical Review of the Literature," *Sociological Review* 52 (2004): 62–89; and Carole Despres, "The Meaning of Home: Literature Review and Directions for Future Research and Theoretical Development," *Journal of Architectural and Planning Research* 8 (Summer 1991): 96–115.

7. Robert Rakoff, "Ideology in Everyday Life: The Meaning of the House," *Politics and Society* 7 (1977): 85–104.

8. Smith, "The Essential Qualities of a Home," 31–46.

9. Mechthild Hart and Miriam Ben-Yoseph, "Shifting Meanings of Home," *Journal of Prevention and Intervention in the Community* 30 (2005): 1–7.

10. John Annison, "Towards a Clearer Under-standing of the Meaning of 'Home,'" *Journal of Intellectual & Developmental Disability* 25 (2001): 251–262.

11. Ibid., 252.

12. U.S. Department of Housing and Urban Development, "Section 11302. General Definition of Homeless Individual [Section 103 of the Act]," http://www.hud.gov/offices/cpd/homeless/rulesandregs/laws/title1/sec11302.cfm.

13. Ronald Hill, "Homeless Women, Special Possessions and the Meaning of 'Home': An Ethnographic Case Study," *Journal of Consumer Research* 18 (December 1991): 298–310.

14. Associated Press, "Arkansas Foreclosures Jump 8.5 Percent in August" (Little Rock, AR: Arkansas Business Journal, September 12, 2008), http://www.arkansasbusiness.com/article.aspx?aID=108187.54928.120332.

15. John Tatum, The U.S. Foreclosure Crisis: A Two-Pronged Assault on the U.S. Economy (Munich, Germany, Munich Personal RePEc Archive, July 31, 2008), http://mpra.ub.uni-muenchen.de/9787/ MPRA Paper No. 9787; Naomi Cytron and Laura Lanzerotti, Homeownership at High Cost: Recent Trends in the Mortgage Lending Industry (San Francisco, CA, Federal Reserve Bank of San Francisco, December 2006), http://www.sf.frb.org/publications/community/investments/0612/cytron_homeownership.pdf.

16. David Sibley, "Spaces of Exclusion: Home, Locality, Nation," in *Geographies of Exclusion: Society and Difference in the West* (London: Routledge, 1995), 90–118.

17. Mike O'Sullivan, "Habitat for Humanity: Jimmy Carter Building Homes in Los Angeles" (Los Angeles, CA, Voice of America, April 3, 2007), http://www.voanews.com/english/archive/2007-04/2007-04-03-voa60.cfm.

18. Allan Pred, "Structuration and Place: On the Becoming of Sense of Place and Structure of Feeling," *Journal for the Theory of Social Behaviour* 13 (1983): 45–68; and David Wasserman, Mick Womersley, and Sarah Gottleib, "Can a Sense of Place Be Preserved?" in *Philosophy and Geography III: Philosophies of Place,* ed. Andrew Light and Jonathan Smith (Lanham, MD: Rowman & Littlefield Publishers, 1998), 191–213.

19. Amos Rappaport, "A Critical Look at the Concept 'Home,'" in *The Home: Words, Interpretations, Meanings and Environments,* ed. David N. Benjamin and David Stea (Aldershot: Avebury, 1995), 25–52.

20. Claire Cooper Marcus, *House as a Mirror of Self: Exploring the Deeper Meaning of Home* (Berkeley, CA: Conari Press, 1996).

21. Lynda Johnston and Gill Valentine, "Wherever I Lay My Girlfriend That's My Home," in *Mapping Desire, Geographies of Sexualities,* ed. David Bell and Gill Valentine (London: Routledge, 1995), 99–113.

22. Ann Dupois and David Thorns, "Meanings of Home for Older Home Owners," *Housing Studies* 11 (1996): 485–501.

23. Peter Somerville, "The Social Construction of Home," *Journal of Architectural and Planning Research* 14 (1997): 225–245.

24. Judith Sixsmith, "The Meaning of Home," 281–298.

25. Smith, "The Essential Qualities of Home," 31–46.

26. Tomoko Doi Hata, "Inference about Resident's Personality in Japanese Home," *North American Journal of Psychology* 6 (2004): 337–348.

27. Suk-Kyung Kim, "Urban Renters and Their Perception of Safety in Gated Residential Communities," in *Proceedings of the Environmental Design Research Association 39th Annual Conference* (Norman, OK: EDRA, 2008).

28. Linda McDowell, "City Life and Differences: Negotiating Diversity," in *Unsettling Cities: Movement/Settlement,* ed. John Allen, Doreen Massey, and Michael Pryke (London: Routledge/Open University Press, 1999), 95–136.

29. From data collected as part of the Arkansas Health and Housing Survey, 2006: Summary Report, authored by Korydon Smith, Jennifer Webb, Nancy Miller, and Brent Williams (2007), data collected by the University of Arkansas Survey Research Center in May 2006. See pages 22–24 of the published report at www.studioaid.org.

30. Charles Tolbert et al., "Civic Community in Small-Town America: How Civic Welfare Is Influenced by Local Capitalism and Civic Engagement," *Rural Sociology* 67 (2002): 90–113.

31. Ade Kearns et al., "'Beyond Four Walls' The Psycho-Social Benefits of Home: Evidence from West Central Scotland," *Housing Studies* 15 (2000): 387–410.

32. Christopher Leonard, "What Price Paradise?" Arkansas Democrat-Gazette On-Line (2005), http://www.ardemgaz.com/ ads/mi/articles/paradise.html.

33. Leon Pastalan and Valerie Polakow, "Life Space over the Life Span," *Journal of Housing for the Elderly* 4 (1987): 73–85.

34. Cooper Marcus, *House as a Mirror of Self.*

35. William Hansen and Irwin Altman, "Decorating Personal Places: A Descriptive Analysis," *Environment and Behavior* 8 (1976): 491–504.

36. Naomi White, "'Not Under My Roof!': Young People's Experience of Home," *Youth Society* 34 (2002): 214–231.

37. Robert Atchley, "A Continuity Theory of Normal Aging," *The Gerontologist* 29 (1989): 183–190; and Somerville, "The Social Construction of Home," 225–245.

38. Carter, *An Hour before Daylight, 33.*

39. Sense of Smell Institute, "SOSI Resources: Glossary," The Fragrance Foundation Research and Education Division. http://www.senseofsmell.org/resources/glossary.php?item=O.

40. Charlayne Hunter-Gault was the first African American woman to attend the University of Georgia. She is a noted journalist and has held positions with CNN, National Public Radio, and *The News Hour* with Jim Lehrer. Her work has been published in the *New Yorker, Trans-Action Magazine,* and the *New York Times Magazine* and she has published several books. Amanda Nash, "Charlayne Hunter-Gault," in *The New Georgia Encyclopedia* (Atlanta: Georgia Humanities Council, 2004), http://www.georgiaencyclopedia.org/nge/Article.jsp?id=h-2433.

41. Charlayne Hunter-Gault, *In My Place* (New York: Random House), 178.

42. Robert Kitchin, "Cognitive Maps: What Are They and Why Study Them?" *Journal of Environmental Psychology* 14 (1994): 1–19.

43. Arthur Reber, *Implicit Learning and Tacit Knowledge: An Essay on the Cognitive Unconscious* (New York: Oxford University Press, 1996).

44. Graham Allan and Graham Crow, "The Postwar Development of the Modern," in *Home and Family: Creating the Domestic Sphere,* ed. Graham Allan and Graham Crow (London: Macmillan Press, 1989), 14–32.

45. Humphrey Osmond and Miriam Sieglar, "The Dying Role—Its Clinical Significance," *Alabama Journal of Medical Science* 13 (1976): 116.

46. Irwin Altman, *The Environment and Social Behavior* (Monterey, CA: Brooks/Cole, 1975).

47. Christopher Sonn and Adrian Fisher, "Psychological Sense of Community in a Politically Constructed Group," *Journal of Community Psychology* 24 (1995): 417–430.

48. Ruth Holliday, "Home Truths?" in *Ordinary Lifestyles: Popular Media, Consumption and Taste,* ed. David Bell and Joanne Hollows (London: McGraw Hill International, 2005), 65–81.

49. Claire Cooper Marcus, "Environmental Memories," in *Place Attachment,* ed. Irwin Altman and Sethna Low (New York: Plenum Press, 1992), 87–112.

50. Ronald Hill and Mark Stamey, "The Homeless in America: An Examination of Possessions and Consumption Behaviors," *Journal of Consumer Research* 17 (1990): 303–321.

51. Ronald Hill, "Homeless Women, Special Possessions, and the Meaning of 'Home': An Ethnographic Case Study," *Journal of Consumer Research* 18 (1991): 298–310.

52. Catherine Wallack and Jennifer Webb, "Territory in Temporary Shelters: Media-Documented Space Claiming Following Hurricane Katrina," in *Proceedings of the Environmental Design Research Association 37th Annual Meeting* (Norman, OK: EDRA, 2006), 163.

53. Atchley, "A Continuity Theory of Normal Aging," 183–190.

54. Linda Price, Eric Arnould, and Carolyn Folkman Curasi, "Older Consumers' Disposition of Special Possessions," *Journal of Consumer Research* 27 (2000): 179–201.

55. Ibid.

56. Kathryn Anthony, "Bitter Homes and Gardens: The Meanings of Home to Families in Divorce," *Journal of Architectural and Planning Research* 14 (1997): 1–19.

57. Mary Douglas, "The Idea of a Home: A Kind of Space," *Social Research* 58 (1991): 287–307.

58. Rappaport, "A Critical Look," 25–52.

59. Carole Despres, "The Meaning of Home: Literature Review and Directions for Future Research

and Theoretical Development," *Journal of Architectural Planning and Research* 8 (1991): 96–115.

60. Sherry Ahrentzen, "Home as a Workplace in the Lives of Women," *Harvard Design Magazine* 8 (1999): 1–6.

61. Tom Rice and Diane Coates, "Gender Role Attitudes in the Southern United States," *Gender and Society* 9 (December 1995): 744–756; and J. Scott Carter and Casey Borch, "Assessing the Effects of Urbanism and Regionalism on Gender-Role Attitudes, 1974–1998," *Sociological Inquiry* 75 (November 2005): 548–563.

62. Douglas, "The Idea of a Home," 287–307.

63. Rakoff, "Ideology in Everyday Life," 85–104.

64. Douglas, "The Idea of a Home," 287–307.

65. Somerville, "The Social Construction of Home," 225–245.

66. Gaines Foster, "Southerners," in *The New Encyclopedia of Southern Culture, Volume 6: Ethnicity*, ed. Charles Reagan Wilson and Celeste Ray (Chapel Hill: University of North Carolina Press, 2007), 90.

67. From data collected as part of the Arkansas Health and Housing Survey, 2006: Summary Report, authored by Korydon Smith, Jennifer Webb, Nancy Miller, and Brent Williams (2007), www.studioaid.org, data collected by the University of Arkansas Survey Research Center in May 2006.

68. Jennifer Webb, Korydon Smith, and Brent Williaims, "Perceptions of Independent Living: Influences on the Relationship Between Disability and Design," *Interdisciplinary Design Research Journal* 1 (2006), http://www.idrp.wsu.edu/ googlefd44a7f0b1456374.html.

69. Jonathan Smith, Andrew Light, and David Roberts, "Introduction," in *Philosophy and Geography III: Philosophies of Place*, ed. Andrew Light and Jonathan M. Smith (Lanham, MD: Rowman & Littlefield Publishers, 1998), 17.

70. Johnny Cash, *Cash: The Autobiography* (New York: HarperCollins, 1997), 187–188.

71. Robert Hay, "Sense of Place in Developmental Context," *Journal of Environmental Psychology* 18 (1998): 5–29.

72. John Shotter, *Cultural Politics of Everyday Life: Social Construction, Rhetoric and Knowing of the Third Kind* (Toronto: University of Toronto Press, 1993), 210.

73. Allan Pred, "Structuration and Place: On the Becoming of Sense of Place and Structure of Feeling," *Journal for the Theory of Social Behaviour* 13 (1983): 45–68; and David Wasserman, Mick Womersley, and Sarah Gottlieb, "Can a Sense of Place Be Preserved?" in Philosophy and Geography III: Philosophies of Place, ed. Andrew Light and Jonathan Smith (Lanham, MD: Rowman & Littlefield Publishers, 1998), 191–213.

74. Charles Wilson, "Sense of Place," in *The New Encyclopedia of Southern Culture, Volume 4: Myth, Manners, and Memory*, ed. Charles Wilson, James Thomas, and Ann Abadie (Ann Arbor: University of Michigan Press, 2006), 254.

75. Jerome Tognoli, "Residential Environments," in *Handbook of Environmental Psychology*, ed. David Stokols and Irwin Altman (New York: Wiley, 1987), 655–690.

76. Alice Walker, *In Search of Our Mother's Gardens* (New York: Harcourt Trade, 2004), 144–145.

77. Smith, "The Essential Qualities of Home."

78. Atchley, "A Continuity Theory of Normal Aging," 183–190.

79. Jeanne Hurlbert and William Bankston, "Cultural Distinctiveness in the Face of Structural Transformation: The 'New' Old South," in *The Rural South since World War II*, ed. R. Douglas Hurt (Baton Rouge: Louisiana State University Press, 1998), 171.

80. Atchley, "A Continuity Theory of Normal Aging," 183–190.

81. Cash, *Cash*, 202.

3. Defining Equality

1. Douglas Baynton, "Disability and the Justification of Inequality in American History," in *The New Disability History: American Perspectives*, ed. Paul Longmore and Lauri Umansky (New York: New York University Press, 2002), 33.

2. Amy Petersen, "An African-American Woman with Disabilities: The Intersection of Gender, Race, and Disability," *Disability and Society* 21 (2006): 721–734.

3. Ibid., 727.

4. Cross's five stages are as follows: (1) *pre-encounter*, where African Americans view race as either negative or unimportant, (2) *encounter*, where personal experiences result in a confrontation with and questioning of racial differences, (3) *immersion-emersion*, where a deep questioning of racial identity occurs, often involving negative attitudes toward whites, (4) *internalization*, where outwardly focused negative attitudes give way to an internal solidifying of identity, and (5) *internalization-commitment*, where outward activism typifies a commitment to race as whole beyond the individual. William Cross, *Shades of Black: Diversity in African-American Identity* (Philadelphia: Temple University Press, 1991).

5. Josselson's four identity types are as follows: (1) *foreclosures*, who (a) possess fairly rigid, lasting identity structures and ideals, often adopted from parents, (b) tend not to experience "identity crises," and (c) gain a sense of identity externally, (2) *achievers*, who, on the

other hand, (a) sever ties with their childhood and familial identities, typically negotiated by future aspirations, (b) typically experience "identity crises" during adolescence, and (c) gain a sense of identity from within, (3) *moratorium* women, who struggle deeply to reconcile positive and traditional vs. negative and transformative views of childhood/familial identities, and may remain in moratorium for extended time periods and/or resolve to *foreclosures* or *achievers,* and (4) *diffusers,* who are the most complex and varied group, frequently characterized by unhealthy psychological functioning and behaviors, sometimes marked by troubled relationships with their parents. Ruthellen Josselson, *Finding Herself: Pathways of Identity Development in Women* (San Francisco: Jossey-Bass, 1987).

6. Dozens of books and journal articles have explored identity development socialization and discrimination for persons with disabilities—especially regarding mobility impairments and visible (not hidden) disabilities—through the lens of "queer theory." See, for example: Steven Onken and Ellen Slaten, "Disability Identity Formation and Affirmation: The Experiences of Persons with Severe Mental Illness," *Sociological Practice: A Journal of Clinical and Applied Sociology* 2 (2000): 99–111.

7. Several scholars have explored the similarities and differences between race-based and disability-based discrimination in recent years. As disability studies is a newer discipline than African American studies, etc., many race and ethnicity theories are often applied to disability studies. See, for example: Adrian Asche, "Critical Race Theory, Feminism, and Disability: Reflections on Social Justice and Personal Identity," *Ohio State Law Journal* 62 (2001): 391–423; Dorothy Dunlop et al., "Racial/Ethnic Differences in the Development of Disability among Older Adults," *American Journal of Public Health* 97 (2007): 2209–2215; Beth Ferri and David Connor, "Tools of Exclusion: Race, Disability, and (Re)segregated Education," *Teachers College Record* 107 (2005): 453–474; Fiona Kumari Campbell, "Exploring Internalized Ableism Using Critical Race Theory," *Disability and Society* 23 (2008): 151–162; Elias Mpofu and Liza Conyers, "A Representational Theory Perspective of Minority Status and People with Disabilities," *Rehabilitation Counseling Bulletin* 47 (2004): 142–151; Elias Mpofu and Debra Harley, "Racial and Disability Identity: Implications for the Career Counseling of African Americans with Disabilities," *Rehabilitation Counseling Bulletin* 50 (2006): 14–23; Daniel Sciarra, Tai Chang, Ron McLean, and Daniel Wong, "White Racial Identity and Attitudes toward People with Disabilities,"

Journal of Multicultural Counseling and Development 33 (2005): 232–242; and Joy Weeber, "What Could I Know of Racism?," *Journal of Counseling and Development* 77 (1999): 20–23.

8. For disability statistics, see Judith Waldrop and Sharon Stern, *Disability Status 2000: Census 2000 Brief* (Washington, DC: U.S. Census Bureau, March 2003), http://www.census.gov/prod/2003pubs/c2kbr-17.pdf. For poverty statistics, see Bernadette Proctor and Joseph Dalaker, *Poverty in the United States: 2002.* (Washington, DC: U.S. Government Printing Office, 2003), http://www.census.gov/prod/2003pubs/p60–222.pdf.

9. Age is the greatest predictor of disability. At age 65 and older, the likelihood of having one or more disabilities is greater than 50 percent, whereas only 9 percent of 0–14-year-olds have a disability. John McNeil, *U.S. Census Brief: Disabilities Affect One-fifth of All Americans: Proportion Could Increase in Coming Decades,* CENBR/97–5 (Washington, DC: U.S. Census Bureau, December 1997), http://www.census.gov/prod/3/97pubs/cenbr975.pdf.

10. Charles Lamb, *Housing Segregation in Suburban America since 1960* (New York: Cambridge University Press, 2005); and Matthew Lassiter, *The Silent Majority: Suburban Politics in the Sunbelt South* (Princeton, NJ: Princeton University Press, 2006).

11. National Fair Housing Alliance, "Unequal Opportunity: Perpetuating Housing Segregation in America," http://www.nationalfairhousing.org/resources/newsArchive/resource_24256802754560627686.pdf. [AU: Accessed date?]

12. Baynton, "Disability," 33.

13. Joseph Shapiro, *No Pity: People with Disabilities Forging a New Civil Rights Movement* (New York: Three Rivers Press, 1994), 41.

14. For information regarding *social identity theory,* see Henri Tajfel and John Turner, "An Integrative Theory of Intergroup Conflict," in *The Social Psychology of Intergroup Relations,* ed. William Austin and Stephen Worchel (Monterey, CA: Brooks-Cole, 1979); Henri Tajfel and John Turner, "The Social Identity Theory of Inter-group Behavior," *Psychology of Intergroup Relations,* ed. William Austin and Stephen Worchel (Chicago: Nelson-Hall, 1986); Henri Tajfel (ed.), *Social Identity and Intergroup Relations* (New York: Cambridge University Press, 1982); Henri Tajfel, *Differentiation between Social Groups: Studies in the Social Psychology of Intergroup Relations* (New York: Academic Press, 1978); and Henri Tajfel, *Human Groups and Social Categories: Studies in Social Psychology* (New York: Cambridge University Press, 1981).

15. See previous note.

16. This quotation is taken a bit out of context. In its original form it is not specific to the rural South. It is recast, however, because of its efficacy regarding concepts prevalent in the rural South. Michel de Certeau, *The Practice of Everyday Life* (Berkeley and Los Angeles: University of California Press, 1984), 29.

17. National Fair Housing Alliance, "Unequal Opportunity: Perpetuating Housing Segregation in America," http://www.nationalfairhousing.org/resources/newsArchive/resource_24256802754560627686.pdf.

18. Ben Johnson, *Arkansas in Modern America, 1930–1999* (Fayetteville: University of Arkansas Press, 2000), 211.

19. Elaine Ostroff, "Universal Design: The New Paradigm," in *Universal Design Handbook*, ed. Wolfgang Preiser and Elaine Ostroff (New York: McGraw-Hill, 2001), 1.4.

20. For more information on "universal access" and the concept of "universal design," see chapter 6.

21. Cliff Hymowitz, "The Current State of Transportation for People with Disabilities in the United States," *Concerned Citizens for Public Transportation in Suffolk County* 4 (2005), www.transitrider.net/newsletter/aug05.doc.

22. U.S. Access Board, "History of the U.S. Access Board," http://www.access-board.gov/about/history.htm.

23. As Lefebvre states, architectural spaces are popularly seen as being "molded from historical and natural elements, but this has been a political process [as well]. Space is political and ideological. It is a product literally filled with ideologies." See Henri Lefebvre, "Reflections on the Politics of Space," *Antipode* 8 (1976): 31.

24. David Wolfe, "The Truth about Boomers' Differences from Previous Generations of Aging People," 2005 White House Conference on Aging, http://www.whcoa.gov/about/policy/meetings/Feb_20/WHCoA_Testimony_wolfe.pdf.

25. For an overview of the processes of code authoring conducted by the International Code Council, go to the ICC/ANSI Web site: http://www.iccsafe.org/cs/codespdf/CD022704.ppt#2.

26. Henri Lefebvre, "Reflections on the Politics of Space," *Antipode* 8, no. 2 (1976): 30–37.

27. Antoine Picon, "The Ghost of Architecture: The Project and Its Codification," *Perspecta* 35 (2004): 9.

28. International Code Council, "ICC Conference Marks Many Firsts," October 10, 2003, http://www.iccsafe.org/news/nr/2003/031003conference.html.

29. Antoine Picon, "The Ghost of Architecture: The Project and Its Codification," *Perspecta* 35 (2004): 9–19.

30. American Institute of Architects, *The New ADAAG: The AIA's Response to the Department of Justice's Advance Notice of Proposed Rulemaking on the New ADA Accessibility Guidelines* (Washington, DC: American Institute of Architects, 2005), http://www.aia.org/SiteObjects/files/adaagcomments.pdf.

31. See chapter 5 in this book.

32. See chapter 6 in this book.

33. See chapter 1 in this book.

34. For information on the "enabler" concept, see Susanne Iwarsson, "The Housing Enabler: An Objective Tool for Assessing Accessibility," *British Journal of Occupational Therapy* 62 (1999): 491–497; Susanne Iwarsson and Å Isacsson, "Basic Accessibility in Modern Housing: A Key to the Problems of Care in the Domestic Setting," *Scandinavian Journal of Caring Sciences* 7 (1993): 155–159; Susanne Iwarsson and A. Stahl, "Accessibility, Usability and Universal Design: Positioning and Definition of Concepts Describing Person-Environment Relationships," *Disability & Rehabilitation* 25 (2003): 57; Agneta Fänge and Susanne Iwarsson, "Accessibility and Usability in Housing: Construct Validity and Implications for Research and Practice," *Disability & Rehabilitation* 25 (2003): 1316–1325; and Agneta Fänge and Susanne Iwarsson, "Changes in Accessibility and Usability in Housing: An Exploration of the Housing Adaptation Process," *Occupational Therapy International* 12 (2005): 44–59.

35. *Historical Tables: Budget of the United States Government, Fiscal Year 2009* (Washington, DC: U.S. Government Printing Office, 2008), http://www.whitehouse.gov/omb/budget/fy2009/pdf/hist.pdf.

36. For information on state spending in Arkansas, see the Arkansas Department of Finance and Administration Web site: http://www.arkansas.gov/dfa/budget/budget_facts_brochure_fy05.html.

37. From data collected by the University of Arkansas Survey Research Center in May 2006 as part of the *Arkansas Health and Housing Survey, 2006: Summary Report,* authored by Korydon Smith, Jennifer Webb, Nancy Miller, and Brent Williams (Little Rock: Arkansas Department of Health and Human Services and Arkansas Rehabilitation Services, 2007), available at www.studioaid.org.

38. Health Policy Institute, "National Spending for Long-Term Care," *Georgetown University Long-Term Care Financing Project* (Washington, DC: Georgetown University, 2007), http://ltc.georgetown.edu/pdfs/whopays2006.pdf. (Accessed May 18, 2007); Gerry Zarb and

Pamela Nadash, *Cashing in on Independence: Comparing the Costs and Benefits of Cash and Services* (Derbyshire, UK: BCODP, 1994), http://www.leeds.ac.uk/disability-studies/archiveuk/Zarb/cashing%20in%20on%20indep.pdf.; Linda Barton, "Comparing the options," *American Demographics* 19 (1997): 48–49; William Mann et al., "The Cost-Effectiveness of Independent Housing for the Chronically Mentally Ill: Do Housing and Neighbor - hood Features Matter?," *Archives of Family Medicine [NLM-MEDLINE]* 8 (1999): 210; Adolf Ratzka, "A Brief Survey on Costs and Benefits of Non-handicapping Environments," *Independent Living Institute* (1994), http://www.independentliving.org/ cib/cibrio 94access.html; and Steven Winter Associates, *Cost of Accessible Housing: An Analysis of the Estimated Cost of Compliance with the Fair Housing Accessibility Guidelines and ANSI A117.1* (Washington, DC: U.S. Department of Housing and Urban Development, 1993).

39. Rob Imrie, "The Impact of Part M on the Design of New Housing," https://www.jrf.org.uk/knowledge/findings/housing/823.asp.

40. GovTrack.US, "H.R. 4202: Inclusive Home Design Act of 2007," 110th United States Congress, http://www.govtrack.us/congress/bill.xpd?bill=h110–4202.

41. *Concrete Change,* a project of the Statewide Independent Living Council of Georgia and directed by Eleanor Smith, is the primary proponent of the concept of "visitability" in housing and primary advocate of the proposed *Inclusive Home Design Act.* For more informa-tion on *Concrete Change,* go to http://www.concrete change.org.

42. James Cobb, *Away Down South: A History of Southern Identity* (Oxford: Oxford University Press, 2005), 261; and James Cobb, *Redefining Southern Culture: Mind and Identity in the Modern South* (Athens: University of Georgia Press, 1999), 125.

43. Jos Boys, "Windows on the World?: Architecture, Identities and New Technologies," in *Digital Desires: Language, Identities, and New Technologies,* ed. Cutting Edge, the Women's Research Group (London: I. B. Tauris, 2000), 125.

44. John Reed, *The Enduring South* (Chapel Hill: University of North Carolina Press, 1972), 12.

45. James Cobb, "Redefining Southern Culture," 128, quoting Thadious Davis, "Expanding the Limits: The Intersection of Race and Region," *Southern Literary Journal* 20 (1988): 3–11.

4. Defining Policy and Practice

1. U.S. Census Bureau, *Historical Census of Housing Tables,* http://www.census.gov/hhes/www/housing/census/historic/owner.html.

2. Herbert Gans, *The Levittowners: Ways of Life and Politics in a New Suburban Community* (New York: Pantheon Books, 1967), 274.

3. Ibid., 254.

4. Ibid., 278.

5. James Adams, *The Epic of America* (Boston: Little, Brown and Co., 1931), 404–405.

6. U.S. Census Bureau, *United States: 1790 to 1990,* http://www.census.gov/population/www/census data/files/table-4.pdf.

7. Robert Beuaregard, *When America Became Suburban* (Minneapolis: University of Minnesota Press, 2006), 42.

8. Gans, *The Levittowners,* 207.

9. U.S. Department of Commerce, Census Bureau, *Structural and Occupancy Characteristics of Housing, 2000: Census 2000 Brief,* ed. Robert Bennefield and Robert Bonnette (Washington, DC: U.S. Census Bureau, 2003), http://www.census.gov/prod/2003pubs/c2kbr-32.pdf.

10. From data collected by the University of Arkansas Survey Research Center in May 2006 as part of the *Arkansas Health and Housing Survey, 2006: Summary Report,* authored by Korydon Smith, Jennifer Webb, Nancy Miller, and Brent Williams (Little Rock: Arkansas Department of Health and Human Services and Arkansas Rehabilitation Services, 2007), available at www.studioaid.org.

11. U.S. Census Bureau, *Housing Characteristics, 2000: Census 2000 Brief,* ed. Jeanne Woodward and Bonnie Damon (Washington, DC: U.S. Census Bureau, 2001), http://www.census.gov/prod/2001pubs/c2kbr01–13.pdf.

12. U.S. Census Bureau, *Home Values: 2000* (Washington, DC: U.S. Census Bureau, 2003), http://www.census.gov/prod/2003pubs/c2kbr-20.pdf.

13. U.S. Census Bureau, *America's Families and Living Arrangements, 2000: Population Characteristics,* ed. Jason Fields and Lynne Casper (Washington, DC: U.S. Census Bureau, 2001), http://www.census.gov/prod/2001 pubs/p20–537.pdf, 3.

14. U.S. Census Bureau, *Population Profile of the United States: 2000* (Washington, DC: U.S. Census Bureau, 2002), http://www.census.gov/population/pop-profile/2000/chap03.pdf.

15. National Association of Realtors, 2008, http://www.realtor.org/.

16. U.S. Census Bureau, *Population Profile of the United States*.

17. John Reed, *The Enduring South* (Chapel Hill: University of North Carolina Press, 1972), 36.

18. Jack Friedman, Jack Harris, and J. Bruce Lindeman, *Dictionary of Real Estate Terms*, 6th ed. (Hauppauge, NY: Barron's Educational Series, 2005).

19. Patrick Hare, "Frail Elders and the Suburbs," *Generations* (1992): 35–39.

20. Qi Wang, *Disability and American Families: 2000* (Washington, DC: U.S. Census Bureau, 2005), http://www.census.gov/prod/2005pubs/censr-23.pdf.

21. Ann Rae, "What's in a Name?," *International Rehabilitation Review* (1989), University of Leeds Centre for Disability Studies Research Archive, http://www.leeds.ac.uk/disability-studies/archiveuk/Rae/Whatsname.pdf.

22. *Laura Butalla,* "Highlands Ranch," *Professional Builder* 17 (2006): 63.

23. Scott Kaminski et al., "The Viability of Voluntary Visitability: A Case Study of Irvine's Approach," *Journal of Disability Policy Studies* 17 (2006): 49–57.

24. John Benjamin, Peter Chinloy, and G. Stacy Sirmans, "Housing Vouchers, Tenant Quality, and Apartment Values," *Journal of Real Estate Finance and Economics* 12 (2001).

25. Bret Kloos et al., "Landlords as Partners for Promoting Success in Supported Housing: 'It Takes More Than a Key,'" *Psychiatric Rehabilitation Journal* 25 (2002): 25–28.

26. Bruce Katz and Margery Turner, "Who Should Run the Housing Voucher Program?" *Housing Policy Debate* 12 (2001): 239–262.

27. Suzanne LaBarre, "Truth in Numbers," *Metropolis Magazine,* October 2008, http://www.metropolismag.com/cda/story.php?artid=3544.

28. John Reed, *One South: An Ethnic Approach to Regional Culture* (Baton Rouge: University of Louisiana Press, 1982), 154.

29. James Cobb, *Redefining Southern Culture: Mind and Identity in the Modern South* (Athens: University of Georgia Press, 1992), 133, quoting Chalmers Archer in *Growing Up Black in Rural Mississippi: Memories of a Family, Heritage of a Place* (New York: Walker & Co., 1992).

30. U.S. Department of Housing and Urban Development, "Economic Benefits of Increasing Minority Homeownership," White House Conference on Minority Homeownership, Washington, DC, 2002.

31. Thomas DeBlack, "The Rights and Rank to Which We Are Entitled: Arkansas in the Early Statehood Period," in *Arkansas: A Narrative History,* ed. Jeannie M. Whayne, Thomas A. DeBlack, George Sabo III, and Morris S. Arnold (Fayetteville: University of Arkansas Press, 2002), 118.

32. U.S. Census Bureau, *State Quick Facts for Arkansas 2006* (Washington, DC: U.S. Census Bureau, 2006), http://quickfacts.census.gov/qfd/states/05000.html.

33. Mark Zandi, "The Growing Mortgage Foreclosure Crisis: Identifying Solutions and Dispelling Myths," written testimony before the House Subcommittee on Commercial and Administrative Law Hearing, January 29, 2008, http://www.responsiblelending.org/pdfs/paulson-brief-final.pdf).

34. RealtyTrac, "Foreclosure Activity Increases 12 Percent in August," http://www.realtytrac.com/ContentManagement/ pressrelease.aspx?ChannelID=9&ItemID=5163&accnt=64847.

35. Woodstock Institute, "There Goes the Neighborhood: The Effect of Single-Family Mortgage Foreclosures on Property Values," June 2005, http://www.woodstockinst.org/content/view/104/47/.

36. CNNMoney, "7.5 Million Homeowners 'Underwater,'" http://money.cnn.com/2008/10/30/real_estate/underwater_borrowers/index.htm?postversion=2008103108.

37. U.S. Census Bureau, *State Quick Facts for Arkansas*.

38. Ibid.

39. Smith et al., "Arkansas Health and Housing Survey."

40. Ann O'Hara et al., *Priced Out in 2006: The Housing Crisis for People with Disabilities* (Boston, MA: Technical Assistance Collaborative, 2007), 1.

41. U.S. Census Bureau, *State Quick Facts for Arkansas*.

42. Harvard University, Joint Center for Housing Studies, *The State of the Nation's Housing: 2007,* http://www.jchs.harvard.edu/publications/markets/son2007/son2007.pdf: 25; and Gregg van Ryzin, Michelle Ronda, and Douglas Muzzio, "Factors Related to Self-Sufficiency in a Distressed Public Housing Community," *Journal of Urban Affairs* 23 (2001): 57–70.

43. Harvard, *The State of the Nation's Housing,* 25.

44. Ibid.

45. Ibid., 28.

46. U.S. Department of Commerce, Department of Economic Analysis, *Regional Economic Analysis,* http://www.bea.gov/newsreleases/regional/gdp_state/2006/gsp1006.htm.

47. Ibid.

48. The Diane D. Blair Center of Southern Politics and Society, "Annual Summaries, 2000–2005," *The Arkansas Poll*, http://www.uark.edu/ua/tshield/projects.htm.

49. Mary Jo Bane and David Ellwood, *Welfare Realities: From Rhetoric to Reform* (Cambridge, MA: Harvard University Press, 1994).

50. Christopher Jencks, *Rethinking Social Policy: Race, Poverty, and the Underclass* (Cambridge, MA: Harvard University Press, 1992); and Greg van Ryzin, Michelle Ronda, and Douglas Muzzio, "Factors Related to Self-Sufficiency," 58.

51. U.S. Department of Labor, Bureau of Labor Statistics, *Current Employment Statistics,* 2007, http://www.bls.gov/ces/home.htm.

52. U.S. Department of Labor, Bureau of Labor Statistics, *Local Area Unemployment Statistics,* 2007, http://data.bls.gov/cgi-bin/surveymost?la+05.

53. U.S. Department of Labor, Bureau of Labor Statistics, *Current Population Survey,* 2007, http://www.bls.gov/emp/emptab7.htm.

54. Min Zhan and Shanta Pandey, "Economic Well-Being of Single Mothers: Work First or Postsecondary Education?" *Journal of Sociology and Social Welfare* 31 (2004): 87–112.

55. Suzanne Robbins and Holly Barcus, "Welfare Reform and Economic and Housing Capacity for Low-Income Households, 1997–1999," *Policy Studies Journal* 32 (2004): 439–460.

56. U.S. Census Bureau, *State Quick Facts for Arkansas.*

57. EPE Research Center, *National Highlights Report: A Special Supplement to Education Week's Quality Counts 2008,* January 2008, http://www.pewcenteronthestates.org/uploadedFiles/National%20Highlights%20Report.pdf.

58. *Lake View School District No. 25 of Phillips County, Arkansas, et al., Appellants v. Governor Mike Huckabee, et al., Appellees,* No. 01–836 (12/11/2006), http://courts.state.ar.us/lake%20view/table.htm

59. James Cobb, *Away Down South: A History of Southern Identity* (Oxford: Oxford University Press, 2005), 327.

60. Bruce Webster Jr. and Alemayehu Bishaw, *American Community Survey, Income, Earnings, and Poverty Data from the 2006 American Community Survey* (Washington, DC: U.S. Census Bureau, 2007), 3, http://www.census.gov/prod/2007pubs/acs-08.pdf.

61. James Spencer, "People, Places, and Policy: A Politically Relevant Framework for Efforts to Reduce Concentrated Poverty," *Policy Studies Journal* 32 (2004): 545–567.

62. Ibid.

63. Ibid.

64. Greg van Ryzin, Michelle Ronda, and Douglas Muzzio, "Factors Related to Self-Sufficiency."

65. Tavia Simmons and Grace O'Neill, *Households and Families, 2000: Census 2000 Brief* (Washington, DC: U.S. Census Bureau, 2001), http://www.census.gov/prod/2001pubs/c2kbr01–8.pdf.

66. U.S. Census Bureau, "Section 12. Labor Force, Employment, and Earnings" (Washington, DC: U.S. Census Bureau, 1995), http://www.census.gov/prod/2004pubs/04statab/ labor.pdf; and Rachel Kleit and William Rohe, "Using Public Housing to Achieve Self-Sufficiency: Can We Predict Success?" *Housing Studies* 20 (2005): 81–105.

67. Yvonne Gist and Lisa Hetzel, *We the People: Aging in the United States* (Washington, DC: U.S. Census Bureau, 2004), http://www.census.gov/prod/2004pubs/censr-19.pdf.

68. John Gist, "Boomer Wealth: Beware of the Median Research Report," *AARP Public Policy Institute* (2006).

69. Erika Steinmetz, *Americans with Disabilities: 2002* (Washington, DC: U.S. Census Bureau, 2002), http://www.census.gov/prod/2006pubs/p70–107.pdf.

70. National Alliance to End Homelessness, "Fact Checker: Rural Homelessness" (Washington, DC: National Alliance to End Homelessness, 2007), http://www.endhomelessness.org/content/article/detail/1613.

71. Paul Lasley and Peter Korsching, "Examining Rural Unemployment," *Journal of Extension* 22 (1984): http://www.joe.org/joe/1984september/index.html.

72. Lorin Kusmin, *Rural Employment Turned down in 2001 as Unemployment Continued to Climb* (Washington, DC: U.S. Department of Agriculture, Economic Research Service, 2002), http://www.ers.usda.gov/publications/ruralamerica/ra171/ra171f.pdf: 40.

73. Ibid., 41.

74. Sylvie Morel et al., "Rural Dimensions of Welfare Reform," *Relations Industrielles* 58 (2003): 343–346.

75. Business and Professional People for the Public Interest, "Myths and Stereotypes about Affordable Housing," http://www.bpichicago.org/rah/pubs/myths_stereotypesNEW.pdf.

76. Richard Green, Stephen Malpezzi, and Kiat-Ying Seah, "Low-Income Housing Tax Credit Housing Developments and Property Values" (Madison: University of Wisconsin Center for Urban Land Economics, 2002).

77. George Galster, *A Review of Existing Research on the Effects of Federally Assisted Housing Programs on*

Neighboring Residential Property Values (Washington, DC: National Center for Real Estate Research, 2002), 41.

78. Ingrid Ellen and Margery Turner, "Does Neighborhood Matter?: Assessing Recent Evidence," *Housing Policy Debate* 8 (1997): 833–866.

79. Ingrid Ellen et al., "Does Federally Subsidized Rental Housing Depress Neighborhood Property Values?" Law and Economics Research paper 05–04 (New York: New York University, 2005); and Tama Leventhal and Jeanne Brooks-Gunn, "The Neighborhoods They Live In: Effects of Neighborhood Residence upon Child and Adolescent Outcomes," *Psychological Bulletin* 126 (2000): 309–337.

80. Nick Brunick, Lauren Goldberg, and Susannah Levine, "Voluntary or Mandatory Inclusionary Housing?: Production, Predictability, and Enforcement," *Business and Professional People for the Public Interest* (November 2003), http://www.bpichicago.org/rah/pubs/voluntary_vs_mandatory.pdf.; and Jack Goodman, "Houses, Apartments, and the Incidence of Property Taxes," *Housing Policy Debate* 17 (2005).

81. U.S. Census Bureau, *American Housing Survey, 2000* (Washington, DC: U.S. Census Bureau, 2006), http://www.census.gov/prod/2006pubs/h150-05.pdf.

82. Mark Obrinsky and Debra Stein, "Overcoming Opposition to Multifamily Rental Housing," National Multi Housing Council White Papers, Washington, DC, January 2007, http://www.nmhc.org/Content/ServeFile.cfm?FileID=5717, 4.

83. Ibid., 5.

84. Ibid., 9.

85. Ibid.

86. Bruce Webster and Alemayehu Bishaw, *Income, Earnings, and Poverty Data from the 2006 American Community Survey* (Washington, DC: U.S. Census Bureau, 2007), http://www.census.gov/prod/2007pubs/acs-08.pdf.

87. Phoebe Liebig, Teresa Koenig, and Jon Pynoos, "Zoning, Accessory Dwelling Units, and Family Caregiving: Issues, Trends, and Recommendations," *Journal on Aging and Social Policy* 18 (2006): 155–172; and Patricia B. Pollak, "Rethinking Zoning to Accommodate the Elderly in Single Family Housing," *Journal of the American Planning Association* 60 (1994): 521–531.

88. City of Fayetteville Planning Division, "Accessory Dwelling Unit (ADU)," http://www.accessfayetteville.org/government/neighborhood_resources/documents/Information_and_Resources/ADU_Info_Flyer.pdf.

89. Nicholas Brunick, "The Inclusionary Housing Debate: The Effectiveness of Mandatory Programs Over Voluntary Programs," *Zoning Practice* 9 (2004): 2–7.

90. Ibid., 6.

91. Ibid., 4.

92. David Rusk, "Nine Lessons for Inclusionary Zoning," National Inclusionary Housing Conference, Washington, DC, 2005, http://www.gamaliel.org/DavidRusk/keynote%2010-5-05.pdf.

93. Cobb, *Redefining Southern Culture,* 154, quoting Eric Hobsbawm, "Introduction: Inventing Traditions," in *The Invention of Tradition,* ed. Eric Hobsbawm and Terence Ranger (London: Cambridge University Press, 1983), 4.

94. Centers for Disease Control and Prevention, "Falls among Older Adults: An Overview," http://www.cdc.gov/ncipc/factsheets/adultfalls.htm.

95. Reyner Banham, "A Home Is Not a House," *Art in America* 53 (1965): 70–79.

96. See, for example: the General Electric Web site, including product descriptions that offer universal design features, at http://www.geappliances.com/design_center/universal_design/.

97. Gans, *The Levittowners,* 165.

5. Redefining Disability

1. Joseph Shapiro, *No Pity: People with Disabilities Forging a New Civil Rights Movement* (New York: Times Books, 1994), 45.

2. Michael Phelps gold-medal winning attributes have been cataloged by many sportswriters. For example, see Paul McMullen, "Measure of a Swimmer," *Baltimore Sun,* http://www.baltimoresun.com/sports/olympics/bal-sp.phelps09mar09,0,7665681.story. For a summary of environmental factors influencing race times, see Barry Svrluga, "China Joins Fun As Swimmer Liu Sets World Record," *Washington Post,* http://www.washingtonpost.com/wp-dyn/content/article/2008/08/13/AR2008081304180.html (accessed August 14, 2008). Oscar Pistorius's characteristics and successes have also been well documented. For example, see David Epstein, "Pistorius' victory is Inspirational—and Controversial," *Sports Illustrated Online,* May 17, 2008, http://sportsillustrated.cnn.com/2008/writers/david_epstein/05/16/Pistorius/index.html.

3. In his novels set in the Deep South, Eugene Walter uses climate to frame the passions and proclivities of native Southerners. The weather has a tactile presence that evokes memories and beckons the characters home. Eugene Walter, *The Untidy Pilgrim* (Philadelphia: Lippincott, 1954), 135.

4. Rogers Brubaker and Frederick Cooper, "Beyond 'Identity,'" *Theory and Society* 20 (February 2000): 33.

5. U.S. Census Bureau, *Population Division: Racial and Ethnic Classifications Used in Census 2000 and Beyond,* April 10, 2008, http://www.census.gov/population/www/socdemo/race/racefactcb.html.

6. Mary Jordan, "Tiny Irish Village Is Latest Place to Claim Obama as Its Own," *Washington Post,* Sunday, May 13, 2007, A14.

7. Sarah Lidgus, "Custom Jeans for Every Butt," *Salon Magazine,* March 5, 2003, http://dir.salon.com/story/tech/feature/2003/03/05/levis/index.html, and Susan Reda, "The Quest for Levi's," *Stores* 88 (January 2006): 10.

8. The concept of person-environment fit was developed with regard to people and their occupations and vocations. See Robert Caplan, Sidney Cobb, John French, R. Van Harrison, and Samuel Pinneau, *Job Demands and Worker Health* (Cincinnati, OH: National Institute for Occupational Safety and Health, 1975), Publication No. 75–168. The term has since been applied to environments of all types (e.g., physiological, social) and scales (e.g., tools, homes, communities). The relationship has remained concise in the reciprocity between human attributes and environmental characteristics/resources.

9. The concept of environmental press suggests that environmental stimuli will result in change. When environmental demands fall within an individual's functional capacity, the person is able to control, with a degree of facility, his or her actions within the environment. There is a positive relationship between functional capacity and command of actions. This is a positive fit and little or no adaptation is required. Conversely, environmental demands that fall outside of an individual's functionality results not only in decreased performance but also in decreased self-efficacy and reduced activity. Individuals must, at that point, either adapt his/her behavior or change his/her environment. Behavioral change, such as avoidance of particular places or activities, exemplifies a maladaptive outcome of poor person-environment fit. Learned helplessness also undermines expectations that the environment can or will meet the needs of the individual and effort to facilitate change may cease. The original theory was introduced in M. Powell Lawton and Lucille Nahemow, "Ecology and the Aging Process," in *Psychology of Adult Development and Aging,* ed. Carl Eisdorfer and M. Powell Lawton (Washington, DC: American Psychological Association, 1973), 619–674.

10. World Health Organization, *International Classification of Functioning, Disability and Health: IQ* (Geneva, Switzerland: World Health Organization,

2001); and World Health Organization, *International Classification of Impairments, Disabilities, and Handicaps: A Manual of Classification Relating to the Consequences of Disease* (Geneva, Switzerland: World Health Organization, 1980).

11. Irwin Altman and Martin Chemers, "Chapter 1: Introduction," in *Culture and Environment* (CUP Archive, 1984), 8–11.

12. Adaptation level theory was originally introduced by Harry Helson and addresses the range of stimuli, context, and subjectivity. Harry Helson, "Adaptation-Level as a Frame of Reference for Prediction of Psychophysical Data," *American Journal of Psychology* 60 (1947): 1–29.

13. *Diabetes: Fast Facts. Healthy Arkansas: For a Better State of Health.* http://www.arkansas.gov/ha/materials/brochure_diabetes.html. Retrieved December 5, 2008.

14. Lawton and Nahemow, "Ecology and the Aging Process," 619–674.

15. Altman and Chemers, *Culture and Environment,* 10.

16. Ibid., 11.

17. Bio-Ecological Systems Theory describes the interrelationship between micro-, meso-, exo-, and macro-systems. The micro-system resides primarily in the biological, physical, and cognitive make-up of the individual. The meso-, exo-, and macro-systems are used to describe the immediate and larger-scale social contexts of the individual: family, community, world, etc. For a complete discussion of this topic, see Urie Bronfenbrenner, *Making Human Beings Human: Bioecological Perspectives on Human Development* (Thousand Oaks, CA: Sage Publications, 2005).

18. The major innovation the ICF model brought to the international forefront was a classification schema that made it possible to identify environmental factors that act as barriers or facilitate an individual's activities and participation. Although the ICF model was not created to specifically address the implications of design, it can be very useful in providing a common unified lexicon that can further facilitate conceptual communication across a broad range of disciplines and agendas. The primary utility of ICF model for designers may be in its clarification of the relationship between environmental factors, personal factors, and outcomes; i.e., functionality, activities, and participation. The limitations of the ICF model lie in its macro-level orientation. Created for use at the national and international level, the ICF model addresses barriers faced by people with disabilities as populations and has delineated the critical factor of participation by all populations. World Health

Organization, *International Classification of Functioning;* and World Health Organization, *International Classification of Impairments.*

19. Shapiro, *No Pity,* 45.

20. Ann Rae, "What's in a Name?," *International Rehabilitation Review* (1989), Available at the University of Leeds Centre for Disability Studies Research Archive, http://www.leeds.ac.uk/disabilitystudies/archiveuk/Rae/Whatsname.pdf.

21. The theory of Environmental Affordances was developed by the perceptual psychologist James Gibson. Gibson defined "affordances" as what the environment "offers the animal, what it provides or furnishes, either for good or ill." An affordance is a feature of the environment that fulfills a need of the human interacting with the environment and has some significance to human behavior. One key point in the discussion of affordance is that the human must have a need in order for the affordance to be perceived. It is presumable that as effectual functioning decreases (as a result of reduced function of the physical environment, the physical body, or some combination thereof), awareness of the disjunction in the P-E relationship would increase. See James Gibson, "The Theory of Affordances," in *Perceiving, Acting, Knowing: Toward an Ecological Psychology,* ed. Robert Shaw and John Bransford (Hillsdale, NJ: Lawrence Earlbaum Associates, 1977), 174.

6. Redefining Home

1. Andrew Clause, "Eleanor Smith Looks to Affect Concrete Change," interview with Eleanor Smith, Goshen College Alumni Magazine, June 2002, http://www.goshen.edu/news/bulletin/02june/eleanor_smith.php.

2. Rob Imrie, "Disability, Embodiment and the Meaning of the Home," *Housing Studies* 19 (2004): 746.

3. William Mann is among the foremost scholars on the benefits of assistive technology in housing. See William Mann, "The Potential of Technology to Ease the Care Provider's Burden," *Generations* 25 (2001): 44; William Mann, "Proceedings: Technologies for Successful Aging: Assistive Technology for an Aging Population: Factors of Success," *Journal of Rehabilitation Research and Development* 38 (2001): S62; William Mann, "Common Telecommunications Technology for Promoting Safety, Independence, and Social Interaction for Older People with Disabilities," *Generations* 21 (Fall 1997): 28; and William Mann et al., "Effectiveness of Assistive Technology and Environmental Interventions in Maintaining Independence and Reducing Home Care

Costs for the Frail Elderly: A Randomized Controlled Trial," *Archives of Family Medicine* 8 (1999): 210.

4. See, for example, Michael Dear and Jennifer Wolch, *Landscapes of Despair: From Deinstitutionalization to Homelessness* (Princeton, NJ: Princeton University Press, 1987).

5. Substantive work has been published on gender discrimination in design (especially in architecture). These works include, but are not limited to, Diana Agrest, "Architecture from Without: Body, Logic, and Sex," in Kate Nesbitt (ed.), *Theorizing a New Agenda for Architecture: An Anthology of Architectural Theory 1965–1995* (New York: Princeton Architectural Press, 1996), 542–553; Kathryn Anthony, *Designing for Diversity: Gender, Race, and Ethnicity in the Architectural Profession* (Urbana: University of Illinois Press, 2001); Dolores Hayden, *The Grand Domestic Revolution: A History of Feminist Designs for American Homes, Neighborhoods, and Cities* (Cambridge, MA: MIT Press, 1981); Dolores Hayden, *Redesigning the American Dream: Gender, Housing, and Family Life* (New York: W. W. Norton & Co., 1984); Lance Hosey, "Hidden Lines: Gender, Race, and the Body in Graphic Standards," *Journal of Architectural Education* 55 (2001): 101–112; Joan Rothschild (ed.), *Design and Feminism: Re-Visioning Spaces, Places, and Everyday Things* (New Brunswick, NJ: Rutgers University Press, 1999); and Leslie Weisman, *Discrimination by Design* (Chicago: University of Illinois, 1992).

6. Steven Mintz, for example, states that throughout American history children have been the most marginalized, repressed, and exploited demographic group. Steven Mintz, *Huck's Raft: A History of American Childhood* (Cambridge: Belknap Press, 2004).

7. HUD has released several publications related to universal design, for example: *Homes for Everyone: Universal Design Principles in Practice,* published in April 1996, http://www.huduser.org/publications/destech/unidesig.html. States such as Kentucky and Arkansas have also incorporated UD ideals into their housing policies. For information on Kentucky, see the Kentucky Housing Corporation, "Commonwealth of Kentucky 2006 Action Plan," at http://www.kyhousing.org/uploadedfiles/Publications/Consolidated_Plan/2006FinalActionPlan.pdf. For information on Arkansas, see the Arkansas Development Finance Authority "programs" Web page at http://www.state.ar.us/adfa/listing.html.

8. Edward Steinfeld, "Barrier-free Design Begins to React to Legislation, Research," *Architectural Record* 165 (1979): 69–71; Edward Steinfeld, "Designing Adaptable Housing to Meet Barrier-free Goals," *Architectural Record*

167 (1980): 57–65; Edward Steinfeld, "Designing Entrances and Internal Circulation to Meet Barrier-free Goals," *Architectural Record* 166 (1979): 65–67; and Edward Steinfeld, "Designing the Site to Meet Barrier-free Goals," *Architectural Record* 165 (1979): 69–71.

9. Ronald Mace, "Universal Design: Barrier Free Environments for Everyone," *Designers West* (November 1985): 147.

10. Michael Bednar, *Barrier-Free Environments* (Stroudsburg, PA: Dowden, Hutchinson, & Ross, 1977).

11. American Society of Landscape Architects Foundation, *Barrier-Free Site Design* (Washington, DC: U.S. Department of Housing and Urban Development, Office of Policy Development and Research, 1975).

12. Eastern Paralyzed Veterans Association, *Barrier-Free Design: The Law* (New York: EPVA, 1976).

13. U.S. Senate Special Committee on Aging, *A Barrier-Free Environment for the Elderly and the Handicapped:* Hearings, 92nd Cong., 1st sess., October 18–19, 1972.

14. Barbara Knecht, "Accessibility Regulations and a Universal Design Philosophy Inspire the Design Process," *Architectural Record* 192 (2004): 145–150; and Michael Sorkin, "Limping Our Way to Universal Design: Everything Looks Different on Crutches," *Architectural Record* 192 (2004): 85–86.

15. See, for example: John Clarkson, Roger Coleman, Simeon Keates, and Cherie Lebbon (eds.), *Inclusive Design: Design for the Whole Population* (New York: Springer, 2003); George Covington and Bruce Hannah, *Access by Design* (New York: John Wiley and Sons, 1997); G. Scott Danford and Beth Tauke, *Universal Design New York* (New York: City of New York, Office of the Mayor, 2001); Selwyn Goldsmith, *Universal Design: A Manual of Practical Guidance for Architects* (Oxford: Architectural Press, 2000); Rob Imrie and Peter Hall, *Inclusive Design: Designing and Developing Accessible Environments* (New York: Spon Press, 2001); Cynthia Leibrock and James Terry, *Beautiful Universal Design: A Visual Guide* (New York: John Wiley and Sons, 1999); Wolfgang Preiser and Elaine Ostroff (eds.), *Universal Design Handbook* (New York: McGraw-Hill, 2001); and Polly Welch (ed.), *Strategies for Teaching Universal Design* (Boston: Adaptive Environments Center, 1995).

16. See, for example: *Access by Design,* published by the Centre for Accessible Environments, London, UK; *Disability and Rehabilitation,* published by Taylor & Francis, Oxfordshire, UK; *Form and Funktion,* published by the Nordic Cooperation on Disability, Copenhagen, Denmark; and *Ultimate Home Design,* published by Ultimate Home Design, Inc., Temecula, California.

17. Susanne Iwarsson is among the leading international scholars in this area. See, for example: Susanne Iwarsson, "The Housing Enabler: An Objective Tool for Assessing Accessibility," *British Journal of Occupational Therapy* 62 (1999): 491–497; Susanne Iwarsson and Å Isacsson, "Basic Accessibility in Modern Housing: A Key to the Problems of Care in the Domestic Setting," *Scandinavian Journal of Caring Sciences* 7 (1993): 155–159; Susanne Iwarsson and A. Stahl, "Accessibility, Usability and Universal Design: Positioning and Definition of Concepts Describing Person-Environment Relationships," *Disability & Rehabilitation* 25 (2003): 57; Agneta Fänge and Susanne Iwarsson, "Accessibility and Usability in Housing: Construct Validity and Implications for Research and Practice," *Disability & Rehabilitation* 25 (2003): 1316–1325; and Agneta Fänge and Susanne Iwarsson, "Changes in Accessibility and Usability in Housing: An Exploration of the Housing Adaptation Process," *Occupational Therapy International* 12 (2005): 44–59.

18. The UDiD project was sponsored by the National Endowment for the Arts as part of their initiative to expand the public's awareness of universal design. The project ran 2004–2006 and was headed by the Inclusive Design and Environmental Access Center at the University at Buffalo: Beth Tauke and Alex Bitterman were co-PIs for the project.

19. Doris Fleischer and Frieda Zames, *The Disability Rights Movement: From Charity to Confrontation* (Philadelphia: Temple University Press, 2001), 149–150.

20. National Association of Home Builders, "Builder and Remodeler Online Designation Directory," http://www.nahb.org/directory_list.aspx?sectionID=686&directoryID=186&2876=AR&2883=954&proximityLimit=50.

21. International Code Council, Inc., *International Building Code* (Country Club Hills, IL: International Code Council, 2003).

22. International Code Council, Inc., *International Residential Code for One- and Two-Family Dwellings* (Country Club Hills, IL: International Code Council, 2003).

23. Edward Steinfeld, James Lenker, and Victor Paquet, "Anthropometry of Wheeled Mobility," http://www.ap.buffalo.edu/idea/Anthro/index.asp.

24. Karsten Harries, "The Dream of the Complete Building," *Perspecta: The Yale Architectural Journal* 17 (1980): 36–43.

25. Dolores Hayden, *Redesigning the American Dream: Gender, Housing, and Family Life* (New York: W. W. Norton & Co., 1984), 55.

26. Wouter Vanstiphout, "Rockbottom: Maison Bordeaux," *Harvard Design Magazine* (Summer 1998): 66–70.

27. Quotations by Frank Deford and by Charles Wilson, as found in Charles Wilson, "Cult of Beauty," *Encyclopedia of Southern Culture* (Chapel Hill: University of North Carolina Press, 1989), 600.

28. Michael Sorkin, "Limping Our Way to Universal Design: Everything Looks Different on Crutches," *Architectural Record* 192 (2004): 85–86.

29. Lennard Davis, *Enforcing Normalcy: Disability, Deafness, and the Body* (New York: Verso, 1995), 11.

30. See, for example: Lennard Davis, *Bending over Backwards: Disability, Dismodernism, and Other Difficult Positions* (New York: New York University Press, 2002); Rob Imrie, "Disability and Discourses of Mobility and Movement," *Environment and Planning A* 32 (2000): 1641–1656; and Elaine Ostroff, "Universal Design: The New Paradigm," in *Universal Design Handbook,* ed. Wolfgang Preiser and Elaine Ostroff (New York: McGraw-Hill, 2001), 1.2–1.12.

31. See note 17.

32. See note 15.

33. Katherine Ott, "The Sum of Its Parts: An Introduction to Modern Histories of Prosthetics," in *Artificial Parts, Practical Lives: Modern Histories of Prosthetics,* ed. Katherine Ott, David Serlin, and Stephen Mihm (New York: New York University Press, 2002), 1–42.

34. David Serlin, *Replaceable You: Engineering the Body in Postwar America* (Chicago: University of Chicago Press, 2004).

35. For information on the Maison Bordeaux, see Colin Davies, "Machine for Living," *Architecture* 87 (1998): 72–83; "Bordeaux House: Bordeaux, France 1994–1998," *Architecture and Urbanism* 342 (1999): 10–29; Rem Koolhaas, "A One Family Home at Floirac, Bordeaux, France," *Domus* 811 (1999): 46–62; Rem Koolhaas, "Bordeaux House, Bordeaux, France 1994," *Architecture and Urbansim* 314 (November 1996): 124–130; Victoria Newhouse, "Rem Koolhaas in Bordeaux: A Radical Residence in the French Countryside Challenges Ideas about What a House Can Be," *Architectural Digest* 55 (1998): 170–179, 254; and "Rem Koolhaas: Maison a Bordeaux, Bordeaux, France," *GA Houses* 57 (1998): 54–75.

36. Colin Davies, "Machine for Living," *Architecture* 87 (1998): 72–83.

37. Jos Boys, "Windows on the World?: Architecture, Identities and New Technologies," in *Digital Desires: Language, Identities, and New Technologies,* ed. Cutting Edge, the Women's Research Group (London: I. B. Tauris, 2000), 125–126.

38. Philip Tabor, "Striking Home: The Telematic Assault on Identity," in *Occupying Architecture: Between the Architect and the User,* ed. Jonathan Hill (London: Routledge, 1998), 217–228.

39. James Cobb, *Redefining Southern Culture: Mind and Identity in the Modern South* (Athens: University of Georgia Press, 1999), 200.

40. Christine Oldman and Bryony Beresford, "Home, Sick Home: Using the Housing Experiences of Disabled Children to Suggest a New Theoretical Framework," *Housing Studies* 15, no. 3 (2000): 429–442.

41. Adolf Loos, "Ornament and Crime," in *Ornament and Crime: Selected Essays* (Riverside, CA: Ariadne, 1998), 167. First published in 1908.

42. Beatriz Colomina, "The Medical Body in Modern Architecture," in *Anybody,* ed. Cynthia Davidson (Cambridge, MA: MIT Press, 1997), 228–239; and Adrian Forty, "Hygiene and Cleanliness," in *Objects of Desire: Design and Society since 1750* (London: Thames & Hudson, 1986), 156–181.

43. Colomina, "The Medical Body," 230.

44. Forty, "Hygiene and Cleanliness," 160.

45. From data collected as part of the *Arkansas Health and Housing Survey, 2006: Summary Report,* authored by Korydon Smith, Jennifer Webb, Nancy Miller, and Brent Williams (2007), www.studioaid.org, data collected by the University of Arkansas Survey Research Center in May 2006.

46. G. Tonello, "Seasonal Affective Disorder: Lighting Research and Environmental Psychology," *Lighting Research Technology* 40 (2008): 103–110.

47. Johnny Cash, *Cash: The Autobiography* (New York: HarperCollins, 1997), 47–48.

48. Ibid., 149–150.

49. Clare Cooper Marcus, *House as a Mirror of Self: Exploring the Deeper Meaning of Home* (Berkeley, CA: Conari Press, 1995).

50. Imrie, "Disability and Discourses," 1652.

51. Cash, *Cash,* 95–98.

52. *Historical Tables: Budget of the United States Government, Fiscal Year 2009* (Washington, DC: U.S. Government Printing Office, 2008), http://www.whitehouse.gov/omb/budget/fy2009/pdf/hist.pdf.

53. Steve Gold, "Progress since Olmstead: How is Your State Doing?" *Information Bulletin* #231, Topeka Independent Living Resource Center, December 2007, http://www.tilrc.org/assests/news/1207comm10.html.

7. Redefining Equality

1. Tony Dunbar, *Our Land Too* (New York: Random House, 1971), xvi.

2. Robert Coles, "Introduction," in *Our Land Too,* by Tony Dunbar (New York: Random House, 1971), x.

3. U.S. Census Bureau, American Fact Finder, http://factfinder.census.gov/servlet/SAFFFacts?_event=Search&geo_id=04000US05&_geoContext=01000US%7C04000US05&_street=&_county=newton&_cityTown=newton&_state=04000US05&_zip=&_lang=en&_sse=on&ActiveGeoDiv=geoSelect&_useEV=&pctxt=fph&pgsl=040&_submenuId=factsheet_1&ds_name=ACS_2005_SAFF&_ci_nbr=null&qr_name=null&reg=null%3Anull&_keyword=&_industry=&show_2003_tab=&redirect=Y.

4. U.S. Census Bureau, American Fact Finder, http://factfinder.census.gov/servlet/SAFFFacts?_event=ChangeGeoContext&geo_id=05000US05129&_geoContext=01000US%7C04000US05%7C05000US05101&_street=&_county=searcy&_cityTown=searcy&_state=04000US05&_zip=&_lang=en&_sse=on&ActiveGeoDiv=geoSelect&_useEV=&pctxt=fph&pgsl=010&_submenuId=factsheet_1&ds_name=DEC_2000_SAFF&_ci_nbr=null&qr_name=null&reg=null%3Anull&_keyword=&_industry=.

5. Johnny Cash, *Cash: The Autobiography* (New York: HarperCollins, 1997), 193.

6. John Reed, *The Enduring South: Subcultural Persistence in Mass Society* (Lexington, MA: D. C. Heath & Co., 1972), 43.

7. The *Limited Edition House* (*LE House*) is a licensed product of Superbia, LLC, Fayetteville, Arkansas, Darell W. Fields, Chief Technology Design Officer. The text and images of this section of chapter 7 were provided by Darell W. Fields.

8. See, for example: Reed, *The Enduring South;* John Reed, *One South: An Ethnic Approach to Regional Culture* (Baton Rouge: Louisiana State University Press, 1982); John Reed, *Southerners: The Social Psychology of Sectionalism* (Chapel Hill: University of North Carolina Press, 1983); and John Reed, *Surveying the South: Studies in Regional Sociology* (Columbia: University of Missouri Press, 1993).

9. See the previous note.

10. As quoted from the William Faulkner scholar and English professor Fred Hobson, at USADeepSouth.com, Winter 2005, http://usadeepsouth.ms11.net/winter05.html.

8. Redefining Quality and Practice

1. Allan Osborne Jr. and Charles Russo, *Essential Concepts and School-Based Cases in Special Educational Law* (Thousand Oaks, CA: Sage Publications, 2007), 320.

2. Johnny Cash, *Cash: The Autobiography* (New York: HarperCollins, 1997), 86.

3. Charles Lamb, *Housing Segregation in Suburban America since 1960: Presidential and Judicial Politics* (Cambridge: Cambridge University Press, 2005).

4. Kathryn Lawler, *Aging in Place: Coordinating Housing and Health Care Provisions for America's Growing Elderly Population* (Cambridge, MA: Joint Center for Housing Studies of Harvard University, Neighborhood Reinvestment Corporation, 2001), 18.

5. Lamb, *Housing Segregation.*

6. Anne Shlay, "Low-income Homeownership: American Dream or Delusion?" *Urban Studies* 43 (2006): 511–531.

7. Cushing Dolbeare and Sheila Crowley, *Changing Priorities: The Federal Budget and Housing Assistance 1976–2007* (Washington, DC: National Low Income Housing Coalition, 2002), http://www.knowledgeplex.org/kp/report/report/relfiles/nlihc_changing_priorities.pdf (accessed January 5, 2009).

8. Harvard University, Joint Center for Housing Studies, "The State of the Nation's Housing," http://www.jchs.harvard.edu/publications/markets/son2006/son2006_housing_challenges.pdf (accessed January 5, 2009).

9. Cushing Dolbeare, "Shifting Fortunes: Trends in Housing Policy and Programs," *Shelterforce Online* 110 (2000), http://www.nhi.org/online/issues/110/dolbeare.html (accessed January 5, 2009).

10. Jonathan Buttrick et al., "Priced Out in 2006: The Housing Crisis for People with Disabilities," Technical Assistance Collaborative, http://www.tacinc.org/Docs/HH/PricedOutIn2006.pdf (accessed January 5, 2009).

11. Alvin Schorr, *Slums and Social Insecurity: An Appraisal of the Effectiveness of Housing Policies in Helping to Eliminate Poverty in the United States* (Washington, DC: U.S. Department of Health, Education, and Welfare, Social Security Administration, Division of Research and Statistics, 1963).

12. Suzanne M. Robbins and Holly R. Barcus, "Welfare Reform and Economic and Housing Capacity for Low-Income Households, 1997–1999," *Policy Studies Journal* 32 (2004): 439–460.

13. Shlay, "Low-Income Homeownership," 511–531.

14. Dolbeare, "Shifting Fortunes."

15. Charles Connerly, "Fair Housing in the US and the UK," *Housing Studies* 21 (2006): 343–360.

16. Buttrick et al., "Priced Out in 2006."

17. Robert Bennefield and Robert Bonnette, *Structural and Occupancy Characteristics of Housing, 2000: Census 2000 Brief* (Washington, DC: U.S. Census Bureau, 2003), http://www.census.gov/prod/2003pubs/c2kbr-32.pdf (accessed January 5, 2009).

18. Cash, *Cash,* 129.

19. Robbins and Barcus, "Welfare Reform," 439–460.

20. Ibid.

21. National Alliance to End Homelessness, *Homelessness Counts* (Washington, DC: National Alliance to End Homelessness, 2007), http://www.endhomeless ness.org/content/article/detail/1440 (accessed January 5, 2009).

22. Well over 90 percent of Arkansans believe they will maintain their independence as they age, though 81 percent also believe their health will decline. Less than half of Arkansans, however, believe that the design of their neighborhood will impact their ability to live independently. This is from data collected by the University of Arkansas Survey Research Center in May 2006 as part of the *Arkansas Health and Housing Survey, 2006: Summary Report,* authored by Korydon Smith, Jennifer Webb, Nancy Miller, and Brent Williams (Little Rock: Arkansas Department of Health and Human Services and Arkansas Rehabilitation Services, 2007), available at www.studioaid.org.

23. Suzanne Belser and Joseph Weber, "Homebuilders' Attitudes and Knowledge of Aging: The Relationship to Design for Independent Living," *Journal of Housing for the Elderly* 11 (1995): 123–137.

24. Rob Imrie, "Housing Quality and the Provision of Accessible Homes," *Housing Studies* 18 (2003): 387–409.

25. Ibid.

26. Chris Allen, "Disablism in Housing and Comparative Community Care Discourse: Towards an Interventionist Model of Disability and Interventionist Welfare Regime Theory," *Housing, Theory and Society* 16 (1999): 3–16.

27. *Olmstead v. L. C.* (98–536) 527 U.S. 581 (1999).

28. Suzanne Crisp et al., "Money Follows the Person and Balancing Long-Term Care Systems: State Examples Medstat," Research Report (Centers for Medicare and Medicaid Services, 2003), http://www.hcbs.org/files/39/1943/mfp92903.pdf (accessed January 5, 2009).

29. Roberto Quercia and George Galster, "Threshold Effects and Neighborhood Change," *Journal of Planning Education and Research* 20 (2000): 146–162.

30. John Kromer, "Special Needs Housing: The Unfinished Policy," *Journal of Housing and Community Development* 57 (2000): 13–20.

31. "Joint Comments from Homeless Advocacy Organizations on Proposed Changes in the Administrative Review Process for Adjudicating Initial Disability Claims," NPRM 05–14845 submitted to the Social Security Administration, October 21, 2005, http://www.nhchc.org/HomelessAdvocatesComments NPRM0514845.pdf (accessed January 5, 2009), 3.

32. Kromer, "Special Needs Housing," 13–20.

33. Robbins and Barcus, "Welfare Reform," 439–460.

34. Jon Pynoos and Christy Nishita, "The Cost and Financing of Home Modifications in the United States," *Journal of Disability Policy Studies* 14 (2003): 69–73.

Conclusion: Drawing the Line

1. U.S. Census Bureau, *State and County Quick Facts,* http://quickfacts.census.gov/qfd/states/05000.html.

2. U.S. Census Bureau, "Census 2000 Summary File 3, Matrices H1 and H34," http://factfinder.census.gov/servlet/ IdentifyResultServlet?_mapX=338&_mapY=297&_latitude=&_longitude=&_pageX=505&_pageY=645&_dBy=380&_jsessionId=0001ShWWlblEs OM8cUl913zC0wB:10e3887qk.

3. James Cobb, *Redefining Southern Culture: Mind and Identity in the Modern South* (Athens: University of Georgia Press, 1999), 196.

4. Ibid., 211.

5. Ronald Mace, "Universal Design: Barrier Free Environments for Everyone," *Designers West* (November 1985): 147.

6. See, for example: Michael Bednar, *Barrier-Free Environments* (Stroudsburg, PA: Dowden, Hutchinson, & Ross, 1977); Edward Steinfeld, "Barrier-free Design Begins to React to Legislation, Research," *Architectural Record* 165 (1979): 69–71; Edward Steinfeld, "Designing Adaptable Housing to Meet Barrier-free Goals," *Architectural Record* 167 (1980): 57–65; Edward Steinfeld, "Designing Entrances and Internal Circulation to Meet Barrier-free Goals," *Architectural Record* 166 (1979): 65–67; and Edward Steinfeld, "Designing the Site to Meet Barrier-free Goals," *Architectural Record* 165 (1979): 69–71.

7. Rob Imrie, "Disability and Discourses of Mobility and Movement," *Environment and Planning A* 32 (2000): 1652.

8. Suzanne Belser and Joseph Weber, "Homebuilders' Attitudes and Knowledge of Aging: The Relationship to Design for Independent Living," *Journal of Housing for the Elderly* 11 (1995): 123–137.

9. *Laura Butalla, "Highlands Ranch," Professional Builder* 17 (2006): 63.

10. Katherine Ott, "The Sum of Its Parts: An Introduction to Modern Histories of Prosthetics," in Katherine Ott, David Serlin, and Stephen Mihm (eds.), *Artificial Parts, Practical Lives: Modern Histories of Prosthetics* (New York: New York University Press, 2002), 5.

11. Ibid.; and Carl Elliot, *Better than Well: American Medicine Meets the American Dream* (New York: W. W. Norton, 2003).

12. National Center for Health Statistics, *Health, United States, 2006: With Chartbook on Trends in the Health of Americans* (Hyattsville, MD: U.S. Department of Health and Human Services, 2006).

13. Karsten Harries, "The Dream of the Complete Building," *Perspecta* 17 (1980): 36–43.

14. William Mann, "The Potential of Technology to Ease the Care Provider's Burden," *Generations* 25 (2001): 44; William Mann, "Proceedings: Technologies for Successful Aging: Assistive Technology for an Aging Population: Factors of Success," *Journal of Rehabilitation Research and Development* 38 (2001): S62; William Mann, "Common Telecommunications Technology for Promoting Safety, Independence, and Social Interaction for Older People with Disabilities," *Generations* 21 (Fall 1997): 28; and William Mann et al., "Effectiveness of Assistive Technology and Environmental Interventions in Maintaining Independence and Reducing Home Care Costs for the Frail Elderly: A Randomized Controlled Trial," *Archives of Family Medicine* 8 (1999): 210.

15. Adolf Ratzka, "A Brief Survey on Costs and Benefits of Non-handicapping Environments," *Independent Living Institute* (1994), http://www.independentliving.org/cib/cibrio94access.html.

16. Steven Winter Associates, *Cost of Accessible Housing: An Analysis of the Estimated Cost of Compliance with the Fair Housing Accessibility Guidelines and ANSI A117.1* (Washington, DC: U.S. Department of Housing and Urban Development, 1993).

GLOSSARY

accessibility. (1) Generic: the level of convenience or ease in entering, approaching, or moving through or toward a space or object. (2) Specific: the level of convenience or ease of design features that accommodate persons with disabilities, especially regarding users of wheeled mobility devices. Related to **usability; barrier-free design; enabler concept; inclusive design; universal design.**

> See **barrier-free design.**

activity. The execution of a task or action by an individual.

> World Health Organization, *International Classification of Functioning, Disability and Health: IQ* (Geneva, Switzerland: World Health Organization, 2001).

activity limitations. Difficulties an individual may have in executing activities.

> World Health Organization, *International Classification of Functioning, Disability and Health: IQ* (Geneva, Switzerland: World Health Organization, 2001).

adaptation. A change in a human behavior that accommodates an environmental demand.

> Harry Helson, *Adaptation-Level Theory* (New York: Harper & Row, 1964).

adjustment. A human changes the physical environment to better suit his or her physical and psychosocial needs.

> See **adaptation.**

barrier-free design. An early phase of the enabler movement and universal design, focusing on the removal of physical obstacles (barriers) that impeded accessibility. Related to **accessibility; enabler concept; inclusive design; universal design.**

> Michael Bednar, *Barrier-Free Environments* (Stroudsburg, PA: Dowden, Hutchinson, & Ross, 1977); Edward Steinfeld, "Barrier-free Design Begins to React to Legislation, Research," *Architectural Record* 165, no. 3 (1979): 69–71; Edward Steinfeld, "Designing Adaptable Housing to Meet Barrier-free Goals," *Architectural Record* 167, no. 3 (1980): 57–65; Edward Steinfeld, "Designing Entrances and Internal Circulation to Meet Barrier-free Goals," *Architectural Record* 166, no. 7 (1979): 65–67; and Edward Steinfeld, "Designing the Site to Meet Barrier-free Goals," *Architectural Record* 165, no. 5 (1979): 69–71; American Society of Landscape Architects Foundation, *Barrier-Free Site Design* (Washington, DC: U.S. Department of Housing and Urban Development, Office of Policy Development and Research, 1975); Eastern Paralyzed Veterans Association, *Barrier-Free Design: The Law* (New York: EPVA, 1976); U.S. Senate Special Committee on Aging, *A Barrier-Free Environment for the Elderly and the Handicapped:* Hearings, 92nd Cong., 1st sess., October 18–19, 1972.

body functions. The physiological functions of body systems (including psychological functions).

> World Health Organization, *International Classification of Functioning, Disability and Health: IQ* (Geneva, Switzerland: World Health Organization, 2001).

body structures. Anatomical parts of the body such as organs, limbs, and their components.

> World Health Organization, *International Classification of Functioning, Disability and Health, IQ* (Geneva, Switzerland: World Health Organization, 2001).

designer. Person or persons responsible for the design and planning of a built structure; credentials and responsibilities vary by state. Related to **architect; interior designer; contractor; builder.**

disability. (1) Any restriction or lack (resulting from impairment) of ability to perform an activity in the manner within the range considered normal for a human being. (2) An umbrella term for impairments, activity limitations, or participation restrictions. Related to **impairments; activity limitations; participation restrictions.**

World Health Organization, *International Classification of Functioning, Disability and Health, IQ* (Geneva, Switzerland: World Health Organization, 2001).

enabler concept. An architectural, industrial, media, and urban design movement evolved from barrier-free design; views disability as an environmental rather than physiological issue; focuses on how the design of the environment can facilitate ("enable") independence for persons with disabling conditions. Related to **accessibility; barrier-free design; inclusive design; universal design.**

> Susanne Iwarsson, "The Housing Enabler: An Objective Tool for Assessing Accessibility," *British Journal of Occupational Therapy* 62, no. 11 (1999): 491–497; Susanne Iwarsson and Å Isacsson, "Basic Accessibility in Modern Housing: A Key to the Problems of Care in the Domestic Setting," *Scandinavian Journal of Caring Sciences* 7, no. 3 (1993): 155–159; Susanne Iwarsson and A. Stahl, "Accessibility, Usability and Universal Design: Positioning and Definition of Concepts Describing Person-Environment Relationships," *Disability & Rehabilitation* 25, no. 2 (2003): 57; Agneta Fänge and Susanne Iwarsson, "Accessibility and Usability in Housing: Construct Validity and Implications for Research and Practice," *Disability & Rehabilitation* 25, no. 23 (2003): 1316–1325; and Agneta Fänge and Susanne Iwarsson, "Changes in Accessibility and Usability in Housing: An Exploration of the Housing Adaptation Process," *Occupational Therapy International* 12, no. 1 (2005): 44–59.

environmental affordance. A quality or attribute of an environment that is perceived when that quality or attribute is needed by the individual; i.e., a chair/log/ledge is perceived as a place to rest when the individual is tired.

> James J. Gibson, "The Theory of Affordances," in *Perceiving, Acting, Knowing: Toward an Ecological Psychology,* ed. Robert Shaw and John Bransford (Hillsdale, NJ: Lawrence Earlbaum Associates, 1977).

environmental assessment. The process by which an individual evaluates the environmental affordances in the context of his/her physical, psychological, and sociological needs.

> Stephen Kaplan, "Aesthetics, Affect, and Cognition: Environmental Preference from an Evolutionary Perspective," *Environment and Behavior* 19, no. 1 (1987): 3–32. Rachel Kaplan and Stephen Kaplan, *The Experience of Nature* (Cambridge: Cambridge University Press, 1987).

environmental preference. The qualities of an environment preferred by the individual that extends beyond simple fulfillment of need; characteristics include mystery, cohesiveness, complexity, and legibility.

> Rachel Kaplan, Stephen Kaplan, and T. Brown, "Environmental Preference: A Comparison of Four Domains of Predictors," *Environment and Behavior* 21 (1989): 509–530. D. E. Berlyne, *Aesthetics and Psychobiology* (New York: Appleton, 1971).

environmental factors. The physical, social, and attitudinal environment in which people live and conduct their lives. Related to **accessibility; barrier-free design; inclusive design; universal design.**

> World Health Organization, *International Classification of Functioning, Disability and Health, IQ* (Geneva, Switzerland: World Health Organization, 2001).

fit. The degree to which the person's needs and the environment's affordances match. Related to **person-environment fit.**

> Kurt Lewin, *Field Theory in Social Science* (New York: Harper, 1951).

green building. An architectural, industrial, and urban design movement that focuses on environmental issues such as utilizing recyclable and renewable materials, reducing energy consumption, reducing construction waste, and utilizing materials with low embodied energy; sometimes referred to as sustainability. Related to **sustainability.**

home. The physical structure in which an individual or a group lives and is imbued with the emotional investment of sense of place, household responsibilities, and personal relationships and contributes to feelings of belonging, safety, and self-expression. Related to **house.**

> Amos Rappaport, "A Critical Look at the Concept 'Home,'" in *The Home: Words, Interpretations, Meanings and Environments,* ed. David N. Benjamin and David Stea (Aldershot: Avebury, 1995), 25–52. Joseph Rykwert, "House and Home," *Social Research* 58, no. 1 (1991): 51. Robert M. Rakoff, "Ideology in

Everyday Life: The Meaning of the House," *Politics and Society* 7, no. 1 (1977): 85–104.

house. The physical structure in which an individual or a group lives and conducts daily activity that provides protection from the elements. Related to accommodation; abode; domicile; dwelling; habitation; living environment; shelter; residence.

impairments. Problems in body function or structure such as a significant deviation or loss.

> World Health Organization, *International Classification of Functioning, Disability and Health, IQ* (Geneva, Switzerland: World Health Organization, 2001).

inclusive design. (1) European: see **universal design.** (2) As used in this book: an architectural, industrial, media, and urban design movement evolved from the concept of universal design that focuses on designing for the widest range of the population possible with an increased focus on economic issues and the caveat that truly "universal" design is impossible. Related to **universal design.**

> See **universal design.**

mobility. One component of usability, which centers on how people navigate and move around, including the level at which design features assist or impede movement. Related to **accessibility.**

> See **usability.**

operability. One component of usability, which centers on how people activate and control fittings and equipments such as doors, windows, and plumbing fixtures, including the level at which design features assist or impede use.

> See **usability.**

participation. Involvement in a life situation.

> World Health Organization, *International Classification of Functioning, Disability and Health, IQ* (Geneva, Switzerland: World Health Organization, 2001).

participation restrictions. Problems an individual may experience in involvement in life situations. Related to **accessibility; barrier-free design; inclusive design; universal design.**

> World Health Organization, *International Classification of Functioning, Disability and Health, IQ* (Geneva, Switzerland: World Health Organization, 2001).

perceptibility. One component of usability, which centers on how people interact with the environment through senses such as sight, hearing, and touch, including the level at which design features assist or impede visual, auditory, or tactile interaction.

> See **usability.**

person-environment fit. The reciprocal relationship between the person and the environment where environmental constraints influence human behavior and human behavior, in turn results in change to the environment. Related to **fit.**

> Kurt Lewin, *Field Theory in Social Science* (New York: Harper, 1951).

privacy. An optimizing process that involves both the opening and closing of the self to others; privacy because it promotes personal autonomy and is a component of home.

> Irwin Altman. *The Environment and Social Behavior (*Monterey, CA: Brooks/Cole, 1975). Leon A. Pastalan, "Privacy as an Expression of Human Territoriality," Paper presented at the Colloquim of Spatial-Behavioral Relationships as Related to Older People (Ann Arbor: University of Michigan, 1968).

security. One component of usability, which centers on how the environment provides or hinders safety or protection, including the level at which design features assist or impede safety or protection.

> See **usability.**

self-actualization. The attainment of basic physical and emotional needs as well as a sense of belonging and a sense of self-esteem.

> Abraham H. Maslow, "A Preface to Motivation Theory," *Psychosomatic Medicine 5* (1943): 85–92.

self-concept. How we think about ourselves and includes beliefs, attitudes, and opinions in addition to physical and cognitive abilities.

> E. Fromm, *The Art of Loving* (New York: Harper & Row, 1956).

self-esteem. How we feel about ourselves and our estimate of our own worth.

> William James, *The Principles of Psychology* (Cambridge, MA: Harvard University Press, 1983). Original work published 1890.

shelter. The physical act of protecting from the elements or from danger; also used to refer to the basic structures created by man to protect self and others.

social role. How an individual is expected to behave in a particular social situation.

status. One's relative position to others in a social standing.

sustainability. (1) Generic: the capacity of an ideological or physical construct to subsist or level of maintenance required for such a construct to subsist (a) economically, (b) socially, and (c) environmentally. (2) Specific: see **green building.** Related to **green building.**

system. Multiple components working in tandem to achieve or produce a desired outcome.

temporarily able bodied. The concept that all persons have the potential to develop disabilities at some point in their lives, due to accidents, illness, late-emerging effects of genetics or age and that being abled bodied is thus a temporary state. Related to **healthy; nondisabled.**

> Rae, A. "What's in a Name?" *International Rehabilitation Review* 12 (1989): 32–45.

territoriality. The claiming and use of space by both humans and animals; the degree of ownership and control varies; territory provides both social mechanisms that modifies territory and psychological security for the individual. Related to personal space; proxemics.

> Irwin Altman I. *The Environment and Social Behavior* (Monterey, CA: Brooks/Cole, 1975). Edward T. Hall, "Proxemics," *Current Anthropologist* 9, no. 2–3 (1968): 83–108. Robert Sommer, *Personal Space: The Behavioral Basis of Design* (Englewood Cliffs, NJ: Prentice-Hall, 1969).

universal design (UD). An architectural, industrial, media, and urban design movement evolved from barrier-free design that focuses on designing for the widest range of the population possible. Variously referred to as "life-span design," "design-for-all," and "inclusive design." Related to **accessibility; barrier-free design; enabler concept; inclusive design.**

> Ronald Mace, "Universal Design: Barrier Free Environments for Everyone," *Designers West* (November 1985): 147; John Clarkson, Roger Coleman, Simeon Keates, and Cherie Lebbon (eds.), *Inclusive Design: Design for the Whole Population* (New York: Springer, 2003); George Covington and Bruce Hannah, *Access by Design* (New York: John Wiley and Sons, 1997); G. Scott Danford and Beth Tauke, *Universal Design New York* (New York: City of New York, Office of the Mayor, 2001); Selwyn Goldsmith, *Universal Design: A Manual of Practical Guidance for Architects* (Oxford: Architectural Press, 2000); Rob Imrie and Peter Hall, *Inclusive Design: Designing and Developing Accessible Environments* (New York: Spon Press, 2001); Cynthia Leibrock and James Terry, *Beautiful Universal Design: A Visual Guide* (New York: John Wiley and Sons, 1999); Wolfgang Preiser and Elaine Ostroff (eds.), *Universal Design Handbook* (New York: McGraw-Hill, 2001); and Polly Welch (ed.), *Strategies for Teaching Universal Design* (Boston: Adaptive Environments Center, 1995); Barbara Knecht, "Accessibility Regulations and a Universal Design Philosophy Inspire the Design Process," *Architectural Record* 192, no. 1 (2004): 145–150; and Michael Sorkin, "Limping Our Way to Universal Design: Everything Looks Different on Crutches," *Architectural Record* 192, no. 4 (2004): 85–86.

usability. The level of functionality of design features, including four types of functions: mobility, operability, perceptibility, and security. Related to **accessibility; mobility; operability; perceptibility; security.**

> Korydon Smith, *Arkansas Usability Standards in Housing: Guidance Manual for Designing and Constructing Inclusive, Functional Dwellings,* http://uark.edu/ua/studio/StudioAID2/content/usability%20standards/usability%20standards.pdf.

visitability. A design movement evolved from barrier-free design that focuses predominantly on access to housing for occupants and visitors using wheeled mobility devices; includes prescriptions of "zero-step entry" and ground floor toileting/washing facilities. Related to **accessibility; zero-step entry.**

zero-step entry. An entrance/exit to a home that allows users of wheeled mobility devices to enter/exit safely and without assistance. Related to **accessibility; visitability.**

CONTRIBUTORS

KORYDON H. SMITH is an associate professor of architecture at the University of Arkansas, where he teaches courses in architectural design and theory, and has received numerous teaching awards. Professor Smith's scholarship focuses on the physical and political roles of design in contemporary society. In addition, Smith is actively involved in continuing education and the transformation of housing policies and design practices throughout the United States. Professor Smith earned a professional M.Arch. degree with a concentration in architectural theory and design at the University at Buffalo and is completing a doctoral degree in higher education leadership at the University of Arkansas.

JENNIFER WEBB, Ph.D., NCIDQ #8049, is an associate professor of interior design at the University of Arkansas. Her professional work has been in the corporate and healthcare sectors and this experience has directly influenced her teaching and research efforts. Dr. Webb has written about the affects of the interior environment on human behavior, particularly regarding older adults in congregate living settings. Her goal is to improve users' health, safety, and welfare in interior settings through teaching and research.

BRENT T. WILLIAMS, Ph.D., C.R.C., is an associate professor and coordinator for the Rehabilitation Education and Research Program at the University of Arkansas. In addition to his research and teaching efforts,

Dr. Williams has over two decades of experience serving the wider community of persons with disabilities as a service provider, agency administrator, and board member. Dr. Williams has authored journal articles and book chapters and has made presentations across a broad spectrum of subjects, including disability and social justice; the role of not-for-profit community-based rehabilitation agencies; and the societal and fiscal costs of noninclusion for persons with disabilities.

DARELL W. FIELDS teaches design and architectural theory. His theoretical provocations have been exhibited at the Whitney Museum of American Art, the Studio Museum in Harlem, and the August Wilson Center for African American Culture in Pittsburgh. He graduated from the University of Texas at Arlington, in his home state, and twice more from Harvard with a Master of Architecture and a Ph.D. Current work involves research and development through his think tank, Superbia.

NANCY G. MILLER, Ph.D., is an associate professor of interior design at the University of Arkansas. Her professional experience includes designing both residential and small commercial spaces with an emphasis on creating sense of place through the use of fine craft. Dr. Miller's research explores the effects of personalization and self-identify through the use of objects in the home and the workplace.

EDWARD STEINFELD, D.Arch., AIA, is founding director of the Center for Inclusive Design and Environmental Access (IDEA), professor of architecture at the University at Buffalo—State University of New York, and a registered architect in New York State. Steinfeld's research focus is universal design, human factors, and social theory and design. He is widely published and has served as an expert accessibility consultant for the World Bank, the U.S. Department of Justice, the U.S. Department of Housing and Urban Development, and other agencies. His awards include a Distinguished Professor Award from the Association of Collegiate Schools of Architecture, a National Endowment for the Arts Design Research Award, and two Progressive Architecture Applied Research awards. Steinfeld completed his doctoral and post-professional studies at the University of Michigan and holds a professional degree in architecture from Carnegie Mellon University.

INDEX

Page numbers in italics refer to illustrations.

Arkansas (AR) Proto-House: background information, 166; benefits, 204–5; common features, 170, 176; Delta Prototype case study, 194–99; design criteria, 169–70, *171*; Ouachita Prototype case study, 186–93; Ozark Prototype case study, 178–85; patterning taxonomy, 170, *172–73*; prototype deployment, 177; site factors, 176–77; typical wall section, *174–75*. See also LE (Limited Edition) Product House

Arkansas City, Arkansas, 177. *See also* Delta Prototype case study

Arkansas Development Finance Authority (ADFA), 140

Arkansas National Guard, 57

Arkansas Supreme Court decisions, 97

Assets for Independence Act (1998), 253

Assisstive Technology Act (1988, 1998, 2004), 252

assisted living environments, xv

assistive technologies, 134, 140, 155, 240–41

astylistic design, 150–51

Atlanta, Georgia, 73, 123, 133, 216, 254

attitudinal barriers, 12–13, 113

Austin, Texas, 73

autonomy, 29–30, 248

baby-boomers: accessible housing, xxvi–xxvii; affordable housing, xiii–xiv; demographic data, xv; disability rights advocacy, 65; healthcare, xv–xvi, 100–101; homeownership, 100–101; state rankings, *xix*; US-Arkansas statistical comparisons, *xxi*. *See also* aging populations

Banham, Reyner, 107

barrier-free design: background information, 135, 236; housing floor plans, 105; policy and practice, xvi. *See also* universal design (UD)

basic activities of daily living (BADL), 10

bathrooms, 105–6

Baynton, Douglas, 49

Bednar, Michael, 137

bedrooms, 105

Beijing Olympic Games (2008), 114

Benton County, 167, 222, 232–34

Bio-Ecological Systems Theory, 268n17

black identity, 49–50

block grants, 210, 212, 214–15

Blount, Roy, Jr., xx, xxii

BOCA National Building Code, 66

Bolingbrook, Illinois, 73, 216, 255

Brown v. Board of Education (1954), 51, 57

Brubaker, Rogers, 115

Bruyn, Henry, 122

building codes, 60–70, 72–74, 89, 127, 143–45

Bush, George W., 73–74

California, 86, 92, 254, 255

capacity qualifiers, 14

Carlin, George, 80

Carter, Jimmy, 21, *22*, 25, 30

Cash, Johnny: autobiographical account, 258n25; autobiographical song, 257n1; boyhood friend, 3–4, 12–13, 18–19; boyhood home, *xii*; characteristics, xvi; clothing choice, 131; housing-well-being relationship, 207; memories of home, 47; personal identity, 159; self-reliance and perseverance traits, 221; sense of belonging, 42, 169; Southern cultural traits, 231; tour bus description, 157–58

Central High School (Little Rock), 57, 97

Certified Aging-in-Place Specialist (CAPS) program, 141–42

"chance-for-success" analysis, 97

Charles, Ray, xviii

chemical exposure risks, 157

Chicot County, 232–34, *233*

childhood obesity, 148–49

Civil Rights Act (1964), 90, 209

Civil Rights Act (1968), 53, 56, 58, 90, 209

civil rights movements, 53, 135

Cobb, James, xx, 18, 74

code creep, 143

cognitive maps, 31

Coles, Robert, 163–64

college students, 38

communities, 27–28, 42, 47–48, 134–35, 243–44

community-based not-for-profit organizations, 215–16

Community Development Organizations (CDOs), 215–16

Community Housing Development Organizations (CHDOs), 215–16

Community Mental Health Centers Act (1963), 90, 134, 209

Concrete Change, 73, 123, 133, 145, 264n41

Connecticut, 97

Consolidated Farm and Rural Development Act (1972), 251

Cooper, Frederick, 115

cost considerations, 59–60, 76, 81

Cranston-Gonzalez National Affordable Housing Act (1990, 1996), 252

Cross, William, 50, 261n4

death rate statistics, 242

Delaware, 219

Delta Prototype case study: aerial perspective, *195*; ground-level floorplan, *198*; model photographs, *197*; site characteristics, 194; site location, *194*; site plan, *196*; wall section, *199*

demographic variables: aging populations, 100–101; appliances and fixture design, 107, 225; construction conventions, 106–7, 157, 224–25, 238; education attainment, 96–98; employment status, 96, 101; homeownership, 93–98; household income, 93–100, 219; planning and zoning factors, 103–4; public perceptions, 102–3, 220–21; race and gender, 98–100; space-making conventions, 105–6

Departments of Veterans Affairs and Housing and Urban Development and Independent Agencies Appropriations Acts (1993–2004), 253

depression, 157
desegregation, 57, 74, 97
design-for-all, 137
design specialization and integration, 139–45, 236
detached, single-family homes: accessibility/usability codes, 89; aging populations, 100–101; American Dream, 88; appliances and fixture design, 225; background information, 78–80; buyers and renters, 89–93; construction conventions, 106–7, 157, 224–25, 238; demographic patterns, 84; demographic variables, 93–107; design and construction, 83; education attainment, 96–98; federal subsidies, 73; housing style, 150–53, *151*; planning and zoning factors, 103–4; policy and practice, 89–90, 223–25; public perceptions, 102–3; site factors, 176–77; The South, 83–94, *88*; space-making conventions, 105–6; traditional construction techniques, 108–9
deviant behaviors, *55–56*
diabetes, 118–19
Direct Homeownership Loan Program, 212, 250
disabilities: assistive technologies, 134, 240–41; biopsychosocial models, 7–17, 268n18; defining concepts, 3–17; government legislation, 90; identity creation process, 32–34, 238–39; ideological changes, 240; International Classification of Functioning, Disability and Health (ICF) model, 7, 12–14, 16–17; medical models, 5–6, 226; Nagi model, 7, 8–11, 13; Person-Environment Fit (P-E Fit) Model, 117–31; personal experience factors, 17–18; race-disability parallels, 49–51, 56–60, 74–76, 152; social models, 6–7; theoretical models, 4–5; wheelchairs, *5*, 6, 105, 159, 216–17, 238. *See also* housing modifications

disability-poverty-race interrelationships, 51, *52*, 53
disability rights movement and legislation, 57–61, 65, 69–71, 74–76, 135, 149, 160–61
disabled population: aging populations, 101, 235–36, 262n9; Arkansas, 167, 169, 235–36; attitudinal barriers, 12–13, 113; demographic data, xv, 51, 53; disability-poverty-race interrelationships, 51, *52*, 53; discrimination practices, 152, 225–26; family activities and rituals, 41–42; flooring surfaces, 106–7; government housing policies, 208–9, 242–43; healthcare, xv, 5–6, 228–29; identity creation process, 32–34, 238–39; inclusion policies and practices, 71–72, 81; independent living, 134–35, 227–28; marginalization, 7; physical barriers, 113; rural areas, 227–28; SSI recipients, 219; state rankings, *xix*
discrete room arrangement, 105
discrimination: disability rights movement and legislation, 74–76; disabled population, 152, 225–26; fair housing legislation, 53, 209–10, 225–26; funding inequities, 97; inter-group conflict, 56–57; race-disability parallels, 53; segregation, 51, 225–26
District of Columbia, 219
diversity-equality dichotomy, 164–65, 241
do-it-yourself (DIY) projects, 155, 239
DuBois, W. E. B., xxiv–xxv
Dunbar, Tony, 163–64
dwelling, 22

earnings gaps, 99–100
education attainment, 96–98
Education for All Handicapped Children Act (1975), 57–58, 90, 209
employment status, 96, 101
enabler design movements, 70, 137, 160–61. *See also* universal design (UD)

Environmental Affordances Theory, 269n21
environmental diversity, 148–50
environmental domains and sub-domains, 14
environmentally conscious building, 69–70, 106, 127, 224–25
equality: defining concepts, 49–51; diversity-equality dichotomy, 164–65, 241
Equal Pay Act (1963), 100

Fair Housing Act (1968), 53, 56–57, 62, 81, 90, 209–10, 251
Fair Housing Amendments Act (1988), 61, 62, 90, 209, 225, 251
Fair Housing Assitance Program (FHAP), 213, 251
Fair Housing Initiatives Program (FHIP), 213, 216, 251
falls, 106–7
family activities and rituals, 39–42, *41*, 47–48
Faubus, Orval E., 57
Fayetteville, Arkansas, 28, 67, 103, 177, 178
Felty, Dana, 54–55
FHA Mortgage Insurance Programs, 212, 250
flooring surfaces, 106–7
Florida: Certified Aging-in-Place Specialist (CAPS) program, 142; homeownership, 86; SSI recipients, 219; visitability legislation, 255
food culture, 39
foreclosures, 25, 95
form and function design concepts, 152–53
Foucault, Michel, 55
Foxworthy, Jeff, 237
framing techniques, 165, 224
free floor plans, 105
functional limitations, 8–11
funding support, 81
furniture, 36–38

Gans, Herbert, 77, 79–80
garage apartments, 103
gender: earnings gaps, 99–100; gender identity development, 50; homeownership, 98–100;

poverty rates, 99; single-mother households, 99; Southern gender roles, *39*

Georgia: accessible housing, 73, 123; Certified Aging-in-Place Specialist (CAPS) program, 142; death rates, 242; single-mother households, 99; SSI recipients, 219; visitability legislation, 133, 216, 254

"ghost" restraints, 65–66

government legislation: accessibility legislation, 56, 58–62, 72–73, 89–90, 236–37; defining concepts, 80–82; disabled population, 57–61; expenditures, 212–13; fair housing, 53, 56–57, 209–10; housing policies, 207–10, 212–13, 242–43; multifamily versus single-family housing, 84; policy transformations, 213–15; program statistics, 250–53; segregation, 51

grab bars, ix, xxvi, 36, 152, 246

granny flats, 103

Great Mississippi Flood of 1927, 166–67

Green, Ernest, 57

"green" building, 69–70, 106, 127, 149, 218, 224

Gropius, Walter, 146

gross domestic product (GDP), 96

Habitat for Humanity, 21

Harries, Karsten, 146, 245

healthcare: aging populations, xv–xvi, 100–101, 106–7; diabetes, 118–19; disabled population, xv, 5–6, 228–29; falls, 106–7; government spending, 70–71, 242–43; housing-well-being relationship, 207–8, 241–42; obesity, 148–49; policy changes, 241–42; rural areas, 84–85, 235

Heumann, Judy, 125

"Highway Headin' South" (lyrics), 115

Hispanic/Latino population, 148

Holmes, Hamilton, 74

home: assistive technologies, 134, 140, 155, 240–41; autonomy, 29–30, 248; color preferences, *35*;

continuity, 44, 47; defining concepts, 21–29, 108–9, 160, 248–49; as a health device, 156–58, *158*; homeland/home country, 28–29; as an identity device, 159–60, *160*, 249; ideological changes, 240–41; memories, 30–31; objects or possessions, 26, 34, 36–38; personal identity, 25–27, 32–34, 133, 159–60, *160*, 248; personalization and protection, *45*, 249; as a prosthetic device, *151*, 154–56, 159; screen doors, *108*; sense of belonging, 23, 28, 34, 42–44; sense of community, 27–28, 42, 47–48; sense of place, 43–44, 248; social aspects, 39–42, *41*, 47–48, 249; temporal aspects, 44, 249; terminology, 258n4(2); territory and space demarcation, *46*, 249; traditional perspectives, 108–9, 160–61. *See also* homelessness; housing modifications

Home and Community-Based Services [HCBS] Waiver Program, 212, 252

home entry modification, *xvii*

homeland/home country, 28–29

homelessness: defining concepts, 23–25; foreclosures, 25, 95; government housing policies, 227; government legislation, 252; objects or possessions, 34, 36, 248; occurrences, 25, 222; rural areas, 101, 104; stereotypical populations, 222

Homeless Veterans Comprehensive Assistance Act (2001), 253

homeownership: aging populations, 100–101; American Dream, 77–80, *79*; demographic variables, 93–98; ownership rates, 86

home values, 86–87, 95, 102

HOPE IV (Elderly Independence) Program, 212, 252

Hot Springs, Arkansas, 177, 186. *See also* Ouachita Prototype case study

house. *See* home

Housing Act (1949, 1954, 1956, 1959, 1964), 90, 250–51

Housing and Community Development Act (1974, 1977, 1978, 1979, 1980, 1981, 1987, 1992), 251

Housing and Urban Development Act (1965, 1968, 1970, 1990), 251

Housing Choice Voucher Program, 212, 219, 250

housing design and construction: accessibility features, 223–25; accessibility legislation, 56, 58–62, 72–73, 89–90, 236–37; accessibility/usability codes, 66–70, 72–74, 89, 127; aluminum can driveway, *229*; American Dream Home, xxv–xxvi, *24*, 62, 245; appliances and fixture design, 107, 225; architectural materials, 106–7, 157, 224–25, 238; assistive technologies, 134, 140, 155, 240–41; building codes, 60–70, 72–74, 89, 127, 143–45; buyers and renters, 89–93; certification programs, 141–42; changing practices, 243–45; collaborative relationships, 143; community planning, 243–44; contrasting examples, *62*, *63*; demographic variables, 93–107; design criteria, 169–70, 244–45; design ideologies, 69–71; framing techniques, 165, 224; "ghost" restraints, 65–66; good design concepts, xvi, 18, 48, 204; "green" building, 69–70, 106, 127, 149, 218, 224; as a health device, 156–58, *158*; housing recommendations, 239–45; housing style, 150–53, *151*; housing trends, 62–63, 71–72, 91–92, 224; iconic example, *xxiii*; identity creation process, 50–51, 159–60, *160*, 249; innovative builders, 217–18; integration and specialization factors, 139–45, 236; invisibility, 165–66; mailboxes, *211*; Modernist perspectives, 146–48, *147*, 156; NAHB designation programs, 141–42; Person-Environment Fit (P-E Fit) Model, 117–31; policy and practice, xvi, 89–90, 219–30,

New Mexico, 97, 254

New Orleans, Louisiana, xiv, 108

Newton County, 167

New York, 254–55, 256

Nigrescence theory, 49–50

Norburg-Shulz, Christian, 147

North Carolina: Certified Aging-in-Place Specialist (CAPS) program, 142; homeownership, 86; SSI recipients, 219

Northeast: education attainment, 97; government housing policies, 77–78; homeownership, 86; home values, 86–87; multi-family versus single-family housing, 84

northwest Arkansas, 167, 169, 222, 232–34

not-for-profit organizations, 215–16

No Where Road, *xxv*

nursing home care, xv, 63

OASDI recipients: state rankings, *xix*; US-Arkansas statistical comparisons, *xxi*

Obama, Barack, 116

objects or possessions, 26, 34, 36–38, 248

odor memories, 30–31

Ohio, 256

Oklahoma: death rates, 242; SSI recipients, 219

Older Americans Act (1965), 251

Olmstead Decision (1999), 62, 71, 74, 81, 134, 225–27

Olymipic Games (2008), 114

one-bedroom housing units, 219

open-air architecture, 156

open floor plans, 105, 224

oppression, 7

Ostroff, Elaine, 58

Ouachita Prototype case study: aerial perspective, *187*; lower-level floorplan, *191*; model photographs, *189*; site characteristics, 186–87; site location, *186*; site plan, *188*; site section, *192*; upper-level floorplan, *190*; wall section, *193*

outdoor activity, 157

Oxo International, 225

Ozark Plateau: Arkansas (AR) Proto-House, 177; Ozark Prototype case study, 178–85; physiographic regions, *168*; regional diversity, 167

Ozark Prototype case study: aerial perspective, *179*; lower-level floorplan, *183*; model photographs, *181*; site characteristics, 178; site location, *178*; site plan, *180*; site section, *184*; upper-level floorplan, *182*; wall section, *185*

Pacific Northwest, 86

paid and unpaid role activities, 10

Pallasmaa, Juhani, 147

paratransit systems, 60, *61*

Part M (United Kingdom), 72

Partnership for Advancing Technologies in Housing (PATH) program, 141

Parton, Dolly, 115

Pasteur, Louis, 156

Pennsylvania, 73, 255, 256

percentage-based building approach, 72–73

performance domains and sub-domains, 13–14

performance qualifiers, 14

Person-Environment Fit (P-E Fit) Model: background information, 268n8; defining concepts, 117–31, 268n9; personal adaptation, 119–20, *121*, 123–24, *124*, *127*, *128*, 128–29, *129*; physical and cultural environment, 120–29, *122*, *124*, *127*, *128*, *129*; physiological and psychosocial characteristics, 118–19, *119*, *121*, *124*, *127*, *128*, *129*; range of fit, *117*, 119–20, *121*, *122*, *124*, *127*, *128*, *129*

personal experience factors, 17–18, 50

personal factors, 14, 16

persons with disabilities. *See* disabled population

Petersen, Amy, 49

Phelps, Michael, 114, 267n2

photographs, *36–37*

physical barriers, 113, 238–39

Picon, Antoine, 65

Pima County, Arizona, 216, 255

Pine Bluff, Arkansas, 96

Pistorius, Oscar, 114, 267n2

planning and zoning factors, 103–4

Plessy v. Ferguson (1896), 51

policy and practice: criticisms, 219–30; defining concepts, 77–83; disabled population, 240–41; government housing policies, 207–10, 212–13, 226–29; government spending, 242–43; housing-well-being relationship, 207–8, 241–42; independent living, 161, 227–29; multifamily versus single-family housing, 84; policy transformations, 213–15; single-family homes, 89–90; universal design (UD), xvi, 223

population increases, xiv, 232–34, *233*

porches, 27, *29*

poverty: Arkansas, 167, 169, 232–36, *233*; demographic data, 51, 53; disability-poverty-race interrelationships, 51, *52*, 53; low-income housing, 102–3, 208–10, 219; race and gender, 98–99; rural areas, 163–64; The South, 94, 98–99, 235–36; SSI recipients, 219; state rankings, *xix*; US-Arkansas statistical comparisons, *xxi*

privacy, 26, 249

private dwellings, 254

prosthetic technology, *151*, 154–56, 159

public buildings, 127–28, *138*, 218

Public Housing Development Program, 212, 250

public housing projects, 102, 208, 210, 226–27, 254

public perceptions, 102–3, 220–21

Pulaski County, 232–34

race: demographic data, 51, 53, *233*, *234*; disability-poverty-race interrelationships, 51, *52*, 53; homeownership, 98–100; poverty rates, 98–99; race-disability parallels, 49–51, 56–60,

74–76, 152; racial identity development, 50, 115–16, 261n4
ramps, *xvii*, *15*, 33–34, 67, *75*, *135*, *144*
real estate industry, 90–91, 93, 108–9, 146
Reed, John Shelton, xx, 177
Rehabilitation Act (1973), 62, 90, 209
Rehabilitation Act (1998), 61, 90
rehabilitative treatment, 5–6
religion, 39
rental properties, 32, 90–93, 219–20, *220*
Residential Energy Assistance Challenge Option [REACH] Program, 212, 252
retrofitting, 134, 136
rituals, 39–42, 47
Roberts, Ed, 53, 113, 115, 122, 131
Rockefeller, Winthrop, 57
rural areas: agri-business competition, *214*; cultural traits, 237–38; demographic characteristics, xiv–xv, 79; healthcare accessibility, 84–85, 235; homelessness, 101, 104; housing design and construction, 243; independent living barriers, 227–28; porches, 27; poverty, 163–64; public buildings, 127–28; ramps, *33*; socioeconomic aspects, 84–85, 235
Rural Housing and Economic Development (RHED) Program, 212, 253
Rural Housing Repair and Rehabilitation Loans and Grants Program, 212, 251
rural pie shop, *98*
Rural Rental Housing Guaranteed Loan Program, 212, 251
Rural Rental Housing Program, 212, 251

Schakowsky, Jan, 72
Schumacher, Tom, 147
Scranton, Pennsylvania, 73
screen doors, *108*
Searcy County, 167
Seasonal Affective Disorder (SAD), 157
secondary housing spaces, 105–6

security, 23, 28, 42
segregation, 51, 53, 56–59, 74, 115, 225–26
self-reliance and perseverance traits, 221
sense of belonging, 23, 28, 34, 42–44, 169
sense of community, 27–28, 42, 47–48
sense of place, 43–44, 248
sensory memories, 30–31
"separate but equal" legislation, 51, 58–59
Separate Car Act (1890), 51
shared identity, 27–29, 34, 47
shelter, 21–22, 24–25, 258n4(2)
short-distance movers, 90–91
sick building syndrome, 157
single-family homes: accessibility/usability codes, 89; aging populations, 100–101; American Dream, 88; appliances and fixture design, 107, 225; background information, 78–80; buyers and renters, 89–93; construction conventions, 106–7, 157, 224–25, 238; demographic patterns, 84; demographic variables, 93–107; design and construction, 83; education attainment, 96–98; federal subsidies, 73; housing style, 150–53, *151*; planning and zoning factors, 103–4; policy and practice, 89–90, 223–25; public perceptions, 102–3; site factors, 176–77; The South, 83–94, *88*; space-making conventions, 105–6; traditional construction techniques, 108–9; visitability legislation, 254–56. *See also* Arkansas (AR) Proto-House; LE (Limited Edition) Product House
single-mother/single-parent households, 99, 224
sinks, xxvi, 11, *75*, 176
Smith, Eleanor, 133
social change, 54–57
social identity theory, 53–55
social ideology, 64–65
socially prescribed roles, 32–33

social mobility versus social change, 54–55
social oppression, 7
Social Security Act (1935, 1965, 1981), 252
sociat activities, 11
Sorkin, Michael, 150
The South: accessible housing, 73; agri-business competition, *214*; cultural traits, xvi–xvii, 18, 231, 237–38; death rates, 242; demographic and geographic variables, 16–17, 232–36; diversity factors, 203–4; housing industry, 141–42, 161; housing policies and practices, 219–30; housing recommendations, 239–45; manufactured housing, 219–20; national perceptions and stereotypes, xviii, xx, xxii, 220–21; poverty, 94, 98–99, 235–36; race-disability parallels, 74–76; rural areas, *235*; single-family homes, 83–94, *88*; single-mother households, 99; social activities, 39–42; traditional perspectives, 108–9, 160–61; undeveloped areas, *237*
South Carolina: Certified Aging-in-Place Specialist (CAPS) program, 142; death rates, 242; single-mother households, 99; SSI recipients, 219
Southern Building Code, 66
Springdale, Arkansas, 29
SSI recipients, 219
starter homes, 91
State Units on Aging (SUAs), 215–16
STEEL model, 247
Steinfeld, Edward, 137
subsidized public housing, 226–27
suburban tract housing, 77–80, *81*, 108–9
Sullivan, Louis, 245
Supportive Housing for Persons with Disabilities Program, 212, 252
Supportive Housing for the Elderly Program, 212, 250
sustainable design, 69–70, 127
Swanson, Louis E., 235